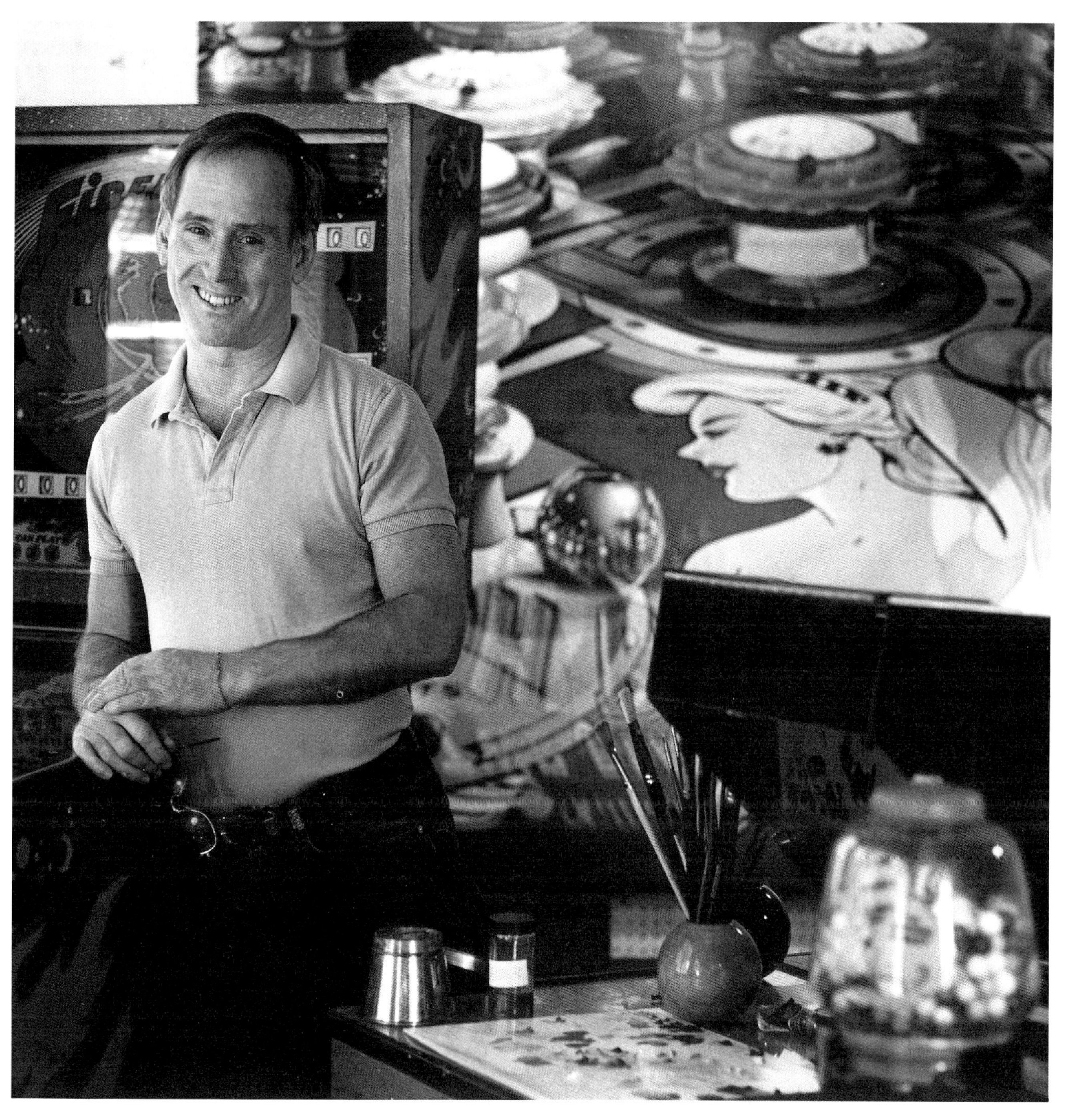

CHARLES BELL

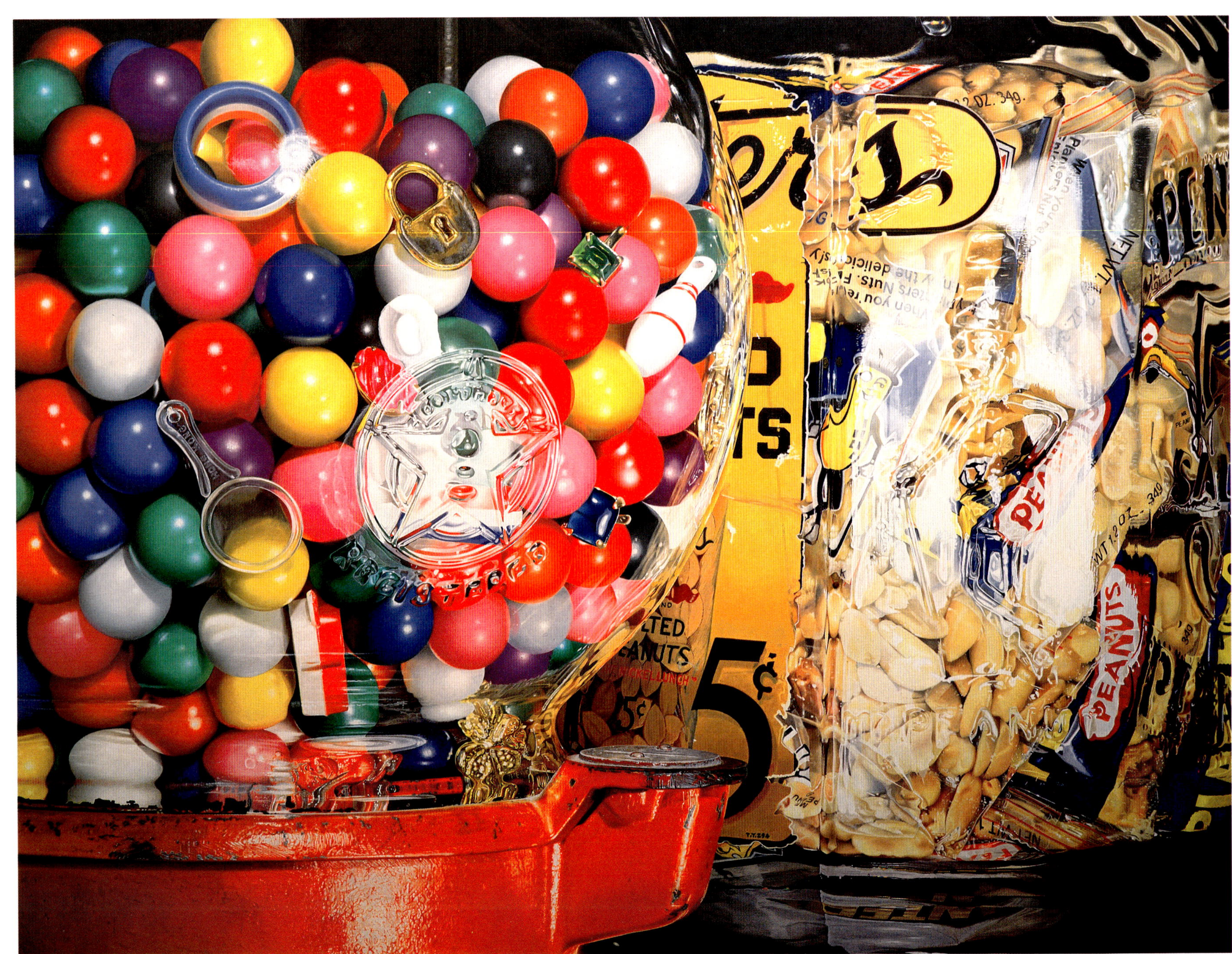

1. *Andy's Mr. Peanut (Major)*. 1991. Oil on canvas, 90 × 120″. Collection Donna and Neil Weisman, New Jersey

CHARLES BELL

THE COMPLETE WORKS 1970–1990

BY HENRY GELDZAHLER

WITH AN ESSAY BY LOUIS K. MEISEL

HARRY N. ABRAMS, INC., PUBLISHERS, NEW YORK

Editor: Margaret Donovan
Designer: Dirk Luykx
Research and Documentation: Aaron Miller, Diane Sena
Photographers: Steven Lopez, Keith Jones, D. James Dee, Aaron Miller

Page 1: Charles Bell in his Soho studio, New York, 1991. © Steven Lopez 1991
Other documentary photographs: Copy Berg (pages 20, 31), Kaz Takahashi (page 10), and Ray Charles White (pages 6, 17)

Figs. 8, 9, and 13: © ARS, N.Y. 1991; fig. 10: © James Rosenquist/VAGA, N.Y. 1991

Library of Congress Cataloging-in-Publication Data
Geldzahler, Henry.
Charles Bell : the complete works, 1970–1990 / by Henry Geldzahler with an essay by Louis K. Meisel.
144 p. 24.8 x 26 cm.
Includes bibliographical references and index.
ISBN 8-8109-3114-1 (cloth)
1. Bell, Charles, 1935- –Catalogs. 2. Photo-realism–United States–Catalogs. I. Bell, Charles, 1935- II. Meisel, Louis K. III. Title.
N6537.B447A4 1991 91-6922
759.13–dc20 CIP

Published in 1991 by Harry N. Abrams, Incorporated, New York
A Times Mirror Company

Printed and bound in Japan

CONTENTS

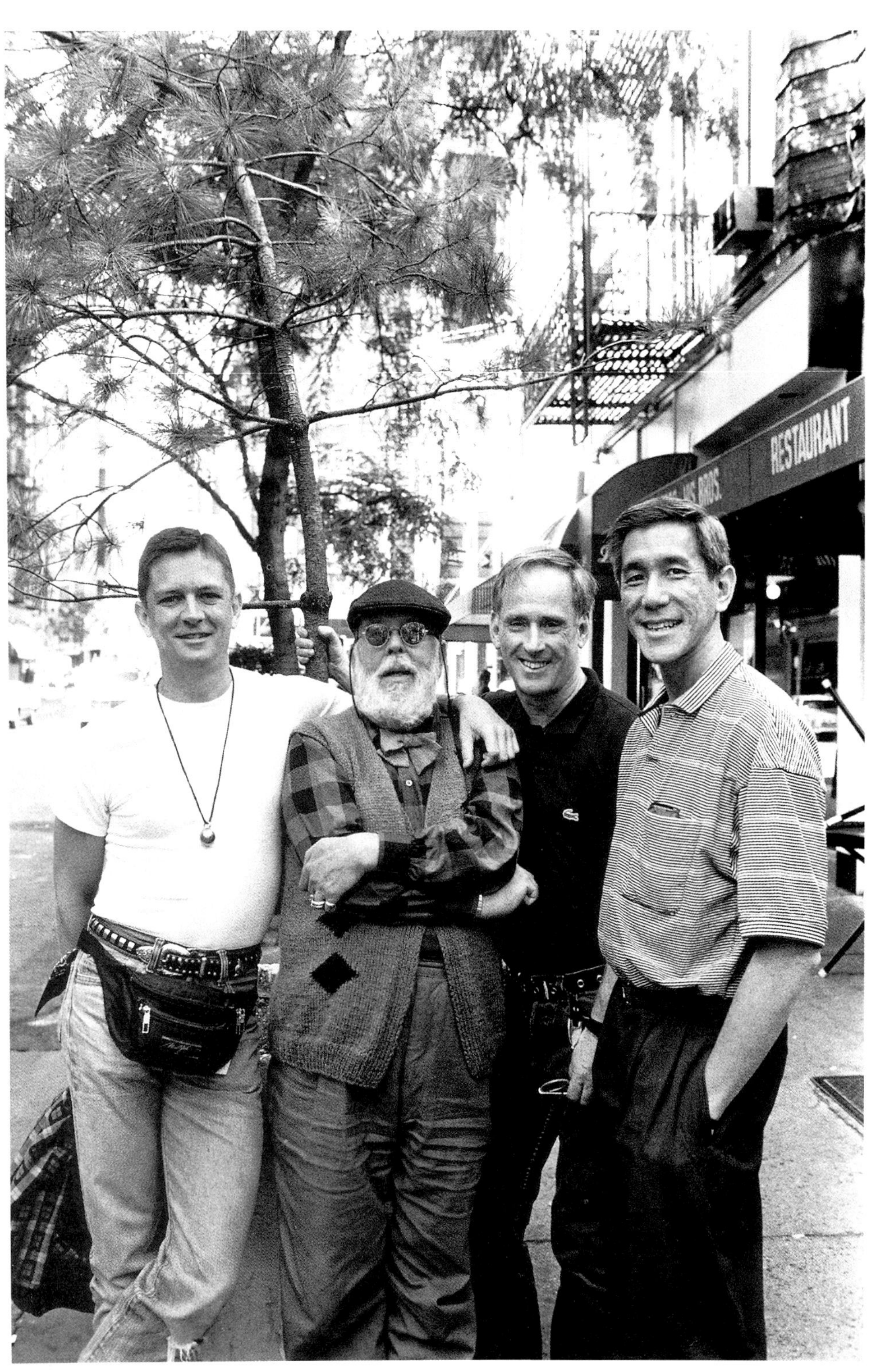

2. Copy Berg, Henry Geldzahler, Charles Bell, and Will Ching, after lunch in Soho, New York, August 1990

FOREWORD

By Copy Berg

I first met Charles Bell in 1976. I was doing graduate work in design at Pratt Institute while at the same time studying drawing at the Art Students League. Charles looked at my work and asked me many questions about my background and plans for the future. He then asked me to draw for him and, after a few minutes, quietly offered to teach me what he knew about painting if I would come to work for him as an apprentice. In this straightforward way we began a working relationship and a friendship that have lasted ever since. Working with Charles has allowed me not only to observe his artistic techniques and progress, but also to participate in decisions and experiments in various media.

Charles believes strongly in the "each-one-teach-one" philosophy of education. He himself learned from a painter who made him promise to teach another. I was not the first or the only student to work with Charles, but I was one of the few who stayed. Once most students see how difficult the work is and how exacting Charles is, they drop out and go back to work that requires less effort and discipline. At our first meeting Charles told me, "I can tell you everything I know in two hours. I can show you everything I know in two weeks. And I can teach you everything I know in two years." He was right in each case almost to the day.

Charles uses primarily classical techniques and proven methods. He works mostly in oil with brush on canvas or in watercolor or pencil on paper. Because his techniques are strongly rooted in tradition, he can feel free to explore more adventuresome subject matter as well as pertinent issues of scale. As I began working with Charles, he had me do everything the hard way. I would boil rabbit-skin glue and apply half-oil ground, build and stretch canvases, mix colors, and in time do underpainting and glazes.

My day started with drawing; each day there was a different subject drawn from life. Charles would select an object that presented some new problem of representation or texture. My first object was a canvas running shoe placed on the drawing board with the toe pointed toward me. The emphasis was thus on the interconnected laces, and Charles pointed out that this made the subject one of the easiest to draw. Each of the many points at which the laces crossed and connected provided a place to triangulate. With numerous points of reference, it was easier for me to keep my place and move from one section of the drawing to another. Each carefully selected object took me further and further toward the most difficult ones—a metal can opener, a teacup, an egg. These have very few points of reference with which to check the drawing. My final drawing in this series of lessons was an antique flatiron, which took a total of eight hours to complete.

In addition to the drawing exercises, there were color-theory and color-mixing studies. For example, I would draw ten adjacent blank squares on canvas paper. Charles would provide two colors, one each for the squares on the ends. The exercise was to mix the two colors and paint, in equal steps of color gradation, the squares between the two ends. From such simple means comes an understanding of hue, chroma, value, relative strength of pigments, subjective responses to color interaction, and nuances of available pigments.

As elementary as these studies may sound, they are actually crucial—many bad paintings have been made from photographs by people who do not understand the principles underlying such exercises. Charles' work is different in this respect: he firmly believes that painting from photographs cannot be successful unless one is fully able to work from life. He frequently says, "The eye cannot truly see what the hand cannot draw." Only when such exercises have been mastered can the artist be free to pursue other styles, mediums, and messages. This is exemplified in the vivid contrast between the traditional techniques Charles employs and his keen interest, based on long years of experience in computer applications, in relating high technology to art. He is now pursuing projects in computer imagery, in computer animation, in video as art, and in interactive instructional programs using laser-storage technology to teach the science and psychology of vision and color theory.

Charles is neither didactic nor pedantic. He once said to me, "You won't honor me unless you go beyond me," for, like the teachers Josef Albers and Hans Hofmann, he never intends to teach replication. His flexibility as a teacher includes experimenting with the use of techniques other than his own—with staining the canvas, colored gessos, and three-dimensional formats. His only concern is that the student master the fundamental techniques before then choosing whether or not to discard them. This is a characteristic he had in common with his friend the Photorealist painter Noel Mahaffey, who shared Charles and Will Ching's brownstone in Brooklyn from 1976 to 1979. Together they created a studio environment conducive to learning and growth. For me, as well as for Noel's students, it was a stimulating and privileged period.

Charles pursues his own work with the same dogged determination that his teaching exercises call for. He employs an intense, self-limited field of vision that has allowed him to explore the myriad complexities found within the globe of a gumball machine or under the glass surface of a pinball machine. I have seen Charles, before ever taking a photograph, spend hours under hot lights, placing charms and gumballs in various combinations inside a machine. We have also spent countless hours together looking at machines of all kinds in bars, warehouses, and amusement parks throughout the world.

Not just any machine or toy contains the material for a successful painting. The object must have a certain kind of architecture to give it enough character to warrant serious two-dimensional examination. This character is further intensified by the large scale of the paintings, which show objects as they would never be seen in real life. Their hugeness plays with and tantalizes our imaginations, draws us into the works. I will never forget the first exhibition of paintings I had actually assisted with. I knew all the works intimately, yet as I walked around the Meisel Gallery, I was shocked by the overwhelming feeling that I was going to fall into the paintings. Like Alice in Wonderland, I had been presented with a world that seemed both very, very real and yet totally impossible.

The first of Charles' large-scale paintings was a Raggedy Ann doll. He had previously been doing small, tabletop still lifes in which interesting objects were juxtaposed in incongruous combinations. These are accomplished, sparkling little gems, but they lack the impact of his later, large-scale works. With the encouragement of interior designer Will Ching, his friend and partner since 1968, Charles decided to use the same tabletop format but jumped the size to six feet. He had seen a similar scale in the works of Harold Stevenson and James Rosenquist, but he had never considered it for his own work until Will's suggestions. The success of this jump in scale was immediate and surprisingly effective, even to Charles. Thus began the body of work for which he is best known and which he still pursues today.

Charles is fond of saying, "The only true art is the art of living." In that regard he holds friendships to be as important as his art, and he has maintained close ties with many people from his past. He cherishes these friends and listens carefully to the advice they provide. Charles had had a career as a naval officer and later as a corporate executive with International Nickel (INCO) Ltd., where he had key responsibilities for computerization and organizational change in the financial area. While he was very successful in this work, he found he was painting with an intensity that continued to grow. Charles' friends, chief among them Will Ching, actively encouraged him to paint full time, yet his determination to succeed in art ultimately came from somewhere deep inside him. The wisdom of this choice is evident in the works presented here, the results of a life now fully dedicated to his art.

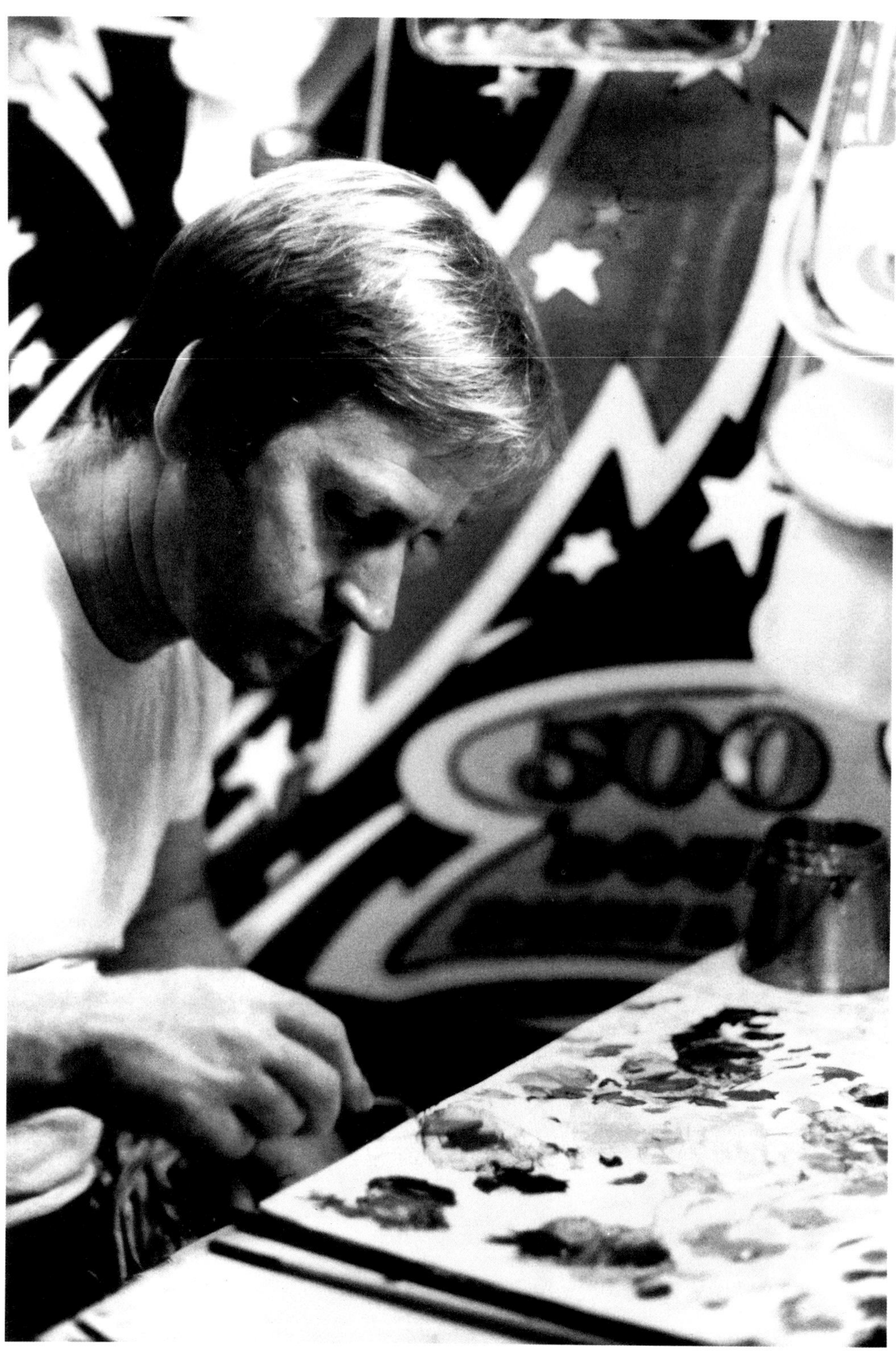

3. Charles Bell working on *Fire Ball 500 No. 1* (fig. 87), 1977

CHARLES BELL: OBSERVATIONS AND CONVERSATIONS

By Henry Geldzahler

Charles Bell's art is about discovery. Although his work is most closely associated with that of the Photorealists, it has a deeply personal intensity that makes him unique within that group. He is included in the Photorealists because of the obvious influence the camera has upon his work, but I find other strong influences as well: Northern European Realism of earlier centuries, American Realism, Pop art, and also obviously Contemporary Realism in America. Bell himself says, "I believe we perceive art today in its plurality: not its rulelessness, but its multiplicity. One can thoroughly appreciate many disciplines and styles, and many of those are from the more distant past as well as from our more recent experience."

The Art World Since World War II

The broader art world, especially during the last half of this century, provides the contextual base from which Photorealism emerged in the late sixties and early seventies. Since World War II, art has, indeed, become increasingly pluralistic; many more possibilities seem to be open to it at every moment. Even though we continue to see the flow of recent history as one movement succeeding another, the length of time in which each movement seems to prevail is shorter all the time. Abstract Expressionism lasted perhaps fifteen to twenty years in its heyday, Pop art about ten years, Neo-Geo five or six, and as we come closer to today, the spans are even shorter, because the games have been worked out so much more quickly.

To mention game theory in this context sounds somewhat unserious, even light-headed, but it's not. Cézanne rewrote the rules, and his game is still in play. Duchamp then rewrote them his way.

Picasso started another game, Miró yet another. After a while, all the positions on the board are occupied and you have to make up a new game, a new set of rules to submit to and then to break with. People forget that everybody doesn't march to the same step, or to the same beat. There are collectors, for instance, who started in the thirties collecting Ben Shahn and still collect Ben Shahn today, others who did the same for Motherwell, and then Warhol, and so it goes. And everybody doesn't stop collecting an artist's work at the same time. The same thing is true of university art departments, art magazines, art galleries, museum curators. They all have points of view that can be seen negatively, as mired in the past, but are actually simply still being propelled by what generated them in the first place. So, although we talk about this quick succession of movements, it's a cover. We really mean only the forward prong, not the army.

Another related factor, one that also generated Pop art, is the rise of the media and their pervasiveness in our daily lives. When I was a graduate student at Harvard in the late fifties, I took my Ph.D. oral exams on twentieth-century art, and I was able to read literally everything that had been written about the subject up to 1958. Ten years later, twenty years later, thirty years later, such a thing has become impossible. Book publishing, magazines, international travel, loan exhibitions from museums, and all kinds of modern technology have been brought to bear on the visual arts, and we all know so much. How deeply we know it is something else: it seems to me that we all merely skate across the surface of something vast. Going back to earlier times, as far back as the Middle Ages, you knew the artist in your town, to whom you could apprentice, and you knew a few itinerant artists who might move fifty to a hundred miles during their entire lives. And you knew famous pictures through some primitive woodblock prints that circulated hand to hand. That was your information and you dug deep with that, as deep as you could. Although, through the succeeding centuries, art information was more widely disseminated, it was not until our century that a sudden, violent change occurred. What happened after World War II was an information glut—or you could call it an information festival, depending on how you feel about it. I think it's wonderful.

Drawing upon this vast wealth of media-generated images, Pop art emerged in the fifties and has exerted a strong influence on the aesthetic perspective of artists ever since. Pop artists, like the Photorealists and other groups that came later, drew energy from the way our modern world looks—from television, newspapers, magazines, billboards, automobiles, suburbia, and the movies—while at the same time providing continuity with prewar American painting and a return to American subject matter. Actually, many of the other stylistic innovations of this century came about similarly, because a new era of subject matter was made the province of art. Physics informed Cubism; Freud's dream theory was behind Surrealism; the art of children and the insane had a profound effect on Klee and Dubuffet. Pop incorporated mass media and consumerism into the fine arts, and that act was so pivotal aesthetically as to force future artists to come to terms with it.

By 1965, surprisingly, the commonality of the movement began to dissipate, and it became clear that there would be no second generation. (Perhaps the mastery the Pop artists displayed left no room for one.) New games began to be played. Of these, interestingly, Minimalism and Photorealism had in common a reaction against the oversaturation of commercialization and ideology as subject matter; both took up positions on a more serene playing field. In the late sixties, we find Charles Bell, along with other artists, making key decisions, coming to terms with an expanding art world. He says, "The mid-sixties art world seemed to muddle in what one felt was nondirection, but now we see it as an expansion of diversity. In that diversity there was room for somebody who would take Pop imagery, place it in the matrix of the traditional still life, and let the two percolate. I set out to push that approach to its logical end."

Photorealism

Along with virtually every other artistic grouping that followed Pop, Photorealism has been classified by one writer or another as Post-Modernist. But consider the origin of that phrase. It's a critic's phrase, something that's meant to help organize the world, rather than an artist's or artlover's phrase. Yet, if you think for a minute, the term is based on a flawed verbal construct. Post-Impressionism supposedly came after Impressionism, but it didn't exactly. It began in 1886 or so, with Van Gogh, Gauguin, Seurat, Bonnard, and Toulouse-Lautrec (to make it simple). But Impressionism didn't stop: Degas lived to 1917, Renoir to 1919, Monet to 1926. It's that cliché again of one thing succeeding another. Not at all—they overlapped.

In addition, while the term Post-Modernism does have a certain resonance, if it means that Modernism is dead, I think it's overstated. The implications of Modernism—the new strategies emanating from the work of Matisse, Picasso, Duchamp, and others since—have not been fully worked out. We haven't walked away from them; we haven't had any change in aesthetic sufficient to alter the rules. We have had great changes in artistic and studio practice and technique, but always in the service of an older tradition like painting, printmaking, sculpture, architecture, or poetry.

It is impossible to discuss Photorealism without coming to terms with the critical anger and controversy it has engendered. Why do some feel so split when it comes to Photorealism? There is first, I think, a guilt at being seduced by its combination of high-level craftsmanship with an undercurrent of wizardry. This is in large part due, in my case anyway, to the astonished admiration I harbor for artists every day of my life—for Vladimir Horowitz playing his version of "Stars and Stripes Forever" as much as for Salvador Dali and Charles Bell painting their bravura set pieces, as if we had been conned into admiring sheer technical facility. Dali got it right when he characterized his Surrealist paintings as "hand-painted dream photographs," a phrase that gives Magic Realism its full due.

Some also have a reluctance to take Photorealism at face value. They feel a lapping of doubt that it is good art, or even that it is really art at all. Good art to them seems as if it shouldn't be so hard to do, shouldn't demand so many sacrifices of the intuitive and the hotly felt, that passion we teach ourselves to honor as the human spirit at its best. Examples in our century of such realized passion might be work as different in intent and effect as that of Hans Hofmann, Paul Klee, and Alberto Giacometti. Yet we don't find the paintings of the Van Eycks or Hans Memling easy or slick—quite the reverse.

It sometimes seems, to listen to the argument, as if Photorealism were a philosophical position rather than the aesthetic catchall that it is. Some say, "Since they all work so closely to photographs, they must all be the same" and "What's so original about copying photographs?" As is so often the case in matters of art, the truth is both more complex and more individual than any such generalization.

First, are all photographs the same? Not only are there various kinds of black-and-white and color films, there are also all kinds of cameras, the whole range of f-stops, and different options in printing, matte and shiny being only two. In addition to the size of the film, there is the relationship in size between the actually used film and the printed or reproduced photograph. This in turn raises another set of possibilities: a Photorealist can use photosensitized canvas, or specially coated paper, or even wood panel or metal to paint images on.

I think the negative implication of leaning on a photograph in order to get a work of art going is disappearing for several reasons. One of them, which became clear through scholarship, is that Degas, Toulouse-Lautrec, and Manet (for three) relied heavily on photographs. The cropping in Manet's paintings, for instance, the radical way in which he changed composition, had a lot to do with photographs and the camera. Now, such uses of the camera have become very much accepted. It's become almost a cliché that everything technological is allowed.

There's no more aura, even among abstract artists, of lack of discipline or failure of courage in working from a photograph. In fact, it's gone beyond that, and there seems to be a kind of battle of cleverness about how many ways an artist can lean on modern technology. If I had to characterize the art of the nineties, I'd say it will be a double one: a return to abstraction and a continuation of game-playing based on new understandings of technology and its relation to the art and thought of the past.

You don't think about photography when you look at a good Photorealist piece. It's painted on canvas. It's a choice of a subject. It's related to the artist's autobiography, to the artist's dream life. It's not just the mechanical or the literal. And of course, going back to Guardi and Canaletto in the eighteenth century and even further back than that, you see that very little has really changed. Such artists used the technology that was available to them to make pictures as correctly as was possible at the time. They wanted to extend the ability of the eye to see and the hand to interpret. They wanted to get more scientific about it, more rational about it.

The Age of Enlightenment is what led to this whole thing. It wasn't enough to just feel, you had to demonstrate. And if you think of the history of the Renaissance, culminating in the Enlightenment, it's about measuring. Everything is about measuring. We discovered America by measuring. We discovered internal medicine and all the ways to help with disease that seem to move faster than we do. We are still spending billions of dollars to get a close-up of Venus, to measure the effect of gravity in space on the arc of a beam of light that supposedly goes straight. Our intellectual curiosity is still best stimulated by questions of measurement. And, in that context, to sneeze at the use of photography is passé.

It is true, however, that if any single characteristic unites the artists who practice Photorealism, it is their continuing fascination with, and in certain cases denial of, the pivotal role of photography in their work. To admit as much is to realize that one of the great attractions art seduces with is the total absence of rules that can be applied in all cases. Every tradition, every characteristic, every rule, is subject to contradictions and objections.

For instance, much has been made of the virtue of abstraction and the vice of Realism. This morning, at Bell's studio, I saw a print, a five-plate etching. It's of a familiar Charles Bell subject, in that it's something that's popular and mechanical and reseen by him. It's something that's fleeting, but made permanent by the fact of his notice of it. Artists put their imprint on the familiar, causing us to focus anew, as Hopper does, for instance, with the Northeast sunlight in his work. And the first thing I thought of, looking at Bell's etching, was how successful it was: a large print of a slot machine, two cherries across and the third one above. (Three cherries across would have been more satisfying, but I think wouldn't have been so engaging.)

It came to my mind that what I was looking at was Charles Bell's image printed on paper rather than painted on canvas. The paper is very much present, but it doesn't in any way mask the vitality of the image. And yet, at every point in the print, if you look at it closely, ink lies on figured paper. The print's vivid image is clearly representational, yet the ink-printed-on-paper aspect of it is abstract. This opposition and others, like Romantic versus Classical and Expressionistic versus Geometric, are all useful guideposts down the road, but they are not the map—and they lie. They lie conveniently if you are trying to teach, inconveniently if you are trying to grapple with the whole matter and grasp its essence.

If Charles Bell didn't know how to organize a picture, how to put things down on canvas in a composition that would read as well abstractly as it does literally, his art wouldn't have the excitement generated by the separation of the image and its ground. It is an abstract quality at work here, a random orderliness in a system in which image and ground are seen to coincide. Bell's success here belies the notion that his is an art that relies too much on photography for its drawing. Photography for an artist is after all only a tool, like a pencil. Each artist finds an individual use for it. It is nonsense to say that Dürer and Miró are alike because they both used pencils.

I once took a connoisseurship course at Harvard Graduate School with Jakob Rosenberg, who had been the director of the prints and drawings department at the Berlin state museum before World War II, and the entire point of the course was to list aesthetic categories. We worked with Rubenses and Rembrandts. We talked about rhythm, variety, and contrast, all the things that are so important in the art of the Renaissance and Post-Renaissance. When we got to the last class, Rosenberg brought in five or six prints and slides of abstract works and said, "Find me a single category that applies to Rembrandt that does not apply here." And that, I think, sums the whole thing up—that Realism and abstraction are not in opposition. The better you know yourself, the better you know the history of art, the better you know your technique and your subject matter, the greater will be the variety and directness characterizing your work. It all has nothing to do with categories like abstraction and Realism.

Conversations with Bell

Charles Bell lies to himself far less than most artists. He is thus a reliable source when it comes to the origins and intentions of his paintings, as you will see from the following notes based on conversations I've had with him over the past year. You will find that he maintains a relentlessness in his own regard, an honesty that allows him no place to hide, no place from which to cop a plea. In fact, Bell's absence of self-delusion earns him an honored place in art-historical autobiography.

Bell sets the scene in art as he saw it early in the sixties, well before a sense of being an "artist" held much glamour for him. His search for a subject and a means of representing it is engrossing. He begins by discussing his own take on and participation in Photorealism.

*Photorealism was the label applied to a particular group of artists, working in the sixties, who made clear reference to photography in their work and took the everyday world as their subject. Incidentally, Photorealist was just one of many descriptive names—*Hyperréal *(French), Hard-Edge, Super-Real, Romantic Real—but it was the one that stuck. There were plenty of other artists using photographs before, during, and after who didn't get called Photorealists; Charles Sheeler and Man Ray come to mind.*

It's difficult to comprehend how pervasive one aesthetic, Abstract Expressionism, was in the art world from the late forties to the mid-sixties. And if you decided to paint anything that was realistic or even slightly representational, you were an illustrator, your work sometimes called calendar art, but whatever it was called, it was just not serious. There were odd artists, as in "odd man out." Walter Murch did ethereal Realist still lifes and was accepted by both art camps. There were people like Fairfield Porter and Hopper. There was always an enormous respect for Hopper; there is something about afternoon light that fascinates the American mind. Edwin Dickinson, Peter Blume, and other artists we don't hear so much about today were respected but not considered the cutting edge.

Photorealism is not a movement in the sense that Surrealism or Fauvism was. Photorealism, to me, is like Cubism. Cubism was not so much an art movement as an intersection in time and spirit. Some people, like Juan Gris, chose to stay in the intersection. Picasso was just passing through, as were many artists who gave Cubism a try. I think of Photorealism that way. It was an intersection at a point in time, and some are still there and some were just passing through.

A big topic of the art world of the sixties was "Is painting dead?" What this referred to was a running battle with sculptors and emerging Performance artists and Conceptual artists on one side versus "old-fashioned" painters on the other—old-fashioned being like paintings on the wall, easel painting. The Conceptual artists, Earth Works artists, sculptors, performers, those people sort of ganged up and declared that easel painting was no longer valid. First off, it had no sense of space, texture notwithstanding. Art couldn't just sit there on the wall and do nothing. It had to get out into space. Personally, I thought,

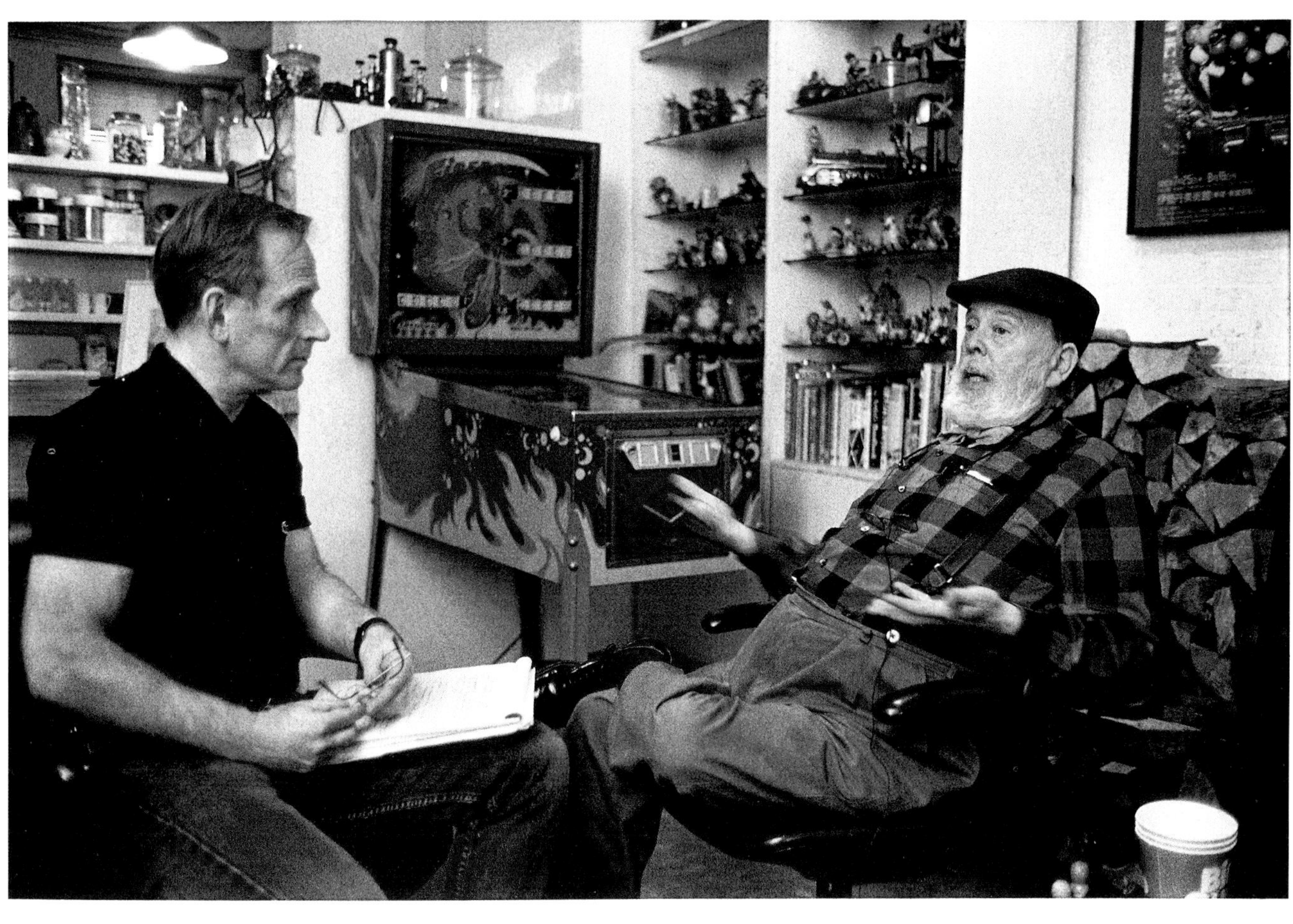

4. Charles Bell and Henry Geldzahler conversing in Bell's studio, 1990

"What's so wrong with illusory space?" Pop artists came along and stuck things on the canvas and said, "Okay, tell me if that's sculpture or if it's painting." The big debate was "Is painting dead?" And I said, "Well, maybe it is," because I did sense that something had run its course, had played itself out.

I had been aware of artists in California who had started bringing figurative work back, Diebenkorn and Park most notably, and of De Kooning's women. However, when Pop came along, suddenly art was a very different thing. Art was no longer the serious work of deadly serious people with their meetings and lectures and arguments and clubiness. Suddenly, art was media and media was art. For me personally, the importance of Pop is that it legitimized the media look, the lens-eye view of the world, in high art. And it made any mode of expression okay. What I mean is: from easel painting to sculpture to tight Realism to blatant advertising and political art, you could co-opt anything in our visual experience and bring it to high art. Many artists started openly using photo-derived source material and unabashedly returned to a kind of classicism; most, except for a few in California, did not know that others were at work in similar ways. In a way, Photorealists were updating Northern European genre painting: I see a similarity between Vermeer's View of Delft *and Robert Bechtle's views of suburbia, between Van Ostade's tavern scenes and Ralph Goings' diners.*

We see the pendulum swing from time to time, and in Photorealism the pendulum swung back from always having to be the newest, most abstract, most intellectually "with it," to embracing the long past as well as the most recent past. I do confess to wishing there were a less restrictive name. "Photorealist" is akin to saying "brush abstractionist" or "masking-tape Neo-Geoist"; it emphasizes only one aspect.

It used to be said that a first-generation Photorealist had to have been in one of three shows: "Twenty-two Realists" at the Whitney, the Documenta of 1972, or Sidney Janis' "Sharp-Focus Realism." There were a couple of prior shows and comments in periodicals, but those three shows in the early seventies caught the world's attention. And by the way, it was electrifying. It was hot news and controversial. I was doing Photorealism by then, but I wasn't known at that time, at least not well enough to be in those shows. I was represented by Lou Meisel, who had a small gallery on 79th and Madison and was also just getting started. Who was going to seek me out? So I was not in those shows, even though I was working with photographs at that time, getting ready for my first one-man show. By sheer persistence, I guess I'm thought of as first-generation, but those shows were indeed important in focusing attention.

Photorealism is still active, but at the same time it's taken a position in history along with all the other movements. There are a lot of overlaps, like with Pop artists or Action painters. Many of these artists are still around making a living, some thriving and in some cases with intense critical attention. We are not in the era of Pop art, but Jasper Johns is doing just fine, as are Roy Lichtenstein, James Rosenquist, and Larry Rivers. There are still people around from earlier periods, like Robert Motherwell and Ellsworth Kelly, who are holding forth. Willem de Kooning still paints. You don't say, "Gee, what's the latest thing in Photorealism?" Instead, you say, "What are the artists who are associated with Photorealism doing now?"

So what are they doing now? Well, most of us who are still working in that sphere are working its outer edges. I could go down the list. Malcolm Morley has completely jumped ship. Audrey Flack is off into a sort of nineteenth-century-style sculpture, which has very little to do with what she was doing before. Don Eddy has gotten much more aesthetic; Ben Schonzeit has become more "painterly," and his new work embraces a Cubist sensibility. Richard Estes is still doing the same thing—same views, same reflections, just better and more refined. Chuck Close, by the nature of his work, is doing the same thing, because he's defined his work as constant reworking, constantly looking for new ways to express repetitive imagery. He's got these eighteen (or some such number) photographs he works from; what he varies is the means to create his images. The Californians are still pretty much in the original mold.

Bell is keenly aware of the process by which photography both informs and alters our daily visual experience. Nonetheless, like David Hockney, he is perceptive to both its potential and its limitations in relation to art. Like Hockney, Bell takes his own photographs, treating them as pages of a sketchbook, having no compulsion to adhere to a particular image. Furthermore, the information contained in the photograph, like that in a diary, is augmented by the memory of the actual subject and the circumstances that led to that particular click of the shutter. While accepting the value of the photograph, Bell is adamant that it is no substitute for the direct experience of looking.

My thesis is that the lens is the premier idiom in this century for communicating visually. The lens-eye view of the world (which is different from the way we see the world with our own binocular vision) pervades our everyday lives. If my aim is to communicate using representational imagery, I can communicate it more persuasively by utilizing the peculiarities of the lens. I've had the progressive realization that the experience of reality is subjective. My paintings look real, but it's a subjective "reality."

People today see more images in one day than people in the Renaissance saw in their entire lives. And what are these present-day images? They are images seen through a lens, the "official" visual reality of this century. Yes, photography was invented in the nineteenth century, and the camera without film (camera obscura and camera lucida) existed long before that, but it came to dominate our visual experience only in the twentieth century. So, if I'm trying to express this culture's reality, I think it's silly not to at least consider the peculiar way that a lens "sees," to at least understand the way the lens distorts our view of reality.

As a means of artistic expression, most photography is limited in its visual staying power. It is the rare exception for an image to stick in our minds. Can you remember a single picture from last Sunday's newspaper? Try this. Recall the imagery of thirty paintings you have seen—not too hard for most of us. Now recall the same number of photographs you have seen—not so easy. Yet the ratio of photos to paintings we have seen must be better than a thousand to one. Another limitation of photography is its one-point fixed perspective and fixed point in time, which is not a lie but rather a half truth. Perhaps this is why many "fine-art" photographers get so excessive with subject matter, seemingly to compensate.

The fact is, it is hard to look at a photo for long, and I feel this has to do with its "split-second" quality. David Hockney does an end run around this with his photo "put-togethers," which approximate the way our eyes naturally dart and explore. In so doing, he adds the element of time, the time it takes to look at different details. In a painting, we intuit a sense of time because of the time it took to make it, and with that knowledge we find ourselves drawn into the painting, more inclined to study it and return to it.

Bell is aware of Renaissance and Newtonian experiments with lenses as well as our common experience with them, and he feels artists can and do use the lens's mechanical attributes to their advantage. He refers to the work of Wayne Thiebaud, an artist he admires, speaking of the radicality of Thiebaud's evocations of San Francisco's streets and hills of houses, their steepness expressed by the look of the telephoto lens. Foreshortening, to be sure, has been around since the Renaissance and is known to every student of traditional art. But it's the telephoto lens, as much as mechanical foreshortening, that we see "behind" these images. Bell cites Thiebaud's paintings as more real than real within the context of our camera-drenched world, the perspective of the telephoto lens allowing us to read them unthinkingly, reflexively. He talks about other aspects of photography as well.

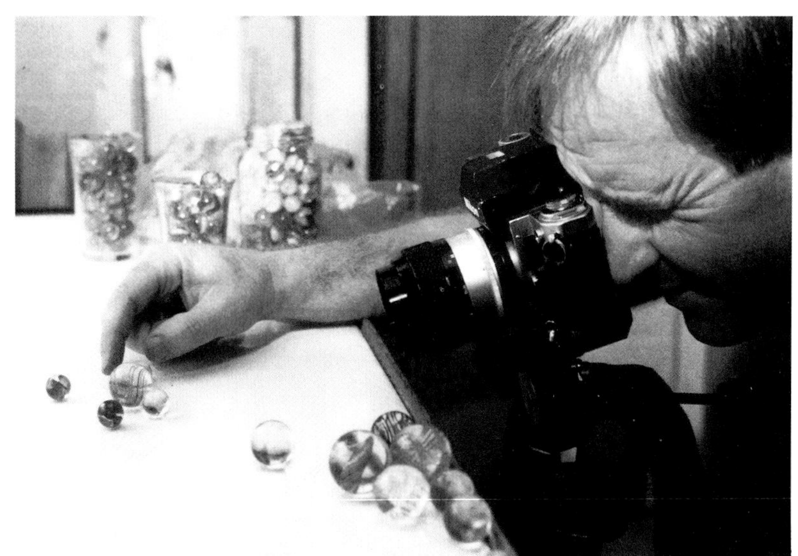

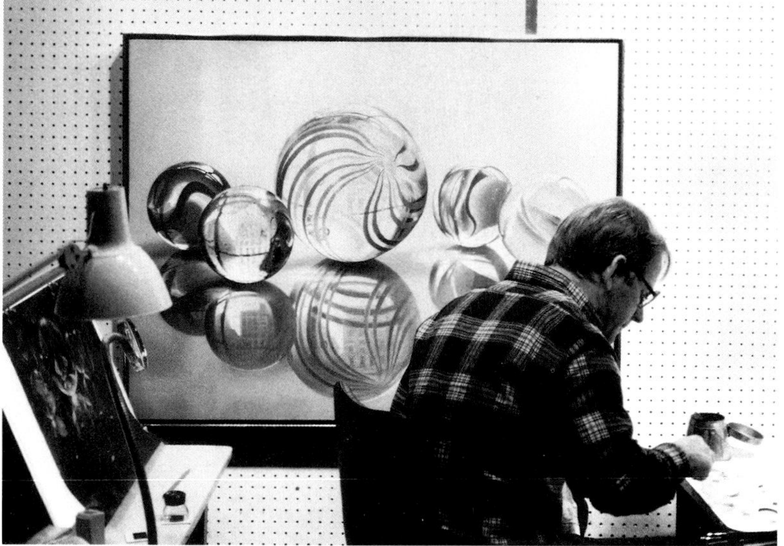

Three steps in the artistic process
ABOVE LEFT: 5. Photographing a setup
ABOVE RIGHT: 6. Working on the canvas from the photograph
BELOW: 7. *Marbles VII* (fig. 109) in progress

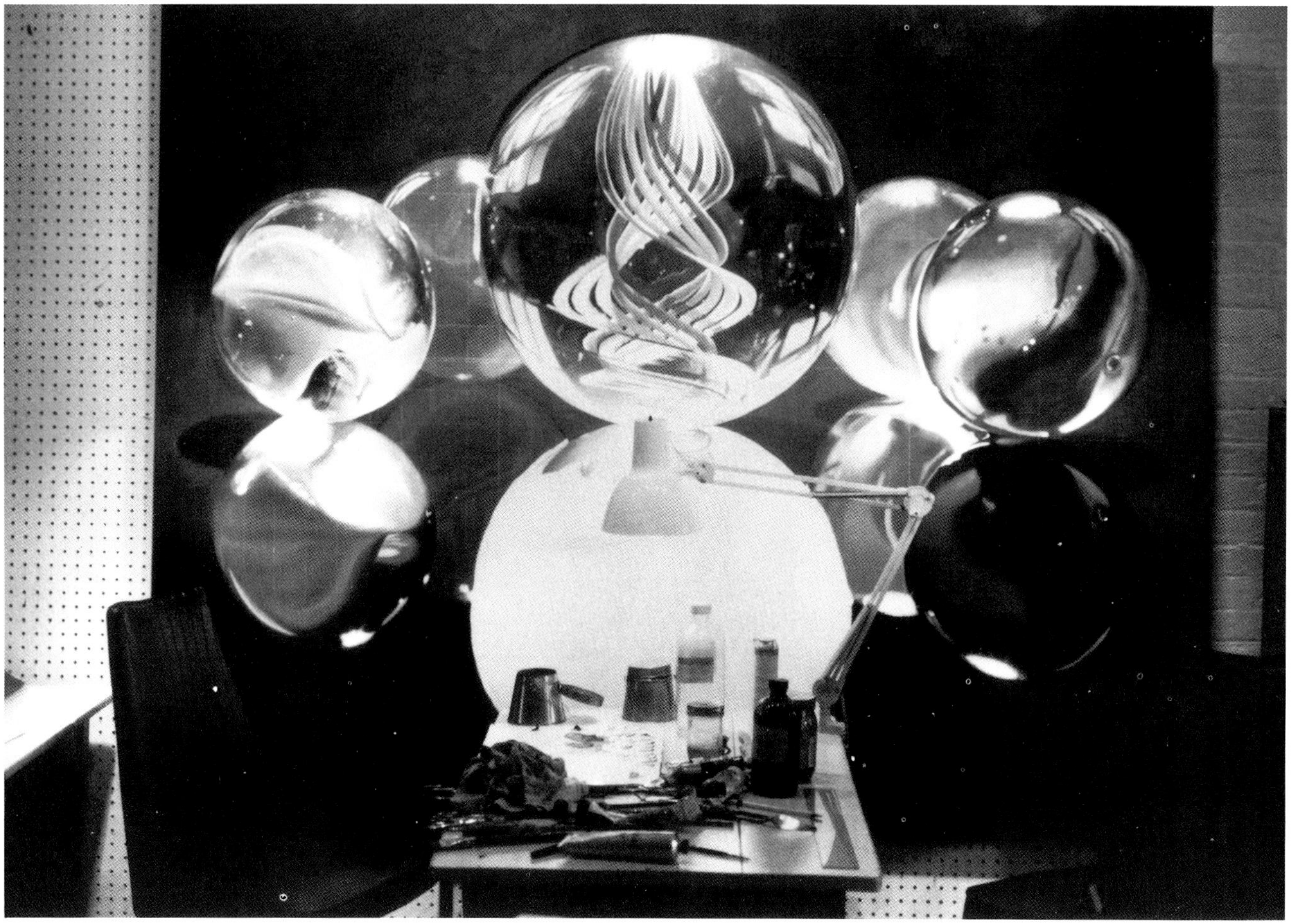

One limitation of photography is the narrow scale of light values it can express. From its darkest to its lightest tone is a range of only three-and-a-half to four f-stops. The eye itself processes a range of light values several times that. On television we've become used to seeing a very limited range of light values, causing shapes and masses in shadows to go abstract. Conversely, in photos, we often see detail in the shadows while accepting burned-out highlights. Also, we've become used to the big *in the compositions we see, big blow-ups in billboard advertisements that are real at a distance but break into abstraction close up. All this becomes to the brain a means of abstraction within the context of reality—even though to say that seems contradictory. For me, these simply become elements for composition.*

I feel a lot of the richness of a painting can occur in the subdued areas and in the shadows, and it can contribute to the overall image. But one time I just decided, what the heck. There was a large section down on the lower right of the photograph, with a shadow in black or some dark, neutral color. I painted it just as it was, thinking I would go in and add detail later. I stood back about twelve or fourteen feet, and I saw that it seemed more real than real. In analyzing why I was getting that feeling, I began to realize how the lens qualifies our visual experience.

The stylized reality that the lens presents dovetails with my own increasing awareness of just how subjective our experience of reality is. Take Chinese perspective (Persian and Indian as well): the person who's in the foreground is just as big or just as little as somebody who's a mile away. It didn't occur to them that anybody would think that was incongruous. Then came the Renaissance and we had perfect three-point perspective. But, for the Chinese, their perspective was just as accurate.

We don't see points of light the same through the lens as through the eye. Take a diamond. Try to photograph a diamond, to make it dazzle the way we see it, and you can't. Besides just the lack of comparative brilliance between the slide and the real thing under light, there are flaws in all lenses; some are better, some worse. Almost all lenses, even with coatings and fine grinding, create Newton Rings, in which all the little highlights have miniature rainbows around them. When I paint them, people say, "Wow, that's so real!" but, of course, it isn't. So in our culture, those things that are idiosyncratic to a lens impinge on our sense of reality, on what looks real to us. But, of course, we know real is subjective, right?

Having given the lens its due, I still feel drawing is the artist's number-one tool. It's a thing an artist has to experience, something like learning to ride a bike. Nobody can tell you. Drawing is like that: you suddenly start seeing a world that you never saw before. Also, if you work from a photograph of a pitcher or a cup and saucer, there may be some sort of aberration in it, a spot or something. I mean I've had students paint the spots on a photograph. I keep saying, "See what is there. See beyond the emulsion to the idea that is there." Drawing is the enabling skill.

People have asked if I ever work without photos and the answer is yes, especially in drawings of people. And I love to spend time down by the West Side Highway drawing things that catch my eye. In my case, the one main reason for the photo is lighting. If I light marbles for a long time in the dramatic way that I like, they will crack, or the refraction may start to burn the cloth or melt the plastic they're on. In the case of the pinballs, the visual raison d'être is to express light coming from within the painting instead of over your shoulder. To give the feeling of a pinball machine glowing in a dark corner of a bar is impossi-

ble, unless I actually put the machine in a dark corner of the studio and I run back and forth fifty feet just to get a look. I can't do that, so I work from a photograph or photographs—I use a composite of many. (And, in fact, I often do have the machine set up in a back corner of the studio.) In the case of the toys, the lighting would be so intense that it would literally blister the paint. You do get a clearer view using your own eyes instead of looking at a picture, but from a practical standpoint I can't be running across the studio fifty feet away and I can't be burning up the subject matter.

Even as a child, Bell was drawing and painting, but the notion of actually making art his lifework did not come until much later. During college (Bell graduated from the University of Oklahoma with a business degree) and in the Navy (as a Reserve Lt., J.G.), he did a lot of looking at and thinking about art, but it was not until about 1964 that he began to take the making of art seriously.

Donti Flores, the artist who taught me briefly in 1965 in his North Beach studio/gallery in San Francisco, told me about an elderly teacher he had studied with. This teacher's thesis was that if you could learn to draw or paint anything you saw, then you could choose to abstract to the degree and in the direction of your choice. His teachings were the antithesis of the "happy-accident" school, the one that says, "Let's enjoy the art experience—thrash around using materials in whatever manner. Come up with something you like, and then if you can repeat it, poof! you've got a style." That was the process of becoming an artist, at least as taught in many schools. The teacher Flores spoke about was just the opposite. He wanted you to do it with control. You want that color? You'd better know exactly how to get it! Donti taught me using the same approach.

My early drawing lessons were an exercise in seeing as much as an exercise in drawing. I devised that saying, "The eye can't truly see what the hand cannot draw," because I found that once you learn to draw with precision, you never see in the same way again. The hand becomes the eye's probe. Later, Flores had me putting my color-mixing exercises and my drawing exercises together. They weren't still lifes for me as much as they were exercises, and yet when I saw what others in San Francisco were doing—artists like Al Proom, an amazing Realist, Jerry Stinsky, Bob Schaefer, and others not well known in New York—I was challenged. So, for three or four years, I was doing still-life paintings on small panels. I was working during the day at a job, a decent job, accounting supervisor at C&H Sugar. I would paint in the evenings and on the weekends, so I couldn't go out in the open air and I really couldn't have models available on a moment's notice. Still life became practical for me: it would be waiting for me when I got home the next evening.

As for early interest in art, I was fortunate to grow up in a school system that taught art each year through junior high. More important, though, were the summer art programs for kids at Tulsa's Philbrook Art Center and family trips to the Gilcrease Museum, where I was mesmerized by the Bierstadts, Morans, and Catlins.

While at the University of Oklahoma, I met Harold Stevenson, who was to become a big influence on me. In the sixties, Harold was doing very large works and exhibiting with Iris Clert in Paris. If he did your portrait, it might be a twelve-foot panel of your elbow. Abstract but real at the same time. I was fascinated by that border. I will always be grateful for his early encouragement of my work. When I finally visited his New York studio, I looked around and decided, "This is where I want to be and what I want to be" and eventually it happened. Harold now shows in New York and Athens and has a studio in Long Island City.

One of my early subjects in San Francisco was water. I'd look down at the reflections of the masts and bows of the boats at Fisherman's Wharf and I'd see the patterns and I'd say that's abstract and yet it's real. I spent many nights and weekends down there photographing the reflections to create these abstract patterns. I loved that. I also like merging imagery, and in that regard Edwin Dickinson and James Rosenquist had a big influence on me.

The decision to come East was a big one—leaving good friends, a good job, and a beautiful city—but my art was becoming increasingly important to me. Having sold a painting for the handsome sum of $350 and having saved $1,200, I decided it was time to plug into the art world and that by definition meant New York. It was 1969. Within days of my arrival, I was showing with Greenwich Gallery in the Village. The following summer, I was invited to show with a new gallery on Upper Madison, the Louis K. Meisel Gallery. I have been with Lou ever since.

In those early days, I was thinking a lot about the kind of art I would throw my energies into. Being here let me see firsthand the work of many artists I had known only through books: Eakins, Homer, Hopper, Sheeler, Vermeer, and Dali among the big names. I spent a good deal of time studying the extraordinary collection at the Frick. I would spend Thursday evenings at the New York Public Library's art reference room. I discovered the work of artists such as Pierre Roy, Aaron Bohrod, Henry Koerner, Walter Murch, John Koch, and especially the "Pajama" group: Paul Cadmus, Jared French, and George Tooker.

The author and critic John Perreault once told me he feels artists use other artists as attractors or deflectors—some pull you into their orbit, some push you away. I felt pulled in by the extraordinary draftsmanship of Dali and Cadmus and Claudio Bravo. I was also drawn to the billboard-sized work of Claes Oldenburg and Rosenquist.

I've never been the kind of artist who feels that what I'm doing is the ultimate aesthetic imperative. I don't feel that what I do invalidates what came before. That very narrow definition of Modernism doesn't appeal to me. One of the better aspects of today's art world is that we can have a wider perspective, one that includes the richness of the past.

I've always had a fascination for objects around me, just like a little boy. Ten-year-old boys always have a pocketful of things, and they'll take them out and say, "Hey, look." It's probably just a little piece of broken glass they found, or a marble, string, or such, yet it's something that fascinates them. I still find wonder in those things. And I like to share that.

Now that I was in New York, I realized it was time to let all these influences coalesce. I had met Will Ching, now my partner, and to give credit where it's due, he was a big influence on my cutting through the quandaries and pursuing what I really wanted to do. My basic decision was, "Maybe painting is *dead, but there's still beauty. And of the things of beauty, I'll choose those in our everyday lives to*

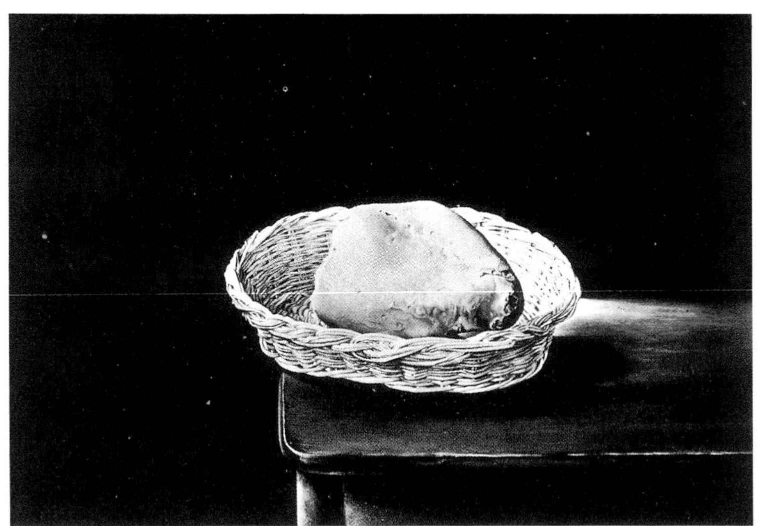

8. Salvador Dali. *Basket of Bread.* 1945. Oil on panel, 13 × 17¾″. Fundación Gala-Salvador-Dali, Figueras, Spain

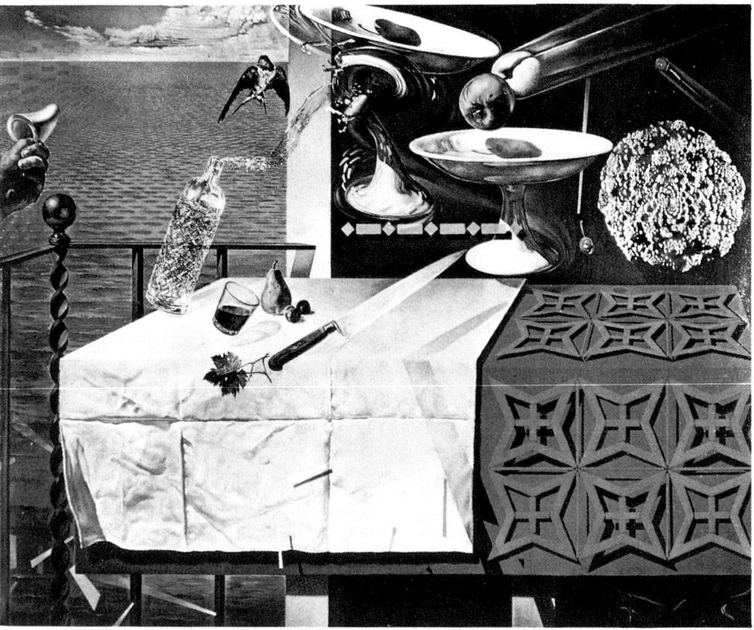

9. Salvador Dali. *Nature Morte Vivante (Still Life—Fast Moving).* 1956. Oil on canvas, 49¼ × 63″. Salvador Dali Museum, St. Petersburg, Florida

Some artists who have influenced Bell's work: Dali, for his great inventive mind coupled with a passion for painting tradition (figs. 8, 9); Rosenquist, for his billboard scale and media-derived subjects (fig. 10); Thiebaud, for his presentation of the "overlooked" common object and radical treatment of traditional foreshortening (figs. 11, 12); Stevenson, for his exploration of scale and the borderline between real and abstract in painting classically oriented subjects (fig. 13); and Sheeler, for his craftsmanship and choice of the unusual and "found" objects as subject matter (fig. 14).

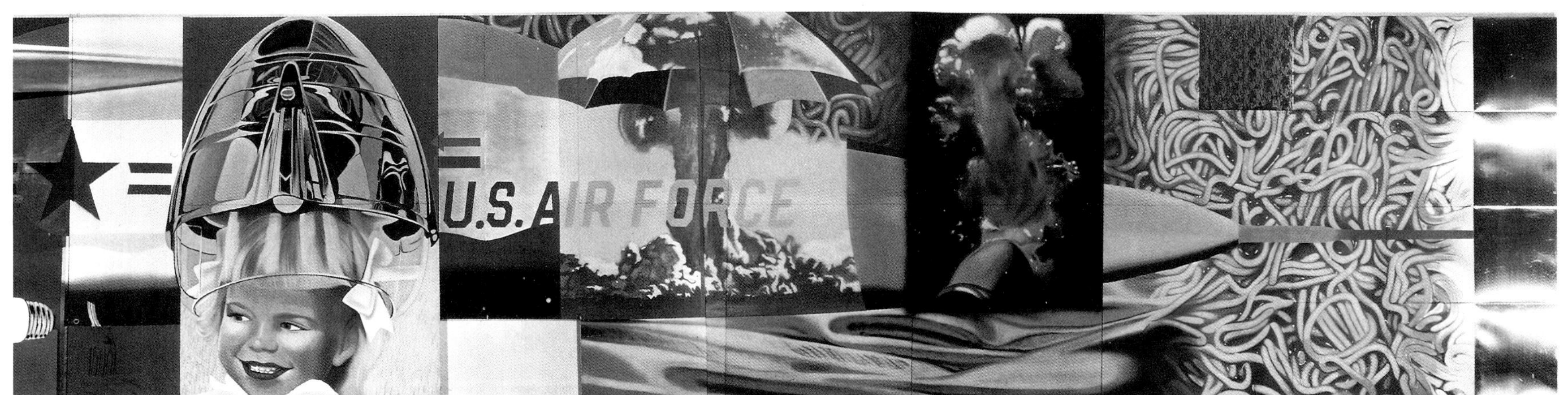

10. James Rosenquist. *F-111* (detail). 1965. Oil on canvas with aluminum, 12 × 86′. Private collection

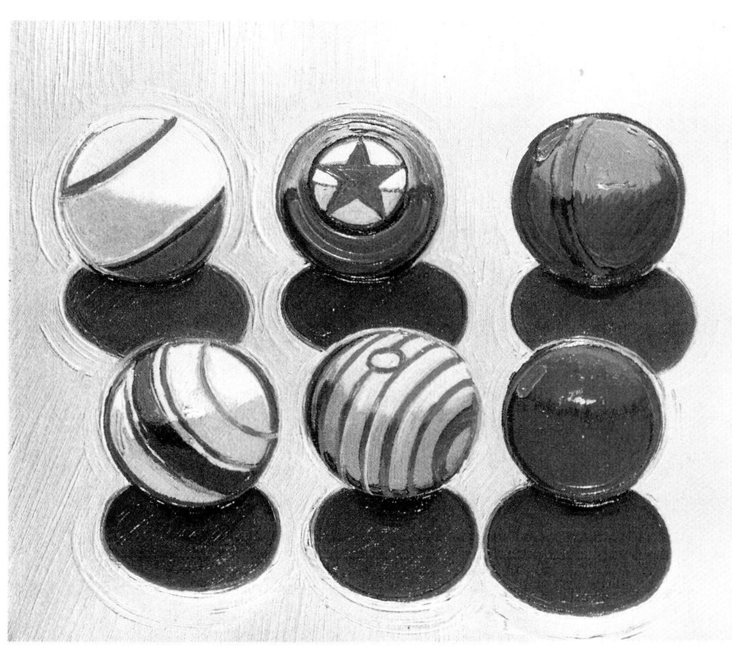

11. Wayne Thiebaud. *Pool Balls*. 1967. Oil on canvas, 12⅛ × 14⅛″. Private collection. Courtesy Allan Stone Gallery, New York

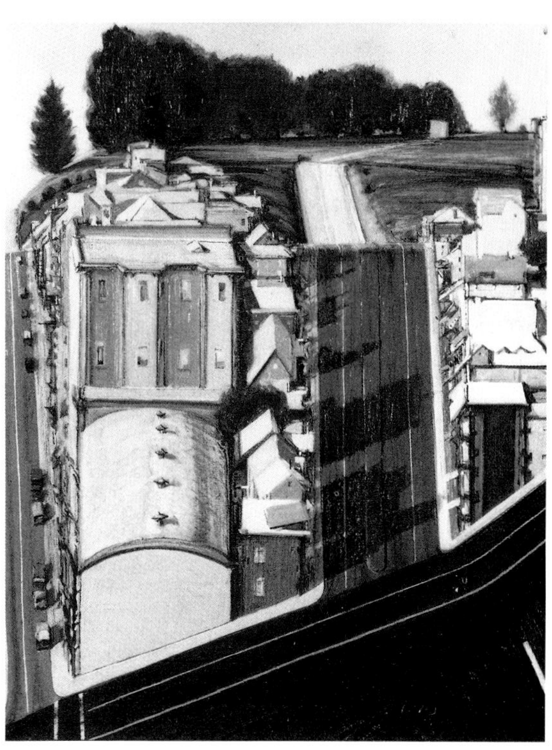

12. Wayne Thiebaud. *Holly Ridge Park*. 1980. Oil on canvas, 28 × 22″. Private collection. Courtesy Allan Stone Gallery, New York

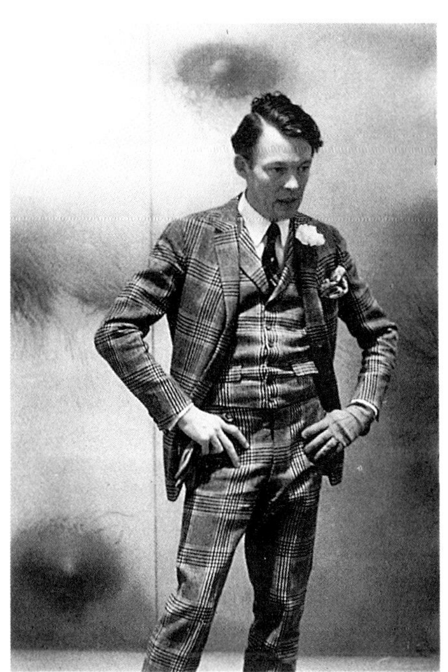

13. Harold Stevenson standing in front of one section of his painting *New Adam* (1962–63, 9 × 48′) at the Richard Feigen Gallery, New York, 1964

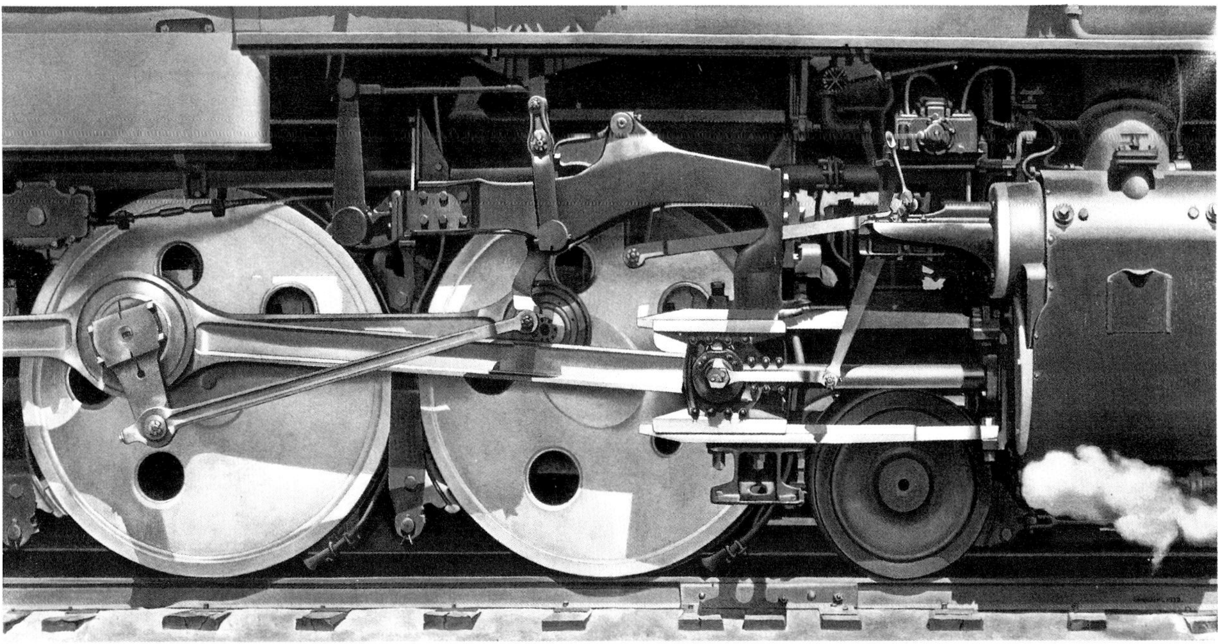

14. Charles Sheeler. *Rolling Power*. 1939. Oil on canvas, 15 × 30″. Smith College Museum of Art, Northampton, Massachusetts. Purchased 1940

portray. I'll paint things we take for granted and often overlook." I was prepared to be an anachronism, not knowing that others were coming to similar conclusions independently. Essentially, I said, "Screw it. I'll do what I want!" The fact is, I think that's what an artist should do—take the risk and follow your own path.

A story Bell relates with both wit and compassion concerns his brief relationship with a currently underestimated artist, Salvador Dali, and his wife, Gala. What follows here is vignetted from several sources, all in Bell's own words, and tells as much about him as a person and an artist as it does about Dali.

For as far back as I can remember (literally), the work of Salvador Dali has fascinated me. Yes, his persona and his work were by their nature "irrational," but his exquisite craftsmanship and his solid embrace of painting traditions made him, for me, one of the very few truly rational artists at work at mid-century. So my meeting him was, I confess, daunting.

In the early days of Photorealism, Dali was still quite active as a painter and doing a lot of artistic exploration. He was very interested in the phenomenon of the New Realism. Hyperréalisme, *he called it. In 1975, Dali, Gala, and their entourage had come to visit an opening of an Audrey Flack exhibition at Lou's gallery. There were about twenty people clustered around him—dealers, models, French businessmen, transvestites in Elizabethan costume, very strange. Dali had his mink cape on and was carrying his large gold cane. Gala, looking regal, was in a floor-length brocade gown.*

Dali asked to see more Hyperréalisme. *So Lou ushered them into the back office, where there was one of my early gumball-machine paintings. Dali turned around and said of my painting,* "Magnifique." *And then twenty other people murmured,* "Magnifique." *So, it was really a hoot—silly, like some sort of caricature of everybody aping the master. While Dali conversed with Lou about Realism in general, Gala grabbed me by the hand, tightly. She had a wrenching grip. She pulled me over to the painting, pointed to a couple of places, and said, "I like this. I like this." She then dragged me out into the gallery, in front of Audrey's pieces, and said, "You must never paint like this" (she didn't like the idea of airbrush at all). Then she said, "Come." And she pulled me back to my painting, saying, "You see this area? You could do better." It was true. She had a fantastic eye.*

Two days later, I was summoned to meet Dali in his apartment at the St. Regis Hotel. Thinking I had been invited to a party, I was surprised when the door opened and it was just Dali. After we talked for a few moments, he told me to look over at an old dresser, upon which he had placed two mirrors and two drawings, each about eighteen inches square, set upright in such a way as to form a W (the two mirrors were the inside panels). He said, "Seet, seet," so I got the idea I was to sit in front of the dresser. He kept pointing at his nose. Finally, I got the message that I was supposed to put my nose at the intersection of these two mirrors. When I did that, one eye could see into one mirror and the other eye into the other. Each mirror reflected one of the two drawings, which were identical insofar as separate drawings from the same photograph can be. Because they were not exactly the same, the new image danced stereoptically.

And because the three-dimensionality had not been planned, there was also something rather serendipitous about it. Being so illusive and fleeting, it was quite a visual experience.

Well, Dali had wanted to assert, in some dramatic way (he was good at that), that he was the grandfather and patron of Hyperréalisme. *He wanted to give me a photograph from which each of us would make a drawing; the drawings would be our own, but their dimensions would be identical for the sake of the stereoptics. They would then be displayed in a show, using the mirrors, with his drawing on one side and my drawing on the other. He asked me if I was interested, to which I replied, "Of course, I would be honored, Monsieur Dali." And he said, "Goood. Goood. If it sells, feefty-feefty." I got a big kick out of that.*

No sooner had he uttered those words than in swept Gala. She stated that it would just not do that I was without coat and tie (my friends having insisted that I go looking like an artist). So I wore one of Dali's ties. And I forget... I think I wore his coat. The three of us went to dinner. I was so nervous that to this day I don't remember where we ate. It was in a hotel dining room quite close to the St. Regis. We walked along Park Avenue in the late evening of a very warm Sunday. She was in another full-length gown of heavy material, he had his cape on and carried his cane. We were proceeding down Park Avenue, and I swear nobody who passed us noticed, not even a fleeting glance of recognition. I thought that was pretty strange.

Dinner turned out to be a banquet of sorts, a menagerie of at least thirty guests. I was seated at Dali's right, so there was much speculation as to my identity. Dali would carry on with his crazy talk, throwing grapes and ordering champagne all around. Interspersed between the antics were questions in straightforward English to me, like "Do you keep your brushes clean?" Or he would say, "What brand of paint do you use? Do you prefer Old Holland over Blockx?" He was delighted that I had read his Fifty Magic Secrets of Painting, *and we discussed a few of the secrets. I realized that he was an old man having a hell of a good time putting people on. He could pop right out of it when needed. It was a show and he loved it.*

As the evening ended, he said, "We will be in touch." But something happened, his plans were changed and he was out of the country for about a year. The next thing I heard, he had done the show by himself, using his own work with the mirrors. And it was stunning.

He seemed to have been fond of my work through the years, enough to say so. Tom Messer [former director of the Guggenheim] *told me that Dali occasionally inquired of my work, inquired of me, and I was flattered to hear it. The last time I saw Dali and Gala, we were at a show of his, the three of us sitting in a huge potted plant on the top ring at the Guggenheim. They were an amazing couple. Dali did not always paint at his best, but when he did, he was one of the great artists of this century.*

In the early eighties, Bell began a series of paintings using toys from his large collection. The purpose of these works was to explore and to express his newfound sense that factual reality and our perception of it are different, indeed. Toys are by their nature symbols; they trigger imagination, memories of stories learned and invented, and cultural myths and values. By this simple means, Bell invoked layers of meaning. The resultant allegories, shaped by the choices of composition, merged the traditions of "history" painting with vestiges of childhood wonder.

Maybe it's the age, or maybe it's my age, but this thing called reality is not very real. It's very, very subjective. And there is no great honesty in a photograph; it's just one way to convey visual information. When you think about it, a photograph is not a whole lot more accurate than language itself. How do we convey ideas in today's world? There's mathematics. Scientists can read and converse directly through equations, but few of us do that. To some extent, music conveys ideas. Just think of the scores of silent films or even current films. They can signal to us what to feel even before the action on the screen does. Actually, most of us are limited in our language ability. Few people express themselves particularly well, few people are multilingual. Yet language is a primary means of communicating with others.

Visual language is, at least, of equal importance as verbal language. How else but through the mechanism of the camera and associated electronic media do we have a recorded image? Yet the photograph is as faulty in conveying ideas as words are. It's not that photographs are really dishonest, but that they present a subjective reality. The painter can utilize that.

Anyway, that's what I mean when I talk about the subjectiveness of reality. Within a painting, everything can be totally false and yet it will be called Realism. I mean false on purpose.

One day, I'd come from seeing my second Kenny Sharf show. His is a daffy Surrealism, based on the Jetsons and monsters with big eyes and stuff like that. I was challenged and upset. I was pissed that it was so powerful, colorful, and vibrant, and I came back despairing I would ever do anything as bright, daffy, and strong all at once. Then I thought, "Toys." Well, there it was, in my own backyard.

I set about to rediscover the toys using their symbolic dimensions. It has to do with the layers of what "real" means. You take a piece of plastic; it's oil out of the ground. You take a piece of pot metal or tin and you shape it into something, and in the shaping of it you assign it a symbolism that exists only in your mind. A piece of tin turns into what we call a duck. Maybe it happens to be a duck that's acting like a person. Well, here's a duck acting like a person and we know it's not a person and we know it's not a duck, yet we know it's a duck acting like a person, but still it's just a piece of metal. So what is real? And then I paint it and that's not real, and I probably change it around so much that it can't possibly exist, even as a piece of tin, and we still call it real. Then people say, "Well, you just took a photograph and you copied it." Wow! What I was exploring was the multilayered nature of "reality" as we experience it.

I put the toys in a tableau just to add another set of meanings. I sometimes used takeoffs on artists or in some cases on particular compositions. Each major painting in the Toy series has its own story. For instance, there's a study on the essence of Rousseau [Nature Study, 1985]. *It's a Godzilla-type metal dinosaur thing with a jutting breast full of plastic rockets, so it's sort of a "living" robot. The dinosaur form harks back to prehistory and yet it's also a robot that refers to the future—neither of which will ever come together in time—and yet the object's just a little piece of pot metal in "reality." Then I stuck it in a setting, a jungle scene that's all made out of plastic foliage; it's not real either. Then I put all of that in front of a postcard of a Rousseau, just for the sake of reference. You see, he had created his own stylized world, too, which he knew never existed. To put this fantasy all together in one still life and to have it called Realism! That was one of my exercises and my fun with what's real and what isn't.*

If I say this is a real flower but the plastic flower that looks like it isn't real, I don't actually mean that literally. They're both real, but one is imitating the other. I was reading a wonderful book called The Transformation of the Commonplace *by the critic Arthur Danto, a brilliant man. In coming to terms with the age-old question of "What is art?" Danto mentions an imaginary warehouse. In it is stored every object that mankind has ever created. Now pick a schoolteacher, a warehouseman, or a kid off the street and send this person in to bring out all of the "art." What would be brought out? But let's take it a step further. If next door to it is another warehouse and in that warehouse is an exact replica of everything that's in the first warehouse, now which is the art?*

If I paint a painting of the Mona Lisa and I show it to Lou Meisel and say, "Lou, this is a terrific painting, I painted the Mona Lisa," he would say, "It's a copy." I say, "Oh no, I painted it." But he'd insist it's a copy, and most people would agree. But wait a minute. Let's say I take a Rodin sculpture and create a painting from it. Now my painting is clearly of the Rodin sculpture. Do I say it's a copy? Well no, but certainly the art in my painting—the "art" in my art—flows from Rodin. But now I paint you and suddenly it's all different. Yet as a painter I painted you, I painted the Rodin, I painted the Mona Lisa. It's all painting. Well, why is some bogus and some not? Where is the art in the art? So, this playing with the toys was a little bit of my exploration into that. Where is the art? Is it here or is it there? Is "real" a quantifiable measurement or only a perception?

An artist finds new directions, new areas to explore, by combining past experiences with energies drawn from the present. Bell is currently reaching out to new subject matter and new media and techniques, particularly printmaking. He is drawing upon his many years of experience with the computer in order to explore its potential in video art, animation, and image manipulation. Yet, his current thinking shows an introspection, a reaching within, a thinking reluctant to draw quick conclusions. Referring to his future work, he says, "I know what it will feel like, I just don't know yet what it will look like."

Right now, most of the major works I'm producing are still in one of my old series, most recently, the pinball-machine paintings. I've found a way to extend that imagery by creating machines that don't exist. It's intriguing for me to pursue that, but my mind is on other things as well. I want to get back to the Surreal context. My best defense of Realism is that I've never dreamed of stick figures. I've never dreamed about a person who looked like a De Kooning woman. I've never, through the means of a dream, entered into the world of Van Gogh's imagery or Kandinsky's or Julian Schnabel's. Dreams are snippets of real experience. I would like to create an art that communicates, but does so at a subverbal, subconscious level. I'm convinced that Realism—and I don't mean pretty pictures or tabletop pictures of apples and oranges, but the fractured imagery that's akin to our dreaming—seems to be the best way to communicate at this level across generations, across cultures. This train of thought is leading me toward Surreal imagery. By that I mean the spirit *of Surrealism and not the visual clichés that have developed over time. I want to get back into and extend the spirit of Surrealism. Of course, Freud was the big influence on the Surrealists, but I'm strongly influenced by Jung. I think that's why I'm so affected by the Joseph Campbell lectures, since he applied and extended Jungian thinking.*

The dream and the art object, or the way we relate to an art object, are very similar. They're both freewheeling. There's a spontaneity and näiveté that one can feel in experiencing both an art object and a dream. Neither is bound by logic or time.

When we dream, we cannot distinguish between that experience and the real experience that we are dreaming. If in the dream I walk through a door, my experience of doing that is no different from walking through that same door while in a waking state. And yet, if I dreamed I was walking through that door right there last night, and this morning I walk through that same door, I will remember the dream and know the difference. There's a paradox there. We can distinguish between our dream world and the real world, and yet at the time of the experience, they are identical. As I said, I have never personally dreamed a stick figure. The realization of that keeps telling me that if my dreams are fragments of reality, then the rather rarefied version of Realism that I am getting into in my art is aesthetically valid.

I have a hunch the computer may be the "sketchbook" that leads to this kind of imagery. Computers, as art tools, in the past were disappointing. Now, with scanners, affordable software, high-resolution and "photoreal" palettes, I see a potential for exploring merged, manipulated, and even perhaps moving imagery.

The toys were a spiraling out, not only with subject matter but also with mediums. I want to embrace all kinds of printmaking—etchings in particular—as well as drawings and watercolors. I love line work and it's a good way to gobble up a lot of images fast. You can get them done "express." Right now, a major painting takes me three to six months. My mind is three years ahead, and my schedule is months behind. I don't particularly want to be the kind of artist who cranks out two paintings a day. I can't imagine the imagery that would interest me and be expressed that quickly. I like what I'm doing. It's just that I'm not keeping up with my mind, and for that reason I want to spiral out.

A student recently asked Charles two questions. First, is art spiritual?

It depends on whether you mean spiritual as religious. Do you mean spiritual as having some centuries-old liturgical symbolism, or do you mean creating a mood that seems transcendental? You know, my feeling is that the best art is a celebration of life—of humanity and the visual experience. There is a spiritual element in that. I've often thought of art as having the quality of haiku poetry. In that connection, I wait for the "aha!" factor, a burst of knowing; it almost makes you laugh. Try channeling your attention down to composing, say, six marbles. You actually open up new worlds of unbelievable combinations and permutations. Through this narrow channeling of attention, visual possibilities open out. Sooner or later, it happens. "Aha!" Now it's right. Now it works. It's subverbal, but you know it when you see it. There is spirituality in that process.

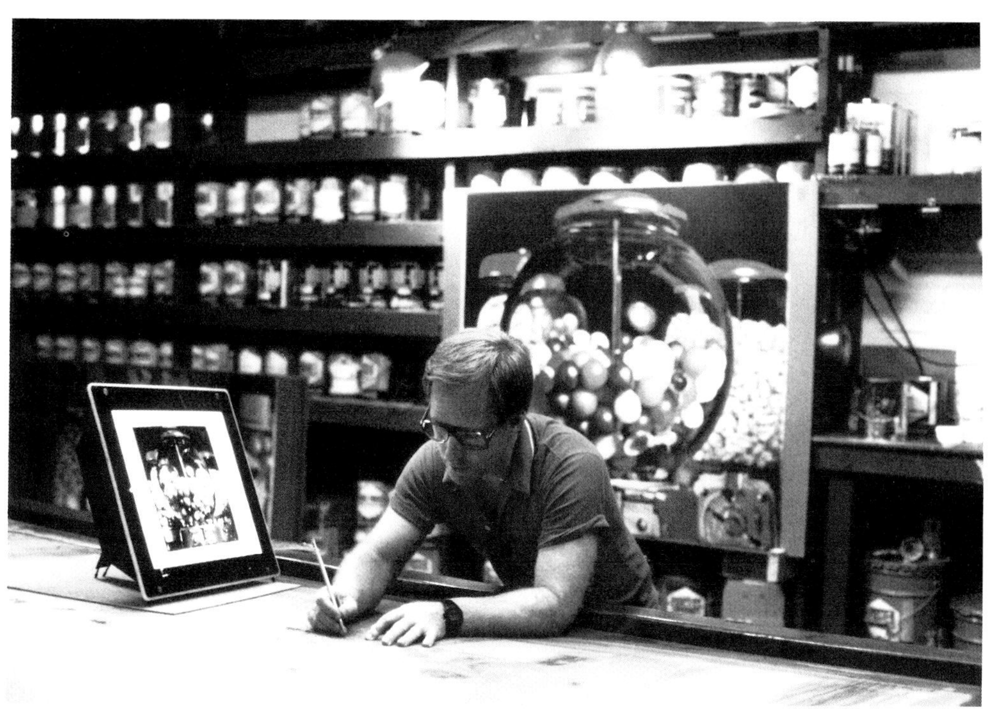

15. Charles Bell working directly on the screen for the *Ultimate Gumball* serigraph (in progress in the background; fig. 192), at Editions Lassiter-Meisel, 1980

And second, how do you determine the best in art?

Judging "the best art" is a tricky one. It's partly a function of one's time in history, one's place, and one's own changing experiences of life. I often wonder if a Bugatti or a Mercedes looks better because it is *better or because I know what it is. Can we judge the Mona Lisa naïvely? Probably not, but I do know this: whenever you are in the presence of a great work of art, you will also sense the strong presence of the artist, even across the centuries.*

For the artist, the goal of art is not to reach the greatest number of people. So, what is it? I think it's a process of self-discovery. It's a way of communicating inner ideas and commenting on the world we find ourselves in. I think art has to be of and about this world.

Art today has to be about our own experience of life. There were times in the past when it was a means of recording history. Those aims have been supplanted by documentary photographs and films. There was a time when art was primarily a means to make spiritual concepts concrete for the masses. All that has been superseded. Today it's a personal journey. In a post-Freudian world, that's what's left to us.

Consider the lifework of the great artists. They were out more to please themselves than you. If they had been out to please you more, then they would have been illustrators, artists working on "assignment." Name a great artist and you'll find someone on a personal journey in life, and the art is just the footprints of that journey. For me, that's it.

All good artists share one strength: they recognize that in their work they have discovered their own individual subject matter. Whether it is Philip Guston, whose subject matter, if you look at his entire career, seems to be his brushstroke, the way he laid down paint, the exploration of his own psyche in his own handwriting. Or whether it's Ellsworth Kelly, whose subject matter is really the distillation to the essential nub of those things he finds around him. If you look at someone like Charles Bell, the exercise there was to find an area that resonated for him but that hadn't been described visually before. And he found himself, rather nostalgically, very much in love with Americana, with the period in which he grew up, as we all are, with the idea that we live in a throwaway culture, yet we don't really throw everything away but instead recycle it in funny ways. And one of the ways we recycle it is through thrift shops, antique shops, and flea markets.

I think what Bell is doing is recycling a whole corner of society—its childhood, its toys, its games—as it grows older. Notice the element of chance in much of the work, the dark corners of bar rooms with billiard tables, the pinball machines, the slot machines, and the casino mentality. These kinds of things, which we are not necessarily particularly proud of or push forward in our lives, are the ones Bell memorializes in some way.

Another clue to understanding an artist's work is by the art traditions drawn upon to ground it. Many of the artists whom Bell feels directly affected by—individuals as diverse as Salvador Dali and James Rosenquist—have already been mentioned. In addition, certain particularly American traditions play a profound part in his work. The fascination with light in paintings by the Luminists, the love of the common object found in William Harnett's and John Frederick Peto's works, and the verisimilitude sought by Thomas Eakins and Charles Sheeler can all be sensed.

Bell's work also reflects a European influence—the opposition between the Northern and Southern sensibilities, especially as expressed during the Early Renaissance. The Southern, the Italian, comes out of Greece and Rome and has much to do with Platonic ideas of perfection, in which you are born knowing everything and spend the rest of your life recognizing it again. Beauty is up there somewhere, and you strive toward it. Think of the whole Renaissance experience in the South, and that's what it's about. In the North—and I think that Bell is more a Northern artist—they begin, as in a Memling or a Van Eyck, with the very reality of what's before them and the attempt to render that. But the spirituality, the search for eternals, doesn't stop at the surface: it's in the way the form is born, the way the form supports the surface.

Somebody once said that the difference between Flemish art and Italian art is that it's cold in Flanders and hot in Italy. In Italy they sleep naked, in Flanders they sleep under the covers with pajamas on; each place has a different kind of sensual idea about the world. I think there's a grain of truth there, too. I don't know how Charles Bell sleeps, but there is a sensuality in his pictures. It's not the sensuality of the naked body or the naked feelings. It's socialized, civilized. It has the aura of the society he grew up in—the rational, modern world rather than the older, prescientific one in which you were buffeted by the vicissitudes of nature. Bell's is an art that's involved in the long term, that has the ambition of being around for a long time, that stems from experiences that began a long time ago.

And, of course, we observe Charles Bell as a living artist at the leading edge of time, functioning in the world that he encounters today. There is no question that it is the "hard-to-do" aspect of Photo-realist paintings that first attracted the eye of the general art public. The heroic stories and legends of Jackson Pollock and Willem de Kooning had done something toward humanizing the art process, but it was undoubtedly Pop art—with its celebration of the common object and its images drawn from the media—that made the idea of art attractive to greater and greater numbers of people.

To put art's newly won popularity in context, we must also allude to the growth of museums in the Western world. The auction market, which has predicted and ridden the crest through a steady, delirious gain in prices (now still high, if less giddy), has dramatized this growth in the media—the very same media that paved the way to legendary status, in the public's mind, for mad Van Gogh, naughty Gauguin, and crippled, courageous Toulouse-Lautrec. To take this process one step further, it must have to do with the wealth, the stored labor, in capitalist economies, which has to find its expression in one way or another.

If we keep tracking the phenomenal success of and need for art in our culture today, we might eventually get to its source. Yet what is undeniably clear is that artists today intuit their own way within a seductive but not altogether ideal world. Bell is not aloof to this world, but neither does he chase the fad. If he was not easily locked into or annihilated by the designation Photorealist in the seventies, neither will he abandon his technique in favor of something current for its own sake in the nineties. It is in his other love, computer science, that I see his likely future innovation: in new ways, to convey information as subject matter by adapting older, probably painstaking (*pains*taking) techniques. Thus, as an artist must, Bell will remain simultaneously both a creature of his times and an individual with his own characteristic manner of observing the world and recording it.

(Incidentally, Bell's great success in Japan has a lot to do both with the Japanese interest in the history of technology and with the fact that his subject matter is immediate but also distant from their own culture. Bell is digging up his past, he's a computer expert, he's technologically very sophisticated, and yet he pulls out of himself a machine that works on electricity and a spring, in which you bing something or bang something. I think, without their realizing it, the Japanese are fascinated by that, without being able to understand why. Gertrude Stein once said about America, "It's the oldest country in the world that entered the twentieth century first." Well, I think Japan might be the oldest country in the world that entered the twenty-first century first.)

In the final analysis—beyond discussions of influences, internal or external—all art is about discovery. I think the interest in Bell's work is the interest in self-discovery, in showing us a corner of the world, a corner of the room, that we never really looked into before. That corner, which we thought of as negligible, in fact can be made monumental and can be made permanent and memorable. In so doing, we find ourselves reconnected to the feelings of discovery and wonder that we all possess and need to share. I think that's what it's about.

THE IMAGES

By Louis K. Meisel

Throughout its history in art, Realism has concerned itself with three subjects: faces, places, and things or, in more conventional art terms, portraits, landscapes, and still lifes. The most notable and innovative form of Realism in the last half of the twentieth century has been, and most likely will remain, Photorealism. And of those working in the Photorealist mode today, Charles Bell is without argument the leading still-life artist: he has defined and staked out an exclusive, highly individual territory.

In 1969, when I first met Bell and he joined my gallery on Madison Avenue, he was painting small pictures (usually no larger than nine by twelve inches) of fruits and vegetables, bottles and glass, shells and butterflies. The work was disciplined and precise and demonstrated an intense understanding of paint and how to manipulate it. Part of his learning experience and formative years, these forty to fifty small paintings from the sixties are pre-Photorealism and relate more to earlier types of American painting, especially the trompe-l'oeil works of Harnett, Peto, Haberle, and Chalfant of a century ago. These paintings by Bell are poorly documented, but about three quarters of them are included herein for reference purposes (figs. 16 to 47; most are oil on board).

These early paintings do have one importance: they are the first in which the artist expressed an interest in how to paint light—light as reflection, light as transparency, and light distorted by diffusion. While such experiments were not innovative in themselves, they did lead Bell to consider how the elusive qualities of light could be portrayed in original ways and eventually enabled him to develop new artistic approaches. Light is, for me, the single most important consideration in discussing Bell's work and in tracing the development of his career; of secondary but obvious significance are the works' large scale and subject matter related to Pop art.

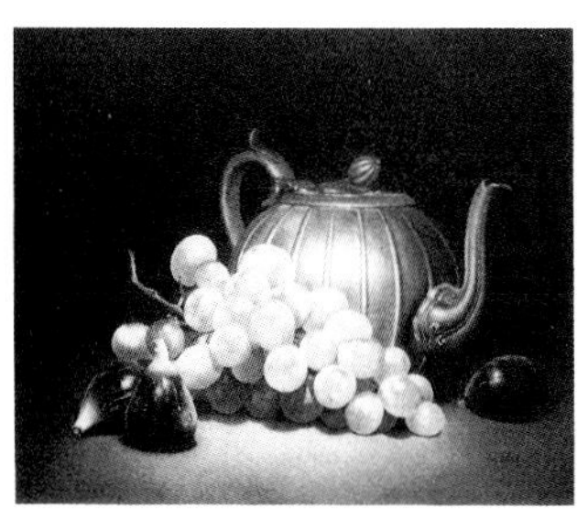
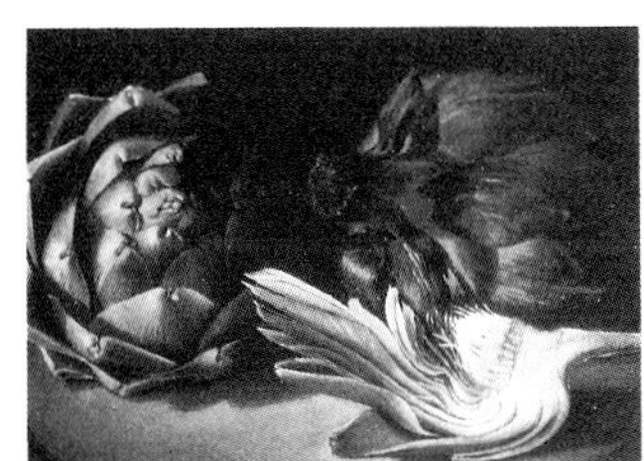
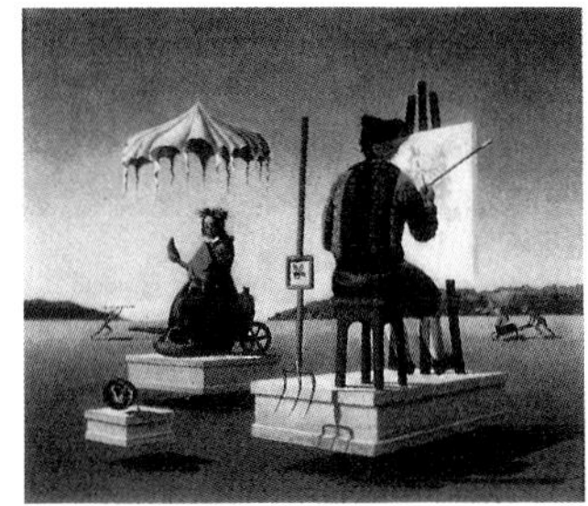
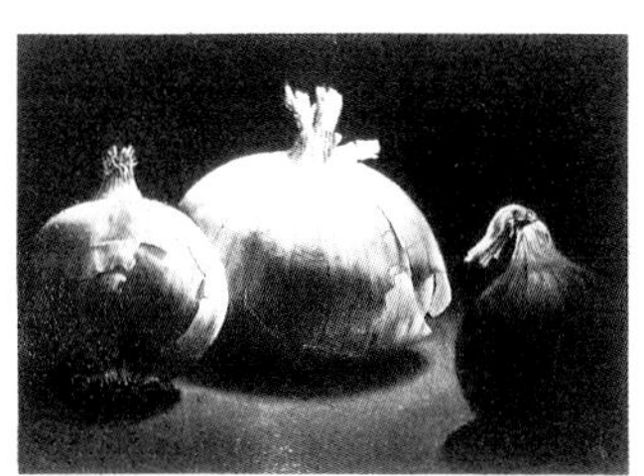
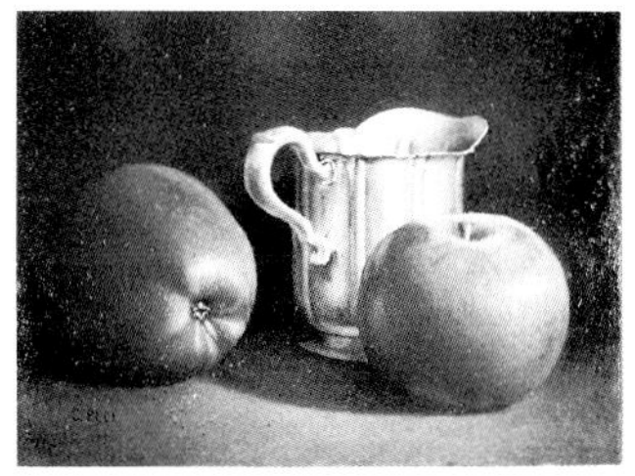
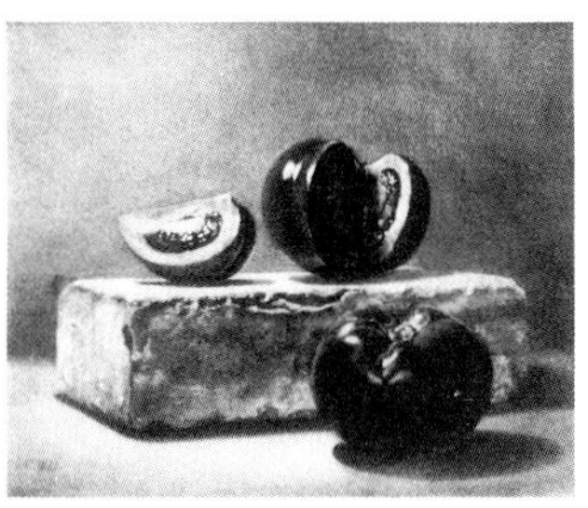
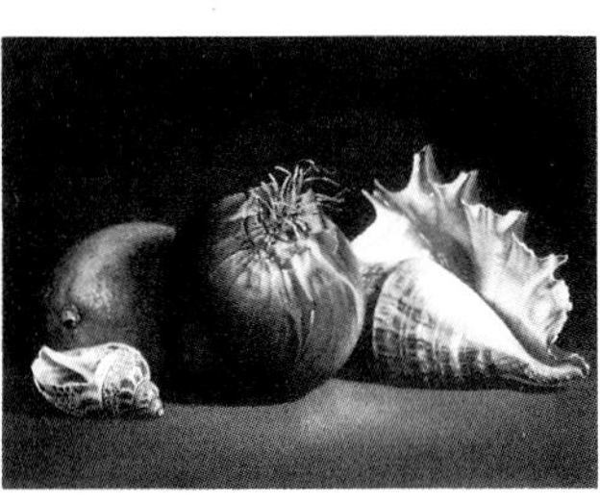
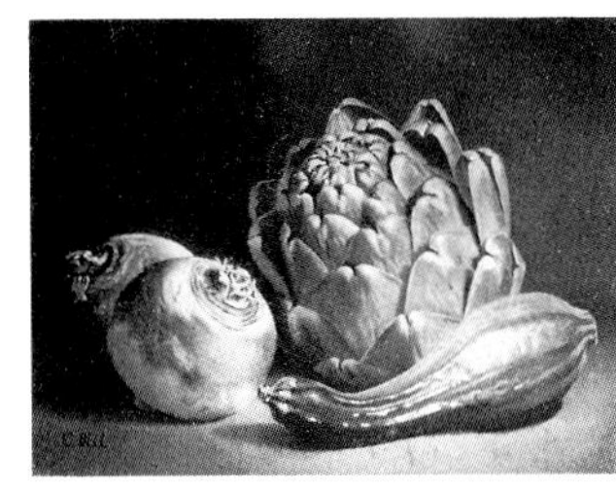
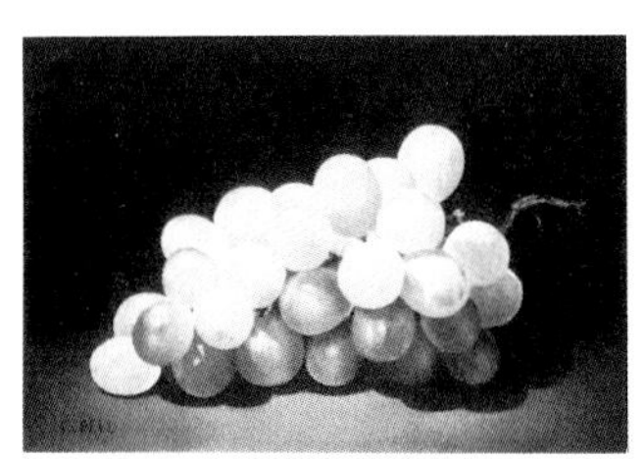
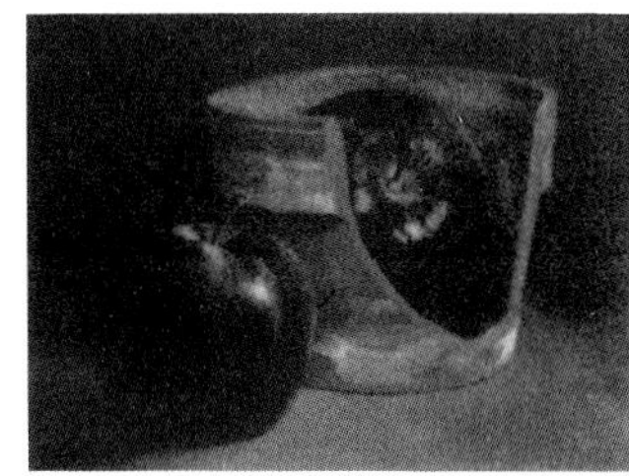

ABOVE AND FOLLOWING TWO PAGES: 16–47. Early works, oil on panel, 1965–69; sizes generally range from 4 × 6″ to 9 × 12″

The first significant step in Bell's artistic evolution was his sudden realization of how scale would help him answer some of the questions he had posed for himself concerning representation. By increasing the size of objects many times, Bell is better able to involve himself in their intrinsic reality. (To carry this process to its furthest extreme would be to use an instrument that would show molecules and atoms and then to reconstruct an object from that level up.) Imparting a great deal of interest and charisma, the enlarged scale in Bell's work is dramatic and captivating to the viewer. His last painting of the sixties, the six-foot-high *Raggedy Ann No. 1* (fig. 48), completed in December 1969, was the first painting of his career as a true Photorealist. It was the first large-scale blowup and the first painting to give a clear prediction of how Bell's career was going to develop.

In the spring of 1970, Bell brought two more versions of this painting to my gallery (1970; see fig. 48 note and fig. 49). At the time, they seemed outrageous and astounding; groups of passersby stopped and stared into the windows. A city bus driver actually halted his bus twice a day in front of the gallery to point the Raggedy Ann out to his passengers. Bell completed this series of images with a seated version holding a baseball (1970; fig. 52).

In 1971 Bell began to focus on the issue of light again. In his new giant format, however, all the tiny details had added so much complexity that he had to find a way of gathering enough information about them in order to make the final work visually convincing. Always interested in technology and particularly in photography, he naturally turned to the camera, its varied lenses and sophisticated darkroom equipment, to capture all that was elusive to the naked eye. With the camera, he could set up and light a still life on a small platform in any way he desired, photograph it in many different focuses

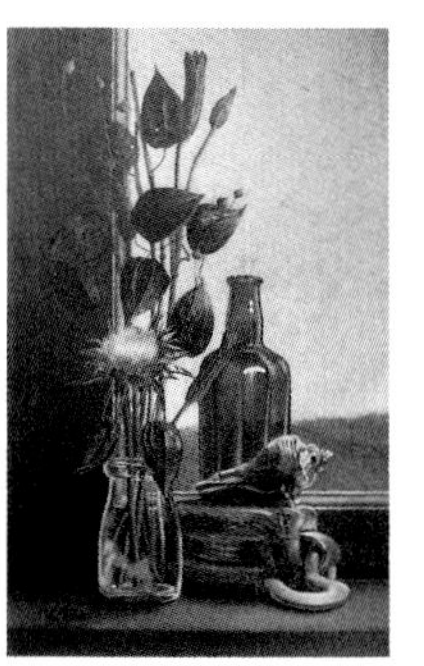
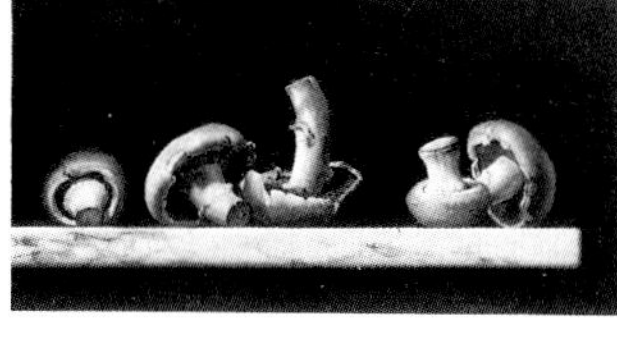
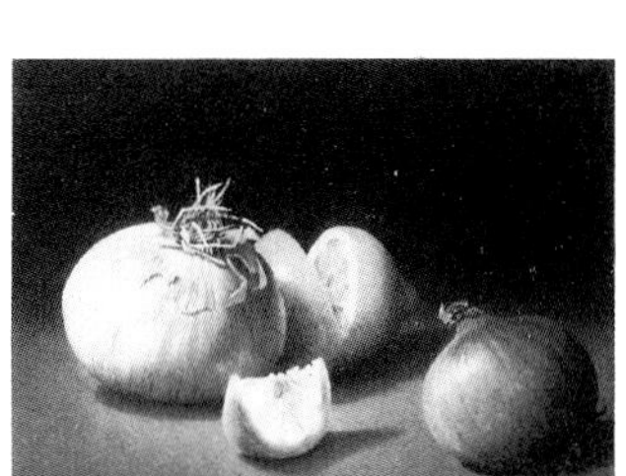
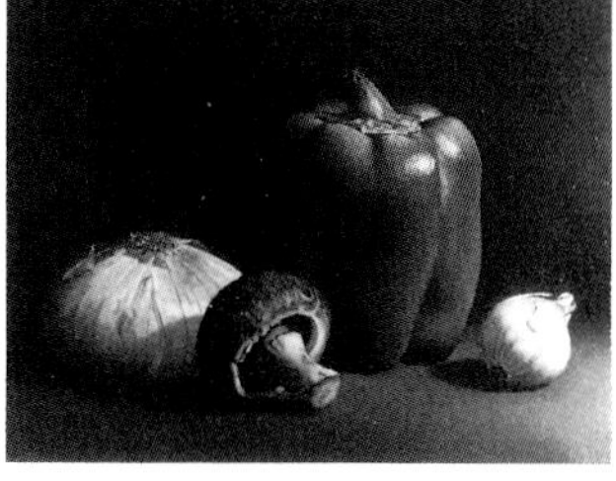
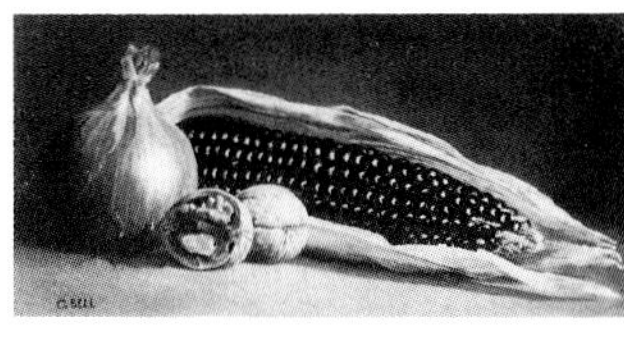
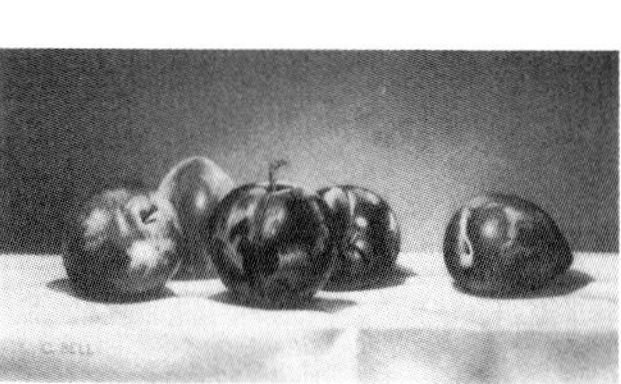
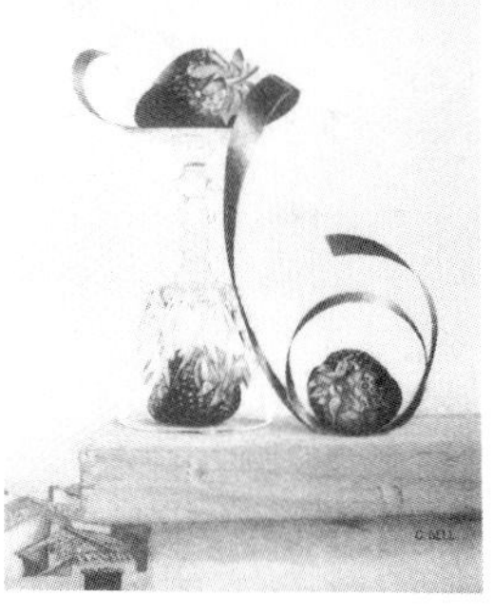
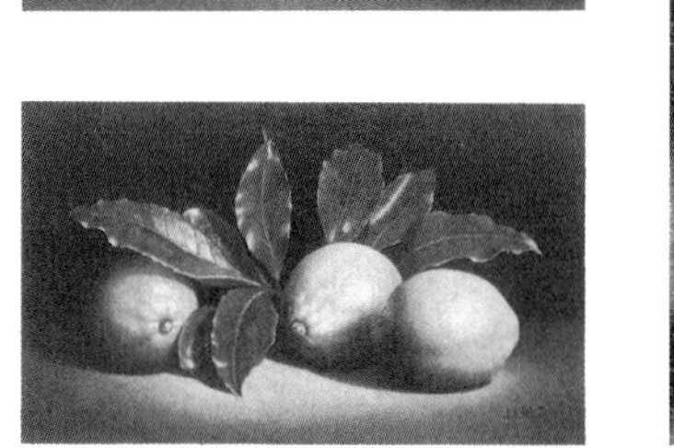
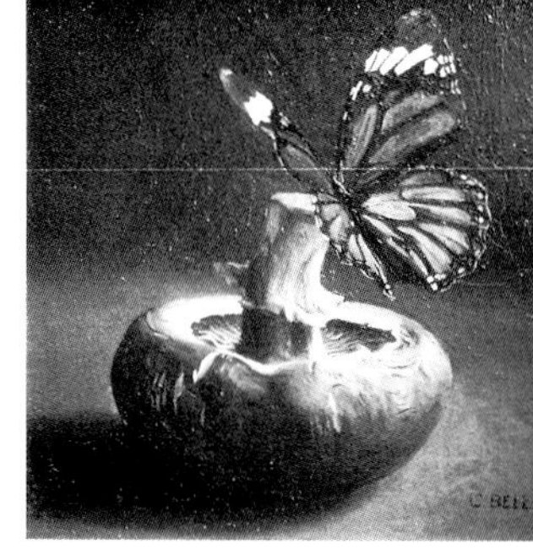
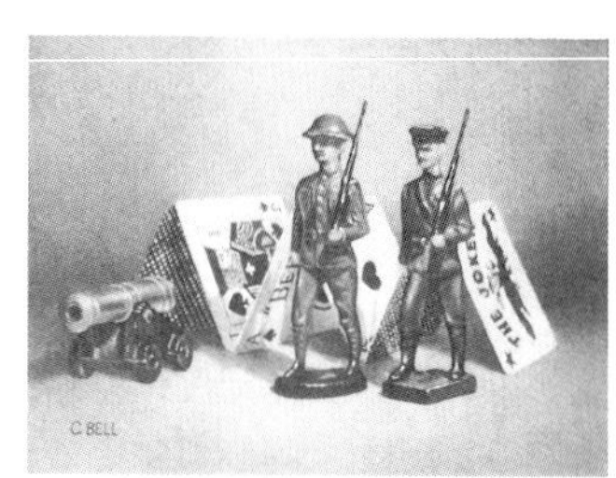
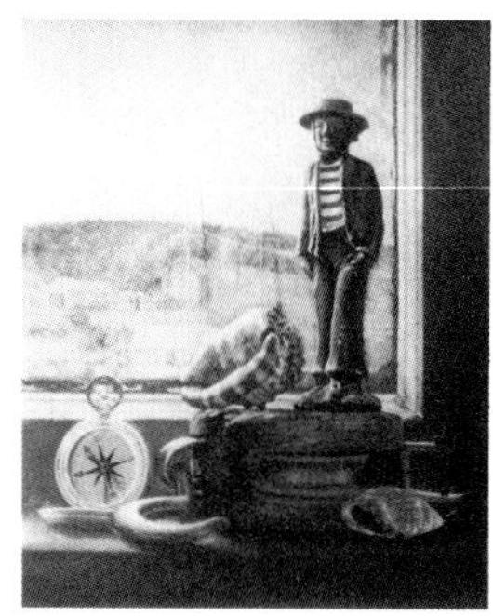

and exposures, and project it to any size and scale before deciding how the final painting would look. In making the painting, he could then refer to the photographs in addition to the original still life.

Since it was light reflections he was looking at, Bell needed many varied surfaces: metals, plastics, paint, wood, paper, glass. His collection of old toys immediately presented itself as a possibility. Not only did it meet the light requirements, it would also introduce original, exciting imagery to the contemporary still life. He also decided that the effective scale would be between six and twelve times life size and planned on paintings with dimensions from five to seven feet.

In 1971 and 1972, Bell made about ten paintings using these toys as subject matter. The first, *Skate* (fig. 51), is interesting to compare with *"Chicago" Pat. No. 1,910,193* (1980; fig. 96) of a decade later. While the artist's technique has improved greatly in the later painting, the impact of the earlier work is still quite powerful. It is very effective compositionally: the low angle of view makes the skate look gigantic and threatening as it straddles the crayons and upstages the box. The image and subject are totally new and fresh. Right after *Skate,* Bell left the toys for a couple of months and painted his first gumball machine, *Gumball I* (1971; fig. 50). He then returned to the toys and did not paint another of the machines—for which he was to become famous worldwide—for another two years.

Bunny Cycle (1972; fig. 59) and *Tops* (1972; fig. 57) are among the best, most classic works in this early Toy series. Again, *Tops* was another of those predictions of things to come, and parallels to this early work may be seen in *"Chicago" Pat.* and in the Marbles series of the eighties.

In 1973 each of the leading Photorealists was offered a commission by Stuart M. Speiser for a major work that contained a reference to aviation in some loosely defined way. One of the world's lead-

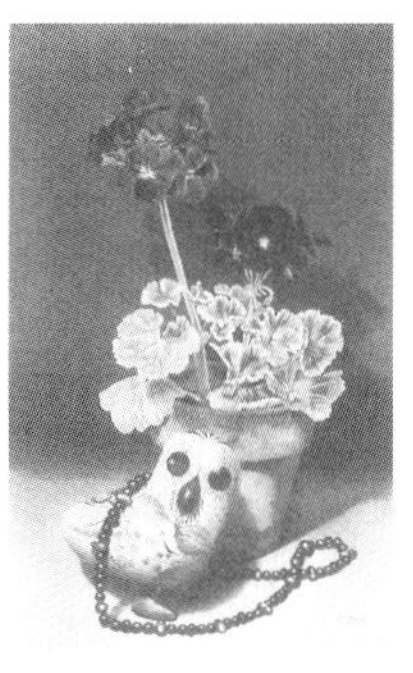
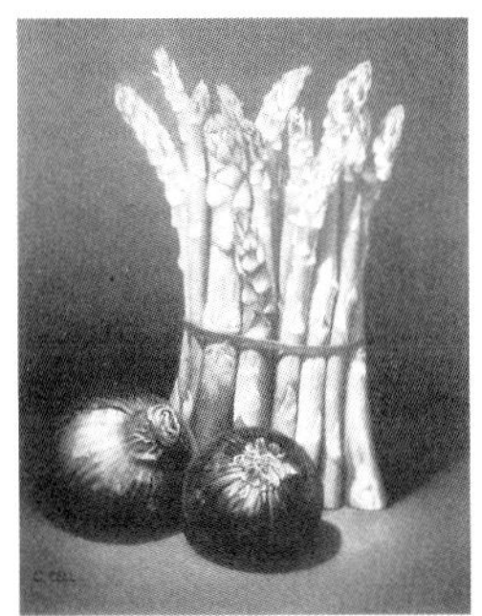
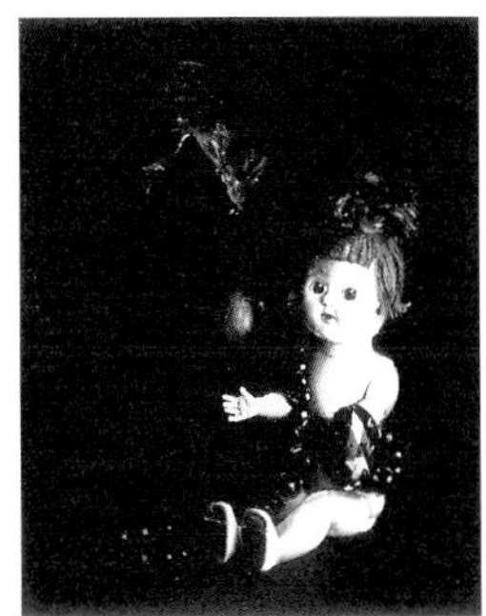
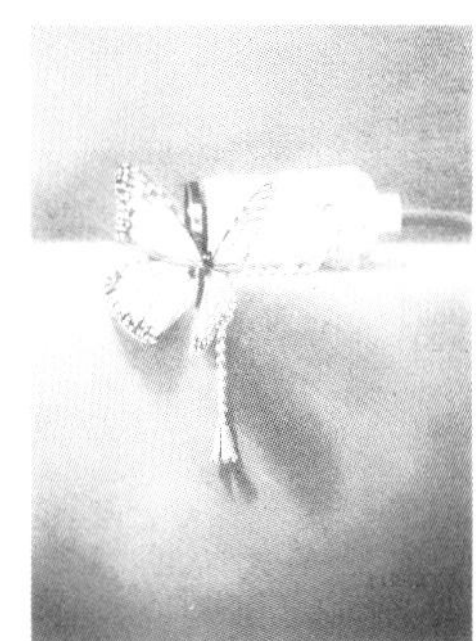
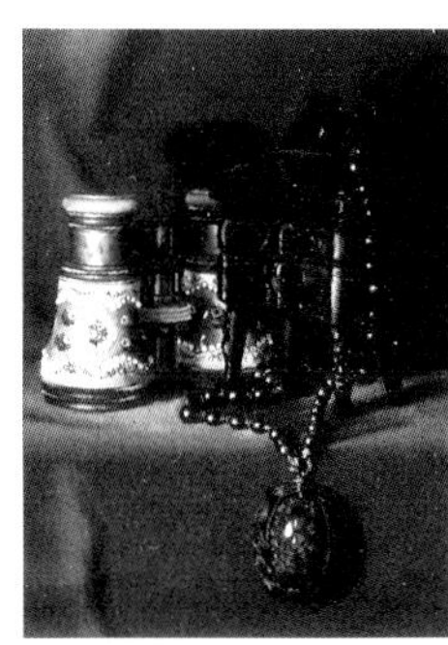
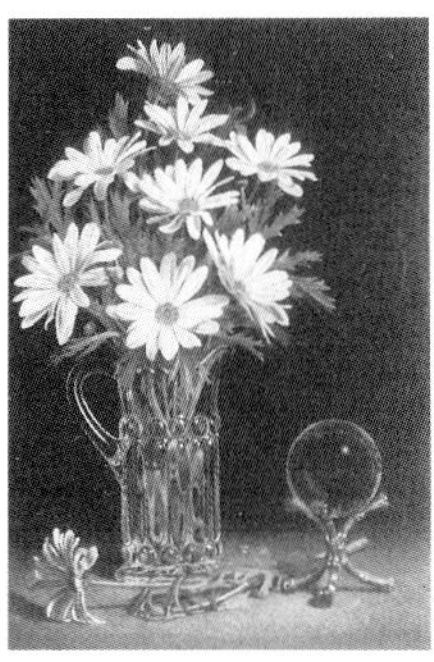
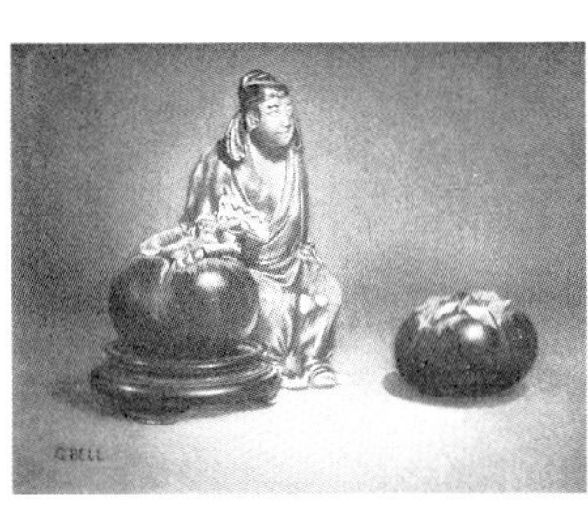
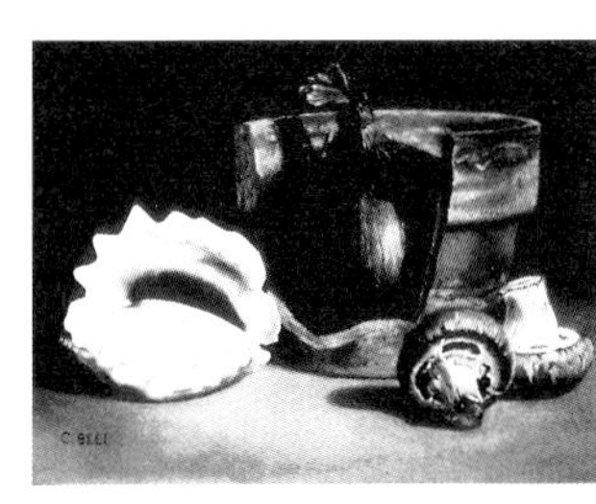
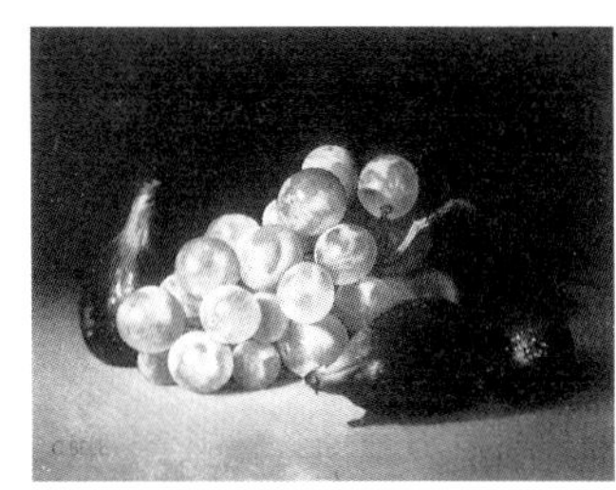
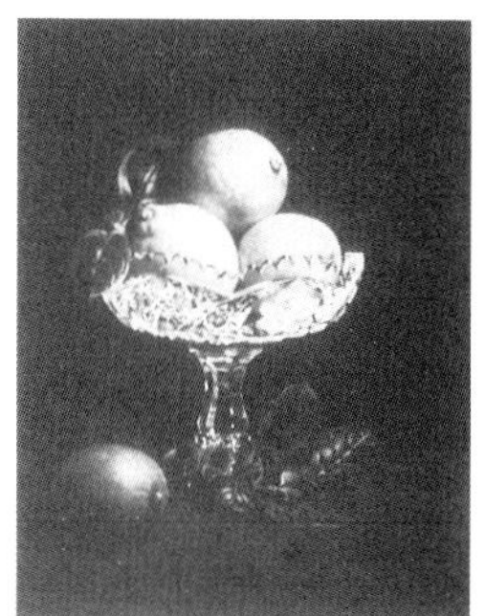

ing attorneys, specializing in aviation law, as well as an art collector, Speiser saw a way to combine his vocation and avocation by commissioning such a collection from the then-up-and-coming Photorealists. (The collection is now owned by the Smithsonian Institution.) Bell's contribution to the collection was *Seaplane in Bathtub* (1973; fig. 62), which cleverly used the aviation theme but was entirely consistent with his earlier toys.

When Bell began to paint the water in the tub for *Seaplane,* it took him to another challenge involving light: how to depict accurately its distortions, diffusions, and reflections. He remembered that a similar problem had arisen when he had worked on the glass globe of his first gumball painting. For the next four years, from 1973 through 1976, he would devote himself totally to addressing this issue. Returning to this visually stimulating image, Bell immersed himself in the endless variations and challenges it presented.

With the globe of the machine filling the entire canvas, *Gumball II* (1973; fig. 63) was the first of the true initial Gumball series (the earlier *Gumball I* was an experimental, smaller-scaled, accidental discovery). *Gumball II* is the only major painting in the series with a light-colored background. Utilizing the physiological dimension of color theory explored by such pioneers as Josef Albers, Bell was to find that the color chosen to make up the background of a painting could serve either to force other colors forward toward the viewer or to allow them to recede. While most of the gumball paintings appear at first to have black backgrounds, closer inspection reveals very dark purples, greens, and browns. A green background (green = blue + yellow) will make a red gumball seem to come forward out of the picture plane. It is also interesting to note here that the colors of all the gumballs were carefully chosen for their visual effect; before photographing them, Bell might spend hours upon hours arranging them with an olive plucker, chopsticks, and wires inside the globes.

Bell is always concerned about building variety within a series, and three works that followed *Gumball II—"Nation's Finest," Gumball IV* (1974; fig. 65), *"Thank You," Gumball V* (1974; fig. 68), and *Gumball VII* (1975; fig. 72)—were tougher and maybe more interesting works of art. *"Nation's Finest,"* the first in the series to be cropped and the precursor of later, more sophisticated compositions, was one of the featured works at the Tokyo Biennial in 1974. *"Thank You,"* the largest of the original Gumball series, introduces an ominous note. *Gumball VII* attains the same menacing tone by de-emphasizing the gumballs behind a flat glass, bringing in the dark, monochromatic peanut jar, and focusing on the grey coin slot; scale, light, and shadow transform a seemingly benign, even playful subject. Two earlier works, *Clown and Monkey* (1972; fig. 60) and *Cat* (1973; fig. 61), have something of the same effect.

Bell's gumball paintings became the classic Photorealist still-life images of the seventies. Among the best-known works are *Gumball II; Gumball IX* (1975; fig. 74); *"Sugar Daddy," Gumball X* (1975; fig. 75), bought by the Solomon R. Guggenheim Museum as one of its earliest Photorealist acquisitions; *"5 Cent Special," Gumball XII* (1976; fig. 77); and *The Ultimate Gumball* (1978; fig. 90), which became the subject of Bell's gumball screen print (1981; fig. 192).

In 1976 Bell discovered the pinball machine as potential imagery. In painting his only pastel of this period, *Pinball No. 1* (fig. 92), he realized that this subject would let him work with yet another sort of light—that which projects from within the canvas. The next year was devoted entirely to five pinball-machine paintings: *The Wizard* (fig. 85), *Gin* (fig. 86), *Fire Ball 500 No. 1* (fig. 87), *Feel Them Bumpers* (fig. 88), and *Double Advance* (fig. 89). The first two were important in Bell's development as an artist, but they were muted in color and not entirely successful in solving the light-projection problem. *Fire Ball,* brilliant in color and graphics but somewhat brash and hard-edged, was successful enough to encourage Bell to pursue the challenge he had set up for himself. *Double Advance* was an experiment, not only with light and dark but with the extreme field-of-focus blur and clarity that only a camera can produce. In this work, Bell was openly answering those who criticized the camera and the photograph as tools by saying, "Hey . . . I *am* using the camera . . . Do the same thing without it if you can, but you could save a lot of time using it!"

By the end of the seventies, the first decade of the Photorealists and of his mature career, Charles Bell had created approximately forty-five works of art: thirty-eight oils, five watercolors, one pastel, and a single black-and-white pencil drawing, *Scenic Overlook* (1976; fig. 83). He had fully established himself in the contemporary art world and had staked out the territory he was to explore more fully in the eighties.

Immediately as the new decade opened, Bell looked back at the old one in an effort to advance and improve on the lessons he had learned. The possibility of combining images occurred to him, and he joined *Skate* and *Tops* in creating the fabulous *"Chicago" Pat. No. 1,910,193*.

Although the marble had been seen earlier as an image in *Tops* and in *Marbles* (1974; fig. 71), it was in *Chicago* that Bell began his serious exploration of this theme. (Ultimately, he was to say that it proved to be for him something like what the square was for Albers.) The Marbles series, which came to be fully equal with those portraying toys, gumballs, and pinballs, is in its essence infinite. Containing the possibility for countless permutations and combinations, this image has led to works that are serene, sophisticated, beautiful, and challenging. Notable early masterpieces are *Marbles I* (1980; fig. 97), *Marbles VII* (1982; fig. 109), and *Marbles VIII* (1982; fig. 118).

In the early and mid-eighties, the toys returned in a major new incarnation. A narrative element and a touch of the Surreal began to enter the paintings, possibly as a result of the artist's friendship with Salvador Dali. *The Critics* (1982; fig. 121), *Troupe* (1983; fig. 125), and *Ta-Daa* (1985; fig. 149) were the most significant works in this new Toy series. *The Critics* is important for its overall size and scale (the two toy birds are perhaps twelve to fifteen times life size). *Troupe* is in my opinion the most beautifully composed and colored painting in the series; note especially the blue glow behind the ballerina, the supporting cast of clowns on the left, the seal on the right. Led by Bell's myriad compositional nuances, the eye flows around and over the painting. *Ta-Daa* involves the most complex conglomeration of objects in any Bell work as well as numerous planes defined by the curtain, the different toys, and the backdrop with its range of shadows. Two other works, *Side Show* (1984; fig. 143) and *Midsummer's Dream* (1986; fig. 158), are particularly notable for their touches of fantasy.

In *The Judgement of Paris* (1986; fig. 156), Bell depicts a Greek myth that has been painted by many artists in the past. In this version of "the first beauty contest," which led to the Trojan War, Minerva, Juno, and Venus are portrayed, respectively, by a Barbie doll, a Miss America doll, and a Marilyn Monroe doll; Mercury is G.I. Joe and Paris is a Ken doll. A great deal of double entrendre and thought-provoking complexity mark this work. Painted six or seven times their actual size, the toys are the size of living people. They are backed by what seems to be a landscape—or perhaps it's a stage set? While the original photograph depicts a still life, is the painting itself one? While the story is a myth, many real issues, including modern-day beauty contests, political intrigue, and bribery, come into play.

Art Angel (1986; fig. 157) and *Nature Study* (1985; fig. 155) are from roughly the same period as *Judgement.* Along with Surrealism, symbolism, and double entendre, they employ a touch of dark humor to make their point. *Nature Study* is, among other things, Bell's second highly individual treatment of the mother-and-child theme, the first being *Manikin Monkey* (1972; fig. 58). It enhances and plays off Henri Rousseau's stylized, artificial reality by including only fake objects.

While all of Bell's subjects had appeared in his work by the end of the seventies, only the gumball machines had been fully developed. The marbles, briefly introduced in the seventies, were deeply explored in the eighties and can continue to inspire the artist indefinitely, providing endless compositions of celestial quietude and simple elegance. The toys of the eighties were related to but totally different in intent from the toys of the seventies: while the earlier works were primarily only still lifes, the later ones had statements to make and touched on political comment.

It is the Pinball series that I consider the artist's greatest achievement—visually, technically, and technologically. This series became his exclusive endeavor in the latter part of the eighties and is continuing today.

In 1987, after completing *Advance Bonus* (fig. 165), the first of several paintings based on the complex Bally machine Paragon, Bell took a giant step toward the successful manipulation of subject matter and imagery. Frustrated by the lack of compositionally interesting machines, he began to alter the available ones. For *Double Bonus* (fig. 167), he first created a painting on plastic, similar to an animation cel, of a seminude girl and then used it to cover the "Fire God" image on Bally's Fireball machine. In this way, he could alter and enhance the color, composition, and interest of the machine's surface. He next photographed the new machine he had created and then painted from those photographs. Viewers, however, are apt to believe that there really is such a machine, since they have long been taught to believe in photographs and, more recently, to believe in Photorealism. Bell's *Double Bonus* adds the artist's own personal comment to the current debate concerning manipulated photography.

After *Double Bonus,* Bell returned to the later-vintage Paragon machine with its more complex plastic bumpers and plastic light sources. He experimented with its details in *Viking Strikes* (1987; fig. 170) and with its angles in *1 to 4 Can Play* (1988; fig. 172). He then produced his final painting of this machine, the remarkable panorama *Paragon* (1988; fig. 171), which summed up all Bell had learned and was able to portray up to that moment.

The final two works of 1988, *Catcher* (fig. 184) and *Dragnet* (fig. 176), were completed for the artist's first West Coast exhibition, which took place at the Modernism gallery in San Francisco. These paintings of details are less complex images than the ones done just before, but because Bell used his own colors rather than the existing color combination on the machines, the finished works are intense and quite imposing.

In his last painting of the eighties, completed in October of 1989 (the only painting that year), Bell created one of the masterpieces of his career, pushing the technical and technological boundaries of Photorealism into entirely new realms. He began with a seventies pinball machine that had a good architecture and composition and a lighting he considered perfect for a major work. Its graphics and colors, however, were awful. At the same time, he came across a fifties machine that had what the other lacked: terrific graphics and good color. He decided, then, to construct the perfect image from the two.

Since the graphics of one machine could not in any way fit the surface of the other, Bell had to create a completely new playing field around all the lights and bumpers of the seventies machine while using the imagery of the fifties board. Of course, he also totally manipulated color to give him the optimum combinations for beauty, composition, and interest. After applying a painting, which he calls a sketch, onto a plastic template, he affixed it to the existing seventies board and spent many days photographing and adjusting. Then, by bringing his computer background fully into his art, he was able to manipulate the image further, to tilt it and invent aspects otherwise unobtainable. One of the problems with creating a nonexistent pinball-machine playing field is that it is almost impossible to figure out what would appear in the distorted reflection on the shiny steel ball, always a focal point in a Bell painting. In a tour de force of computer expertise, Bell skillfully worked with a 3-D program to show him how to wrap the existing image upside down and backwards around the ball to complete the illusion of an actually photographed still life.

The resultant work, *Miami Beach* (fig. 181), took nine months to complete, a period encompassing five months of drawings, photography, and computer experimentation as well as four months of painting, including further intermediate photography. The lessons Bell learned and the theories he proved will have a pronounced effect on all his future work.

The last painting of 1990 was *Oh Boy* (fig. 190). Among the largest of the pinball works, it introduced a new dimension to the series: it is the first machine to be photographed with the glass cover closed and therefore reflecting the back glass superimposed on the playing field. By this means, both the reality and the illusions were heightened.

The first painting Bell completed in 1991 was *Andy's Mr. Peanut (Major)* (fig. 1). The largest painting of his life by a long shot, it is equaled in scale and impact only by the enormous single portraits Franz Gertsch painted in the late seventies and the eighties. The peanut jar in the composition belonged to Andy Warhol, and I think there is more of Andy in the painting than just the jar.

A final note. From the moment I first saw Charles Bell's work, it was obvious to me not only that he was a terrific painter but also that he had seriously studied the history of art and especially the skills and techniques that had been laboriously discovered over the centuries. As his work developed in the next two decades, Bell (and his fellow Photorealists) remained among the few artists anywhere who adhered to traditional standards of quality in art. Elsewhere, pressures arising from the politics of racism and sexism led critics and others in the art schools and museums to question and relax those criteria; as a result, standards gradually but inexorably declined. Artists began to believe that their duty was not to study the past, to learn how to draw, or to know about color, composition, line, and form, but only to express themselves. Ultimately, discipline and craftsmanship were denigrated to such a degree that the eighties produced countless pieces of visual pollution.

Also stemming from his respect for art is Bell's concern for the longevity of the paintings he makes. Looking back, one realizes that the Abstract Expressionists originally had neither the finances nor the technology to be able to work with lasting materials and that, furthermore, they used all sorts of untried materials as part of their obsession with the immediacy of ideas and answers in their totally new kind of painting. By the eighties, it seems as if most artists simply did not know or care about the physical fate of their work. Bell, on the other hand, has a knowledge of paint, canvases, mediums, and varnishes that insures that his work, if properly protected, will remain stable and as he made it for centuries. His colors will not fade like Rothko's, his paints will not ooze like Pollock's, his canvases and paint surfaces will not crack like Kline's. Nothing will fall off a Bell, and a Bell won't rot or disintegrate, as will much of the art created in the last ten years.

As Charles Bell's mastery keeps on growing, the durability of his art will be something to be grateful for. Also to be valued is the fact that he was once told by a teacher, "Each one teach one." Bell has taught many during the course of his career, and his influence will be felt by many, many more, far into the future, as he continues to add to our knowledge of painting.

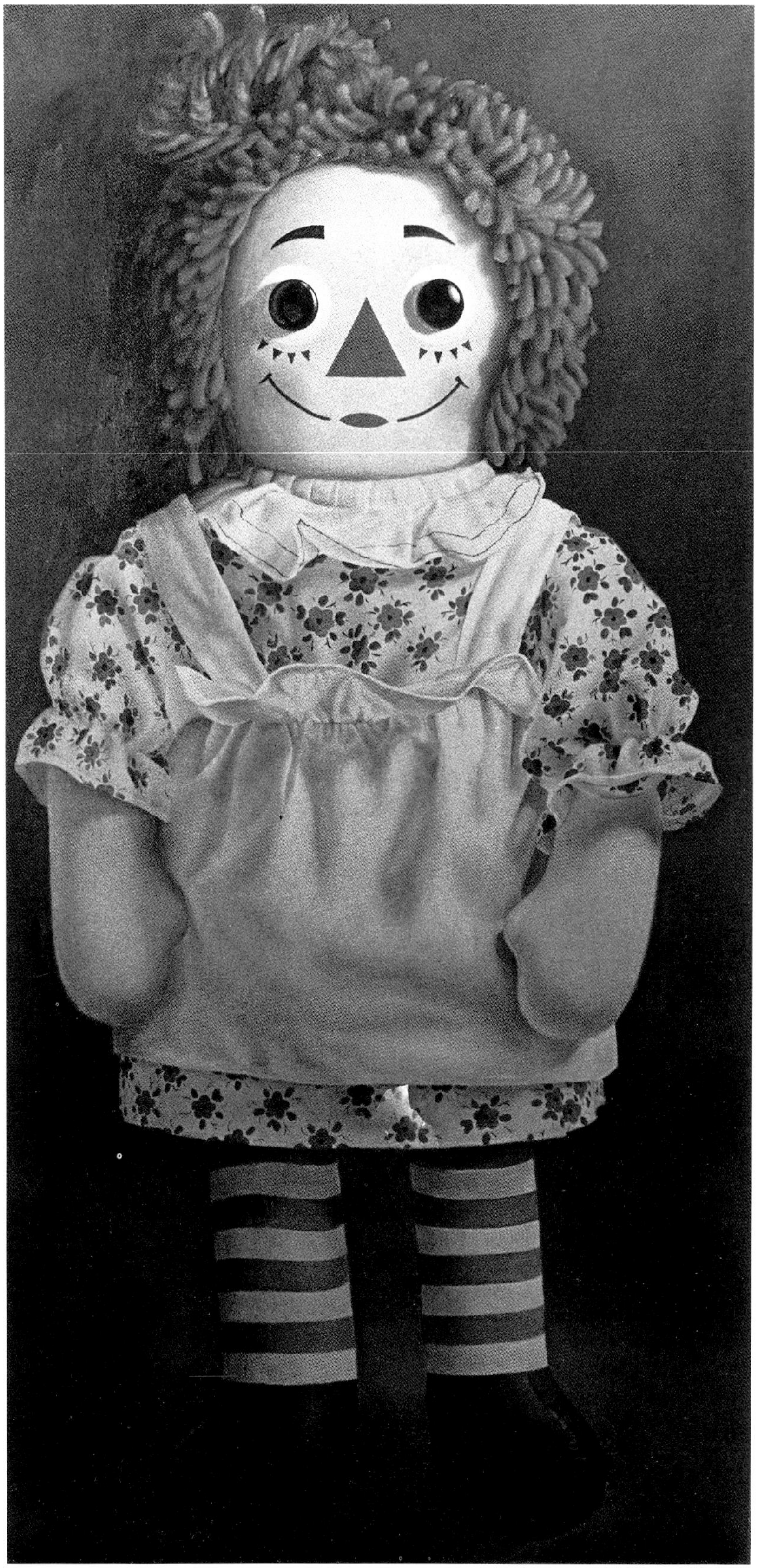

OPPOSITE: 48. *Raggedy Ann No. 1.* 1969. Oil on canvas, 72 × 36″. Private collection, Massachusetts. Another version of this painting—*Raggedy Ann No. 2,* painted in 1970, whereabouts unknown—is virtually identical.

RIGHT: 49. *Raggedy Ann No. 3.* 1970. Oil on canvas, 72 × 36″. Private collection, New Jersey

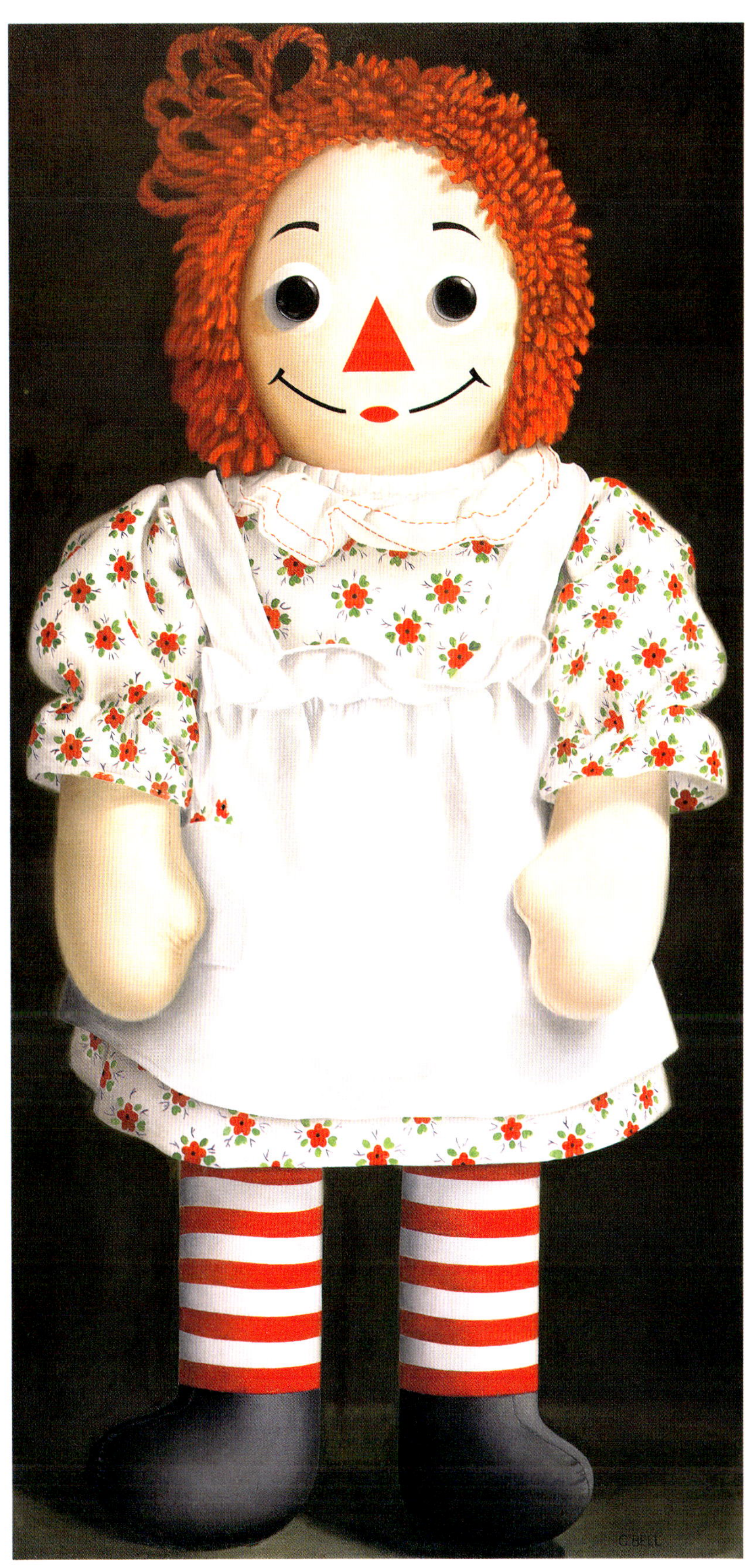

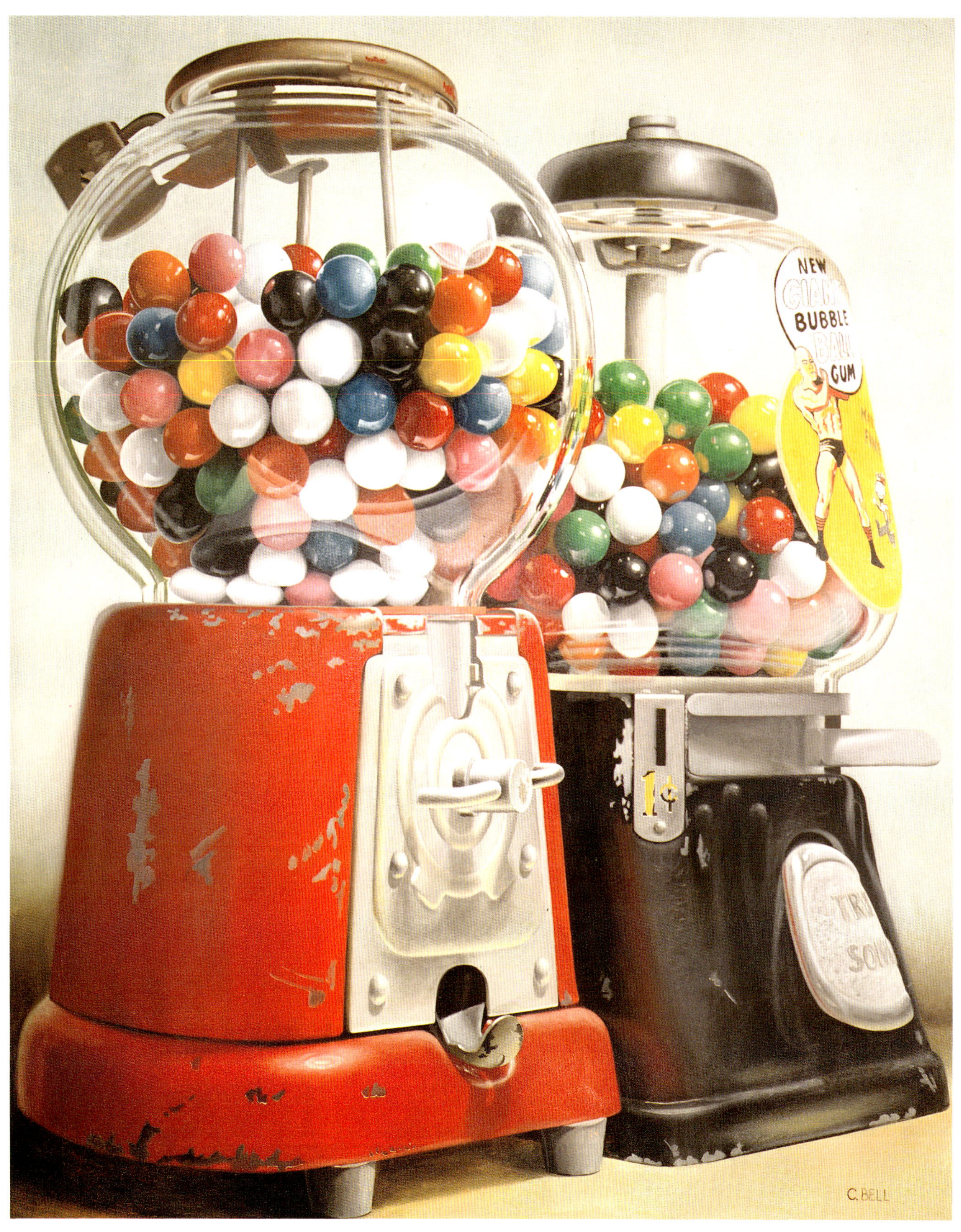
NEW
BUBBLE
GUM
1¢
C. BELL

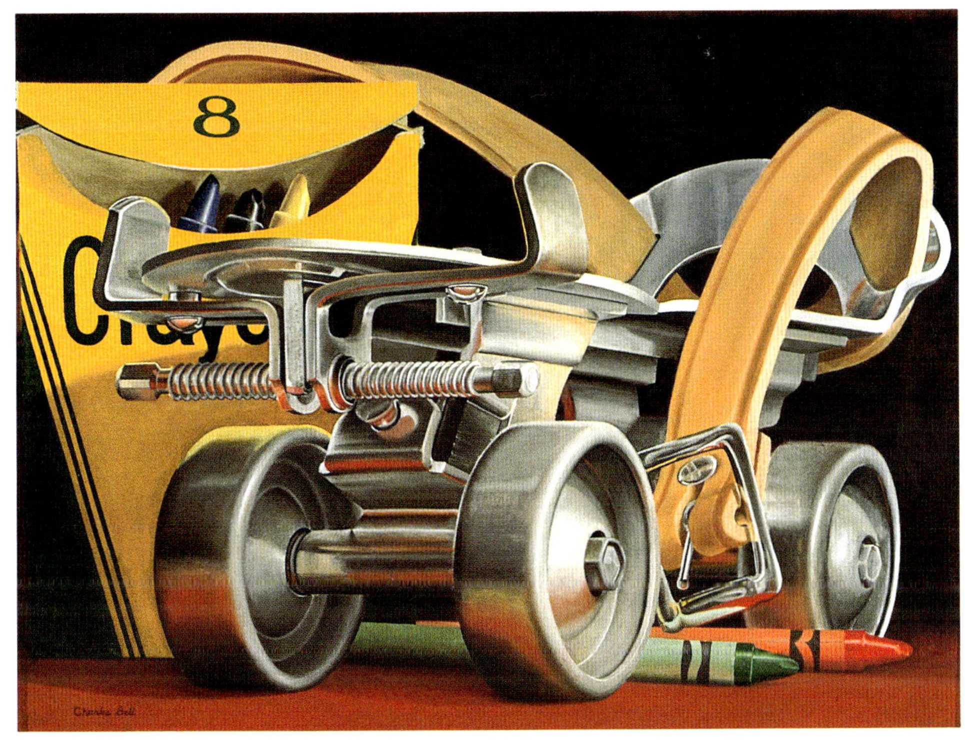

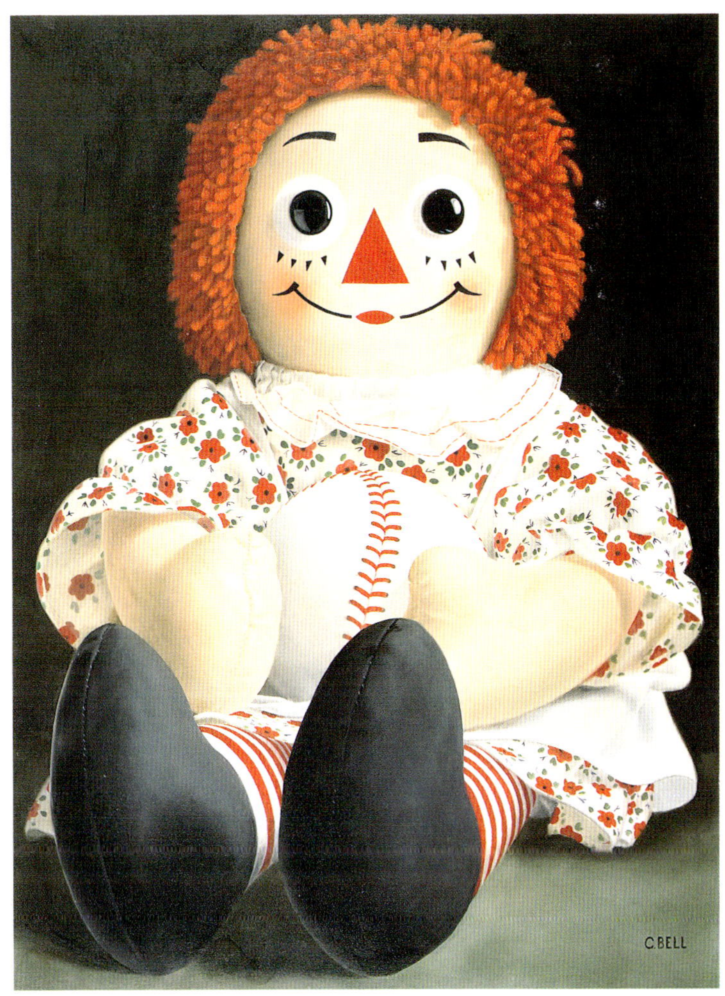

OPPOSITE: 50. *Gumball I.* 1971. Oil on canvas, 72 × 54″. Collection Mr. and Mrs. Arthur H. Morowitz, New Jersey

ABOVE LEFT: 51. *Skate.* 1971. Oil on canvas, 36 × 48″. Private collection

ABOVE RIGHT: 52. *Raggedy Ann With Baseball.* 1971. Oil on canvas, 48 × 36″. Private collection

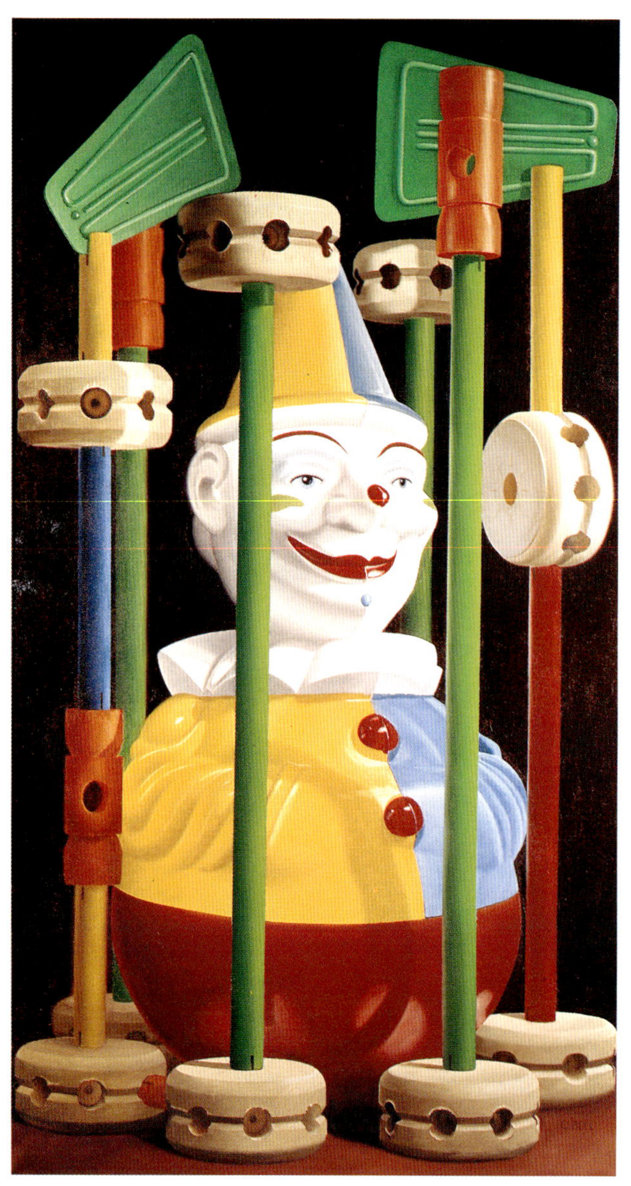

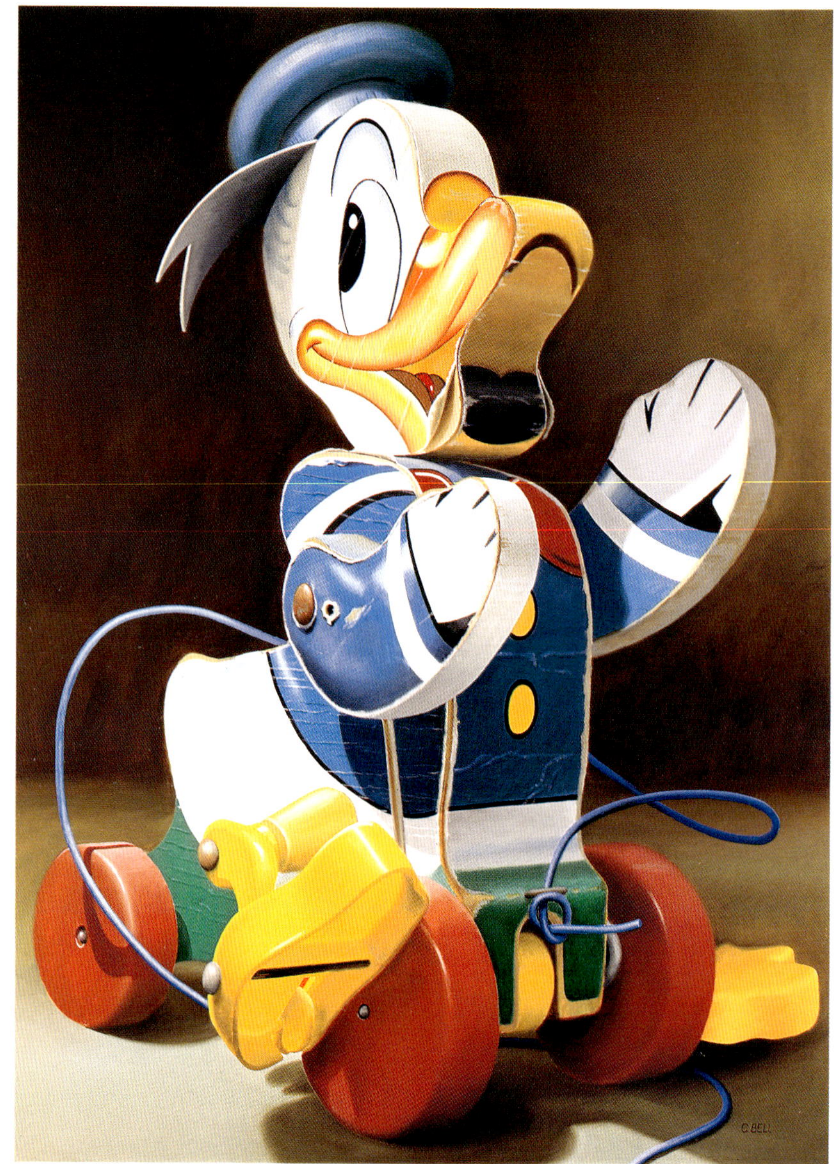
C.BELL

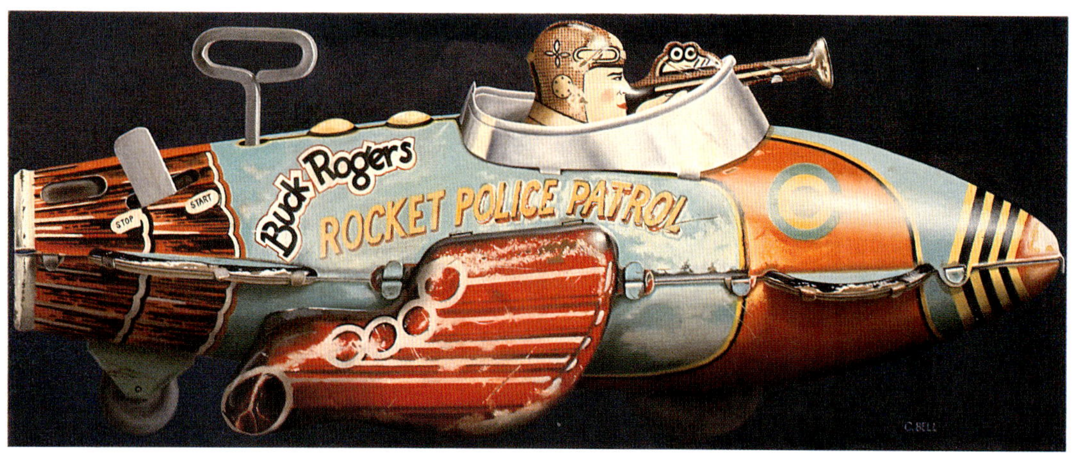
Buck Rogers
ROCKET POLICE PATROL
STOP
START
C.BELL

OPPOSITE, ABOVE LEFT: 53. *Tinker Toy*. 1972. Oil on canvas, 72 × 40″. Collection Herbert Allen, New York

OPPOSITE, ABOVE RIGHT: 54. *Donald Duck*. 1972. Oil on canvas, 54 × 40″. Collection Herbert Allen, New York

OPPOSITE, BELOW: 55. *Buck Rogers*. 1972. Oil on canvas, 24 × 60″. Collection Patricia Field, New York

RIGHT: 56. *Lionel*. 1972. Oil on canvas, 84 × 48″. Private collection, Paris

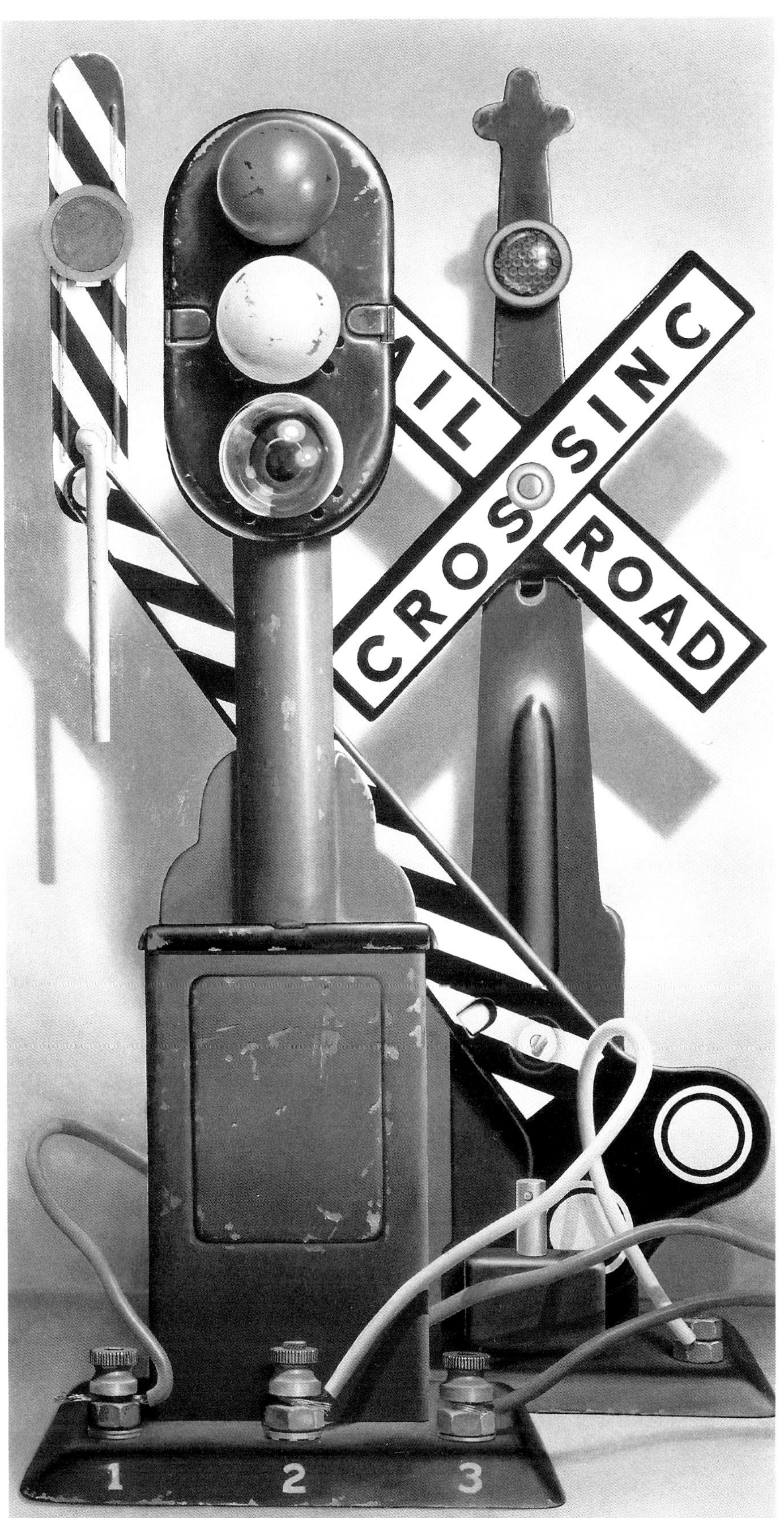

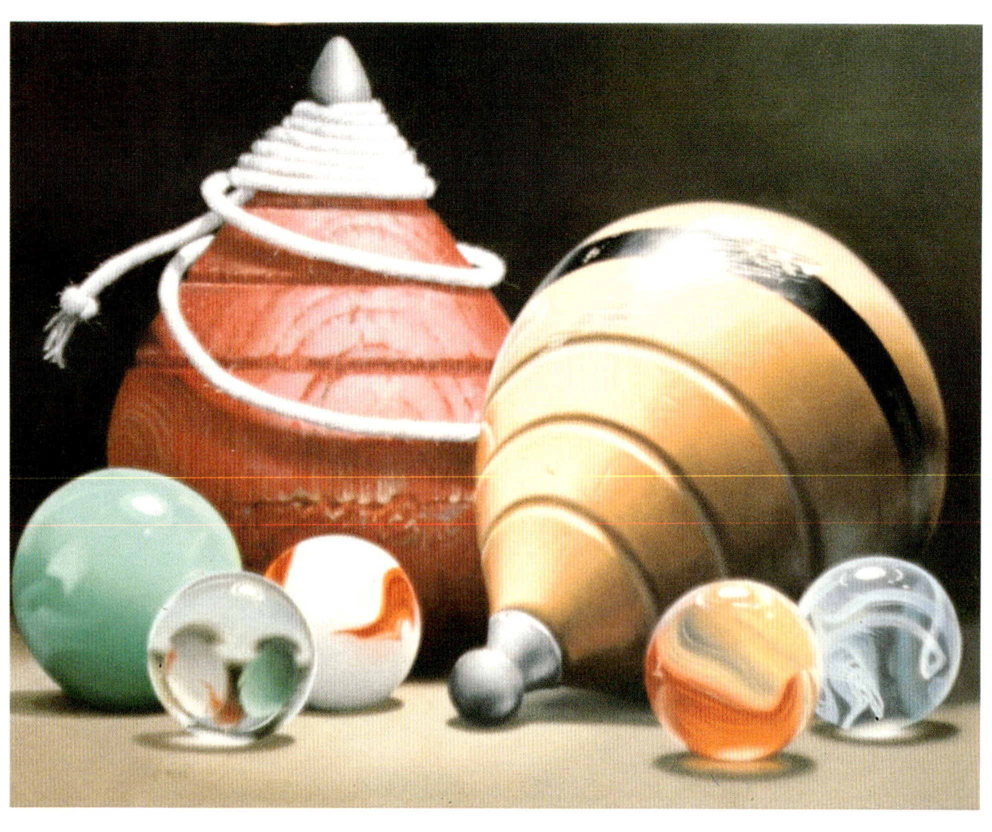

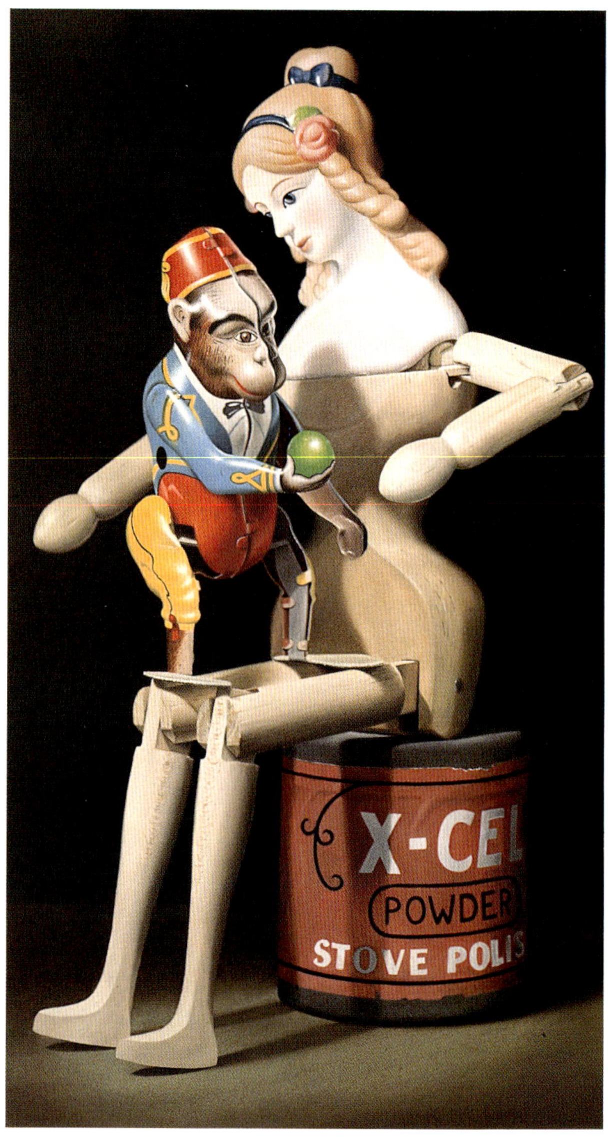
X-CEL
POWDER
STOVE POLIS

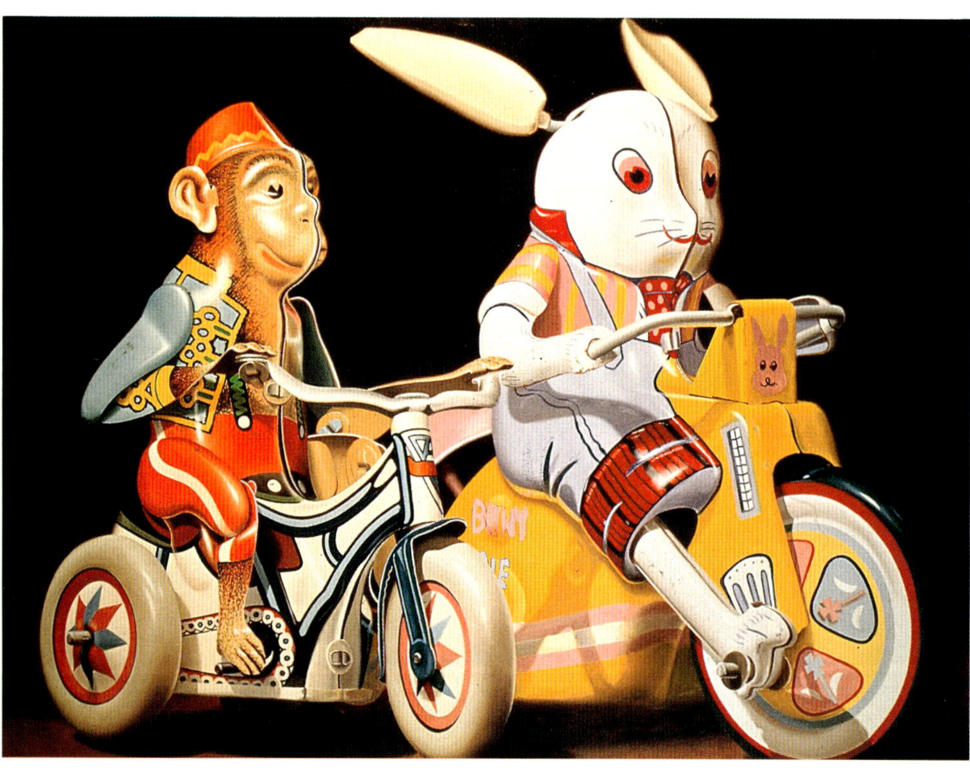

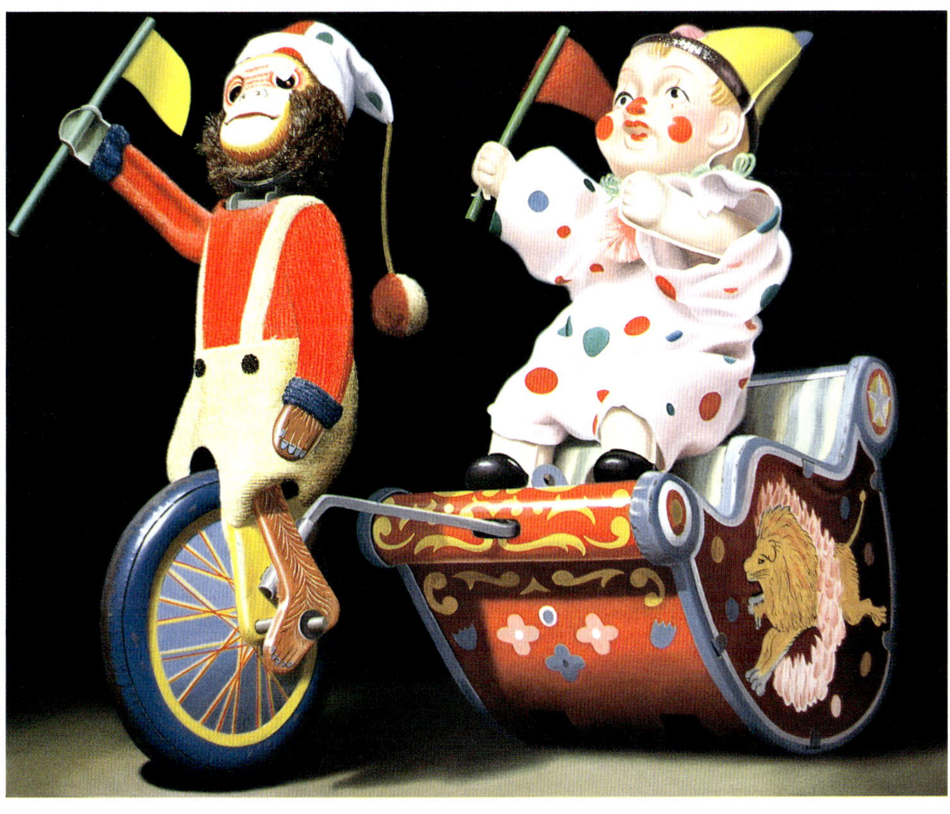

OPPOSITE, ABOVE LEFT: 57. *Tops*. 1972. Oil on canvas, 44 × 58″. Collection Ms. Carmel Roth, New York

OPPOSITE, ABOVE RIGHT: 58. *Manikin Monkey*. 1972. Oil on canvas, 72 × 40″. Collection Richard Clair, California

OPPOSITE, BELOW LEFT: 59. *Bunny Cycle*. 1972. Oil on canvas, 50 × 66″. Private collection

ABOVE: 60. *Clown and Monkey*. 1972. Oil on canvas, 50 × 62″. Collection Richard Chestnov and Harvey Gold, New York

RIGHT: 61. *Cat*. 1973. Oil on canvas, 44 × 36″. Private collection, Sweden

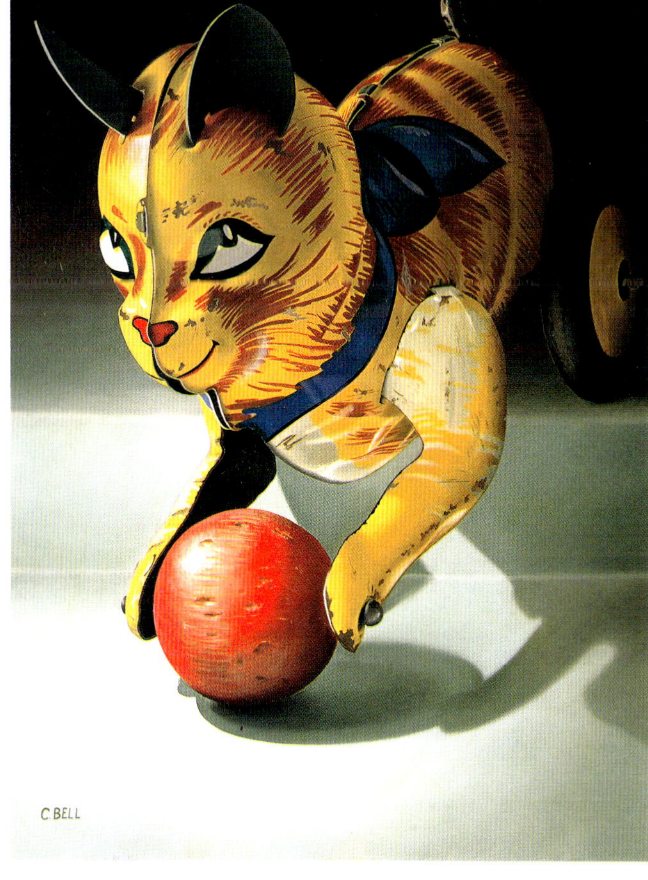

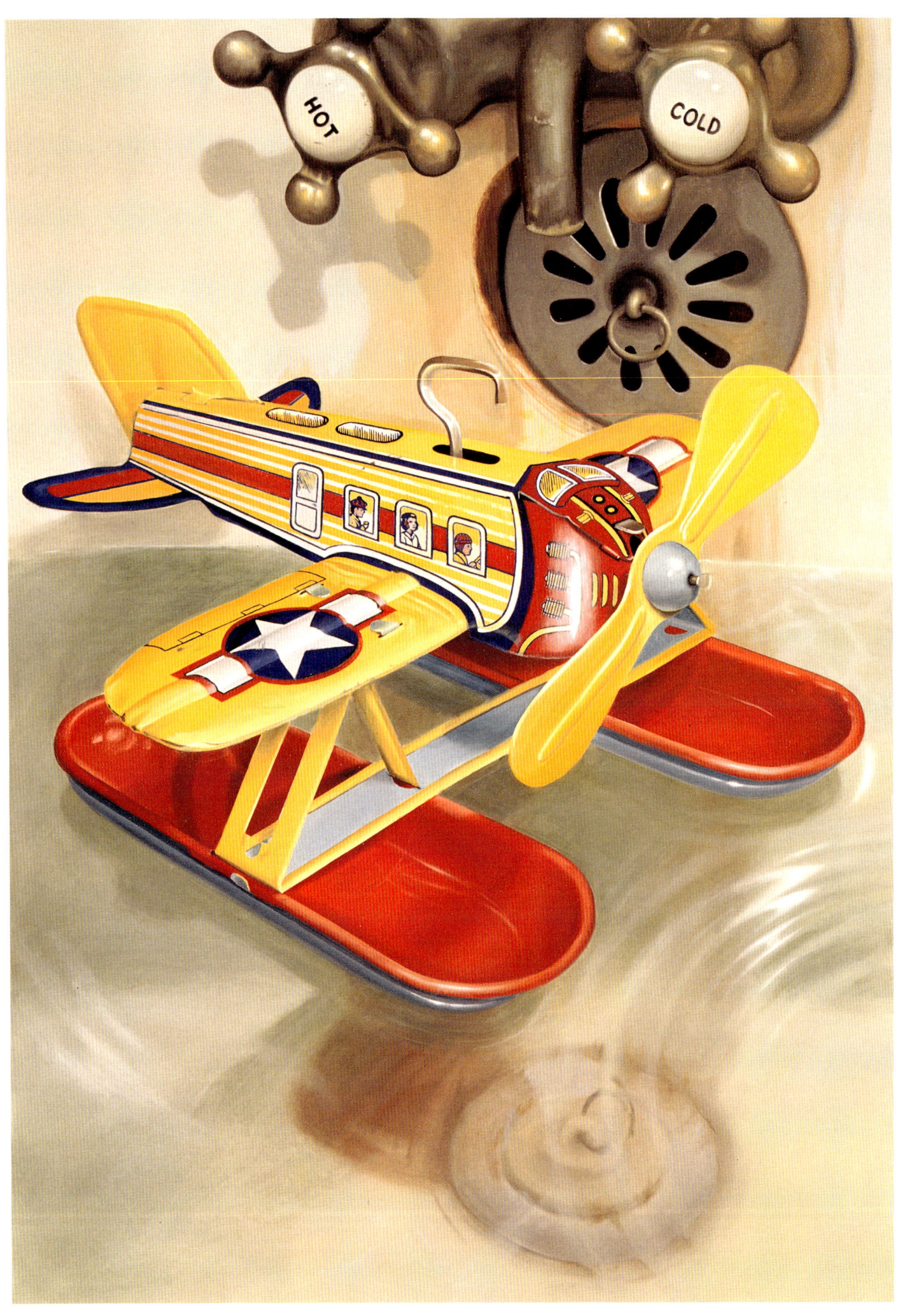
HOT
COLD

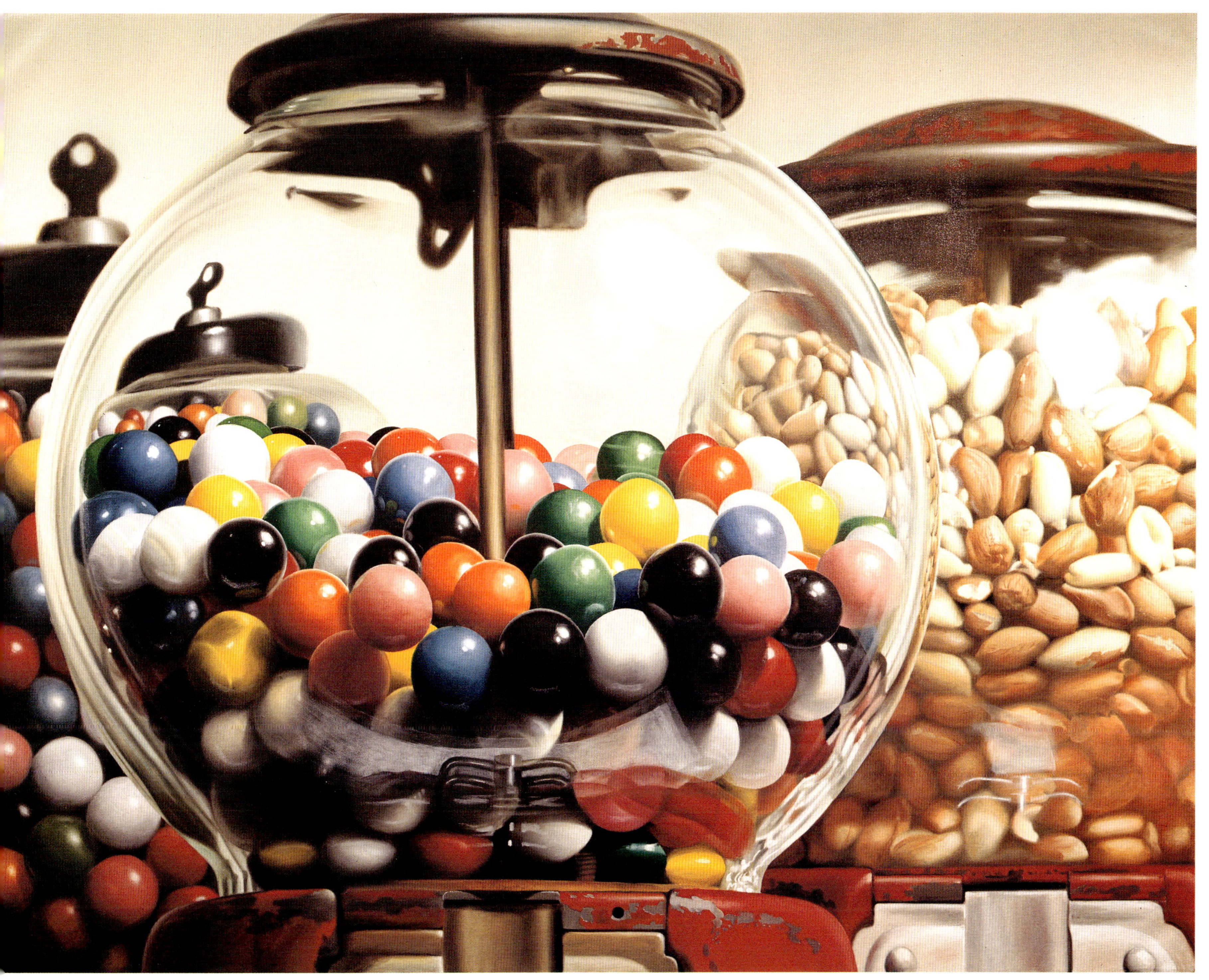

OPPOSITE: 62. *Seaplane in Bathtub*. 1973. Oil on canvas, 68 × 48″. Smithsonian Institution, Washington, D.C. Stuart M. Speiser Collection

ABOVE: 63. *Gumball II*. 1973. Oil on canvas, 60 × 78½″. Collection Louis K. and Susan Pear Meisel, New York

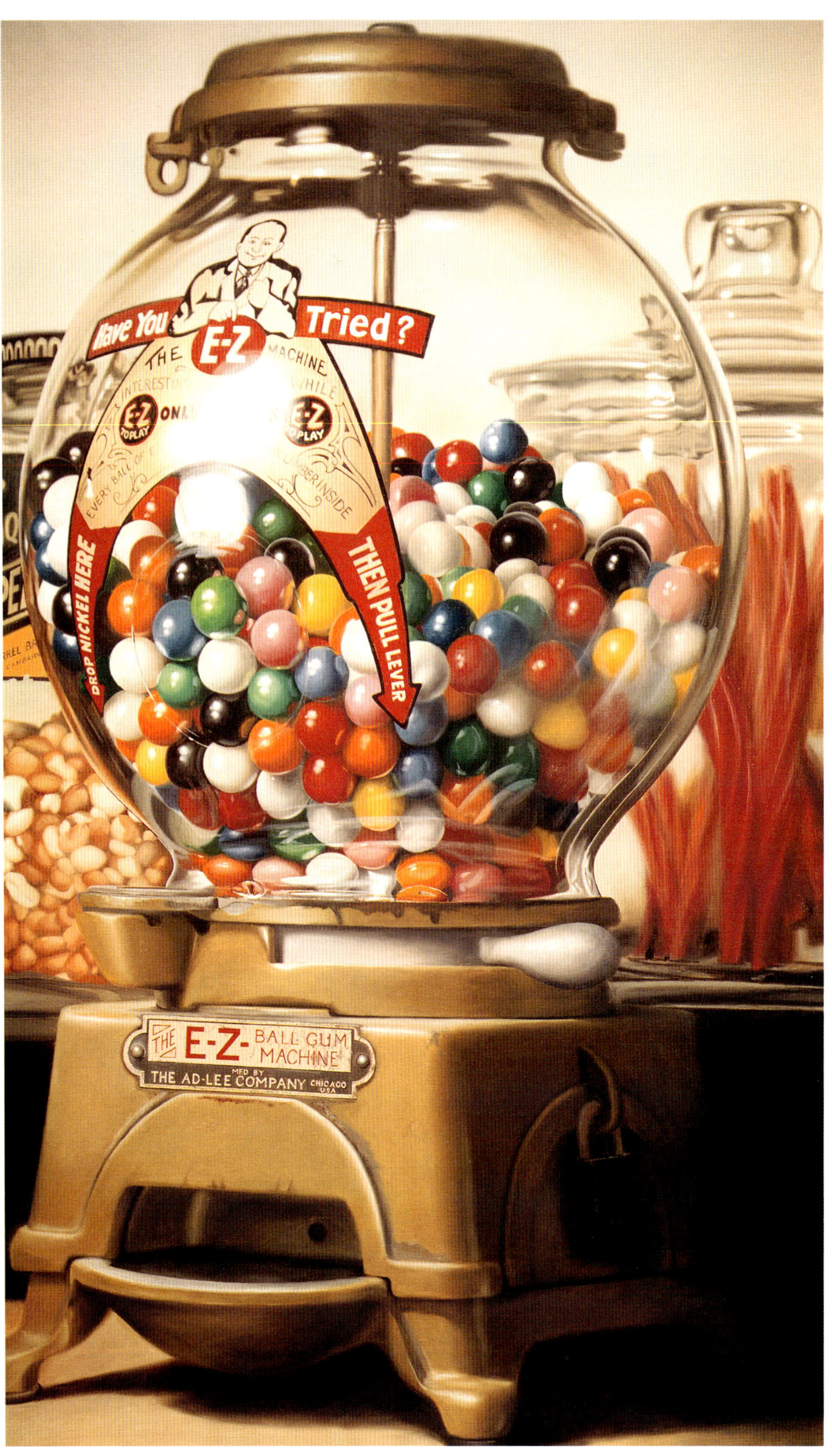
Have You
Tried?
THE E-Z MACHINE
DROP NICKEL HERE
THEN PULL LEVER
THE E-Z- BALL GUM MACHINE
MFD BY
THE AD-LEE COMPANY
CHICAGO USA

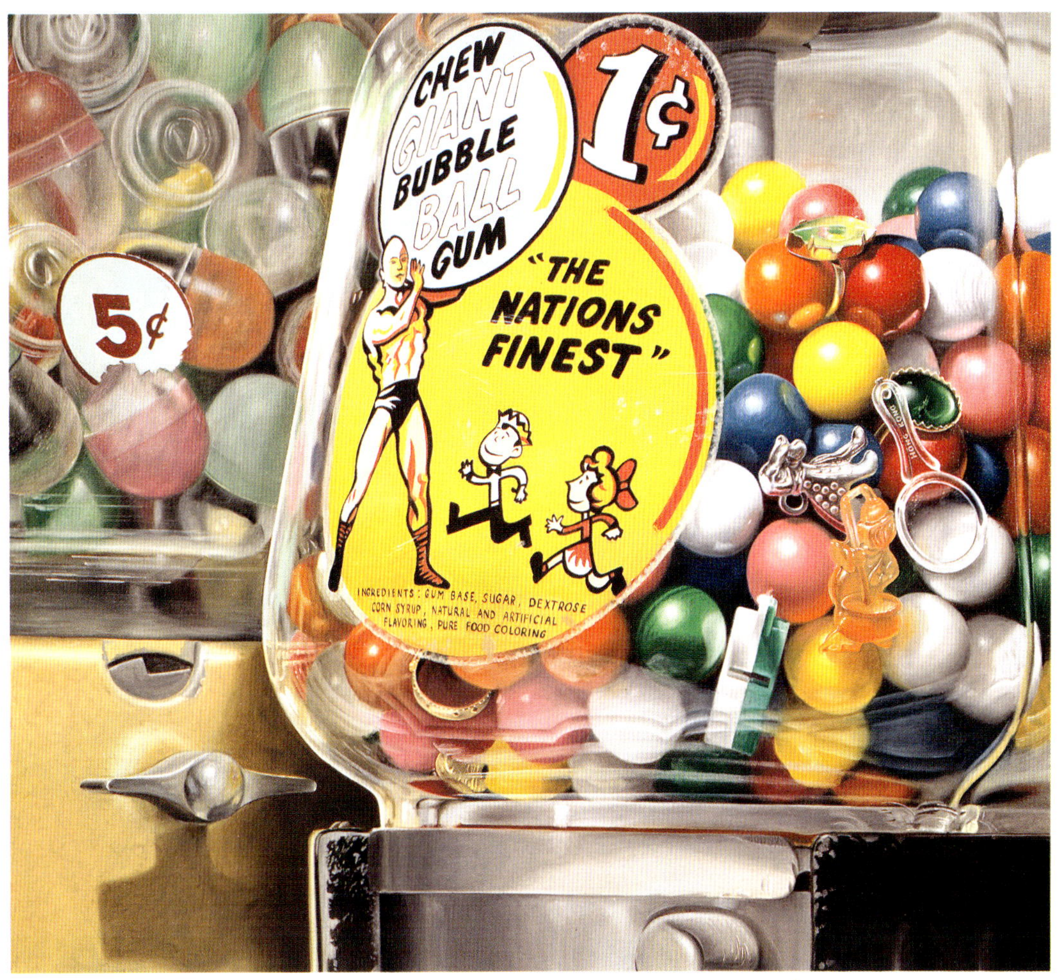

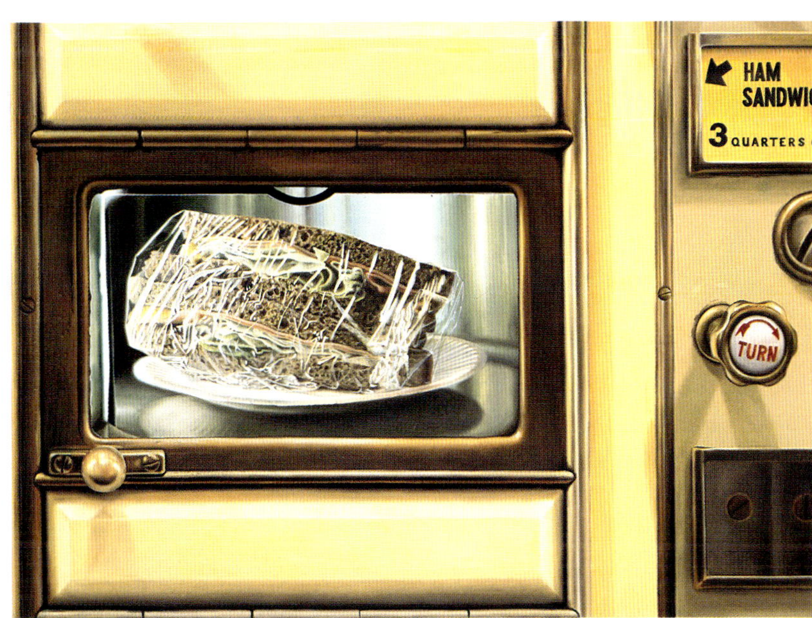

OPPOSITE: 64. *Gumball III*. 1973. Oil on canvas, 84 × 52″. Private collection, Paris

ABOVE: 65. *"Nation's Finest," Gumball IV*. 1974. Oil on canvas, 54 × 60″. Collection Meryle Samuels, New York

RIGHT: 66. *Horn and Hardart*. 1974. Oil on canvas, 52 × 72″. Private collection, New York

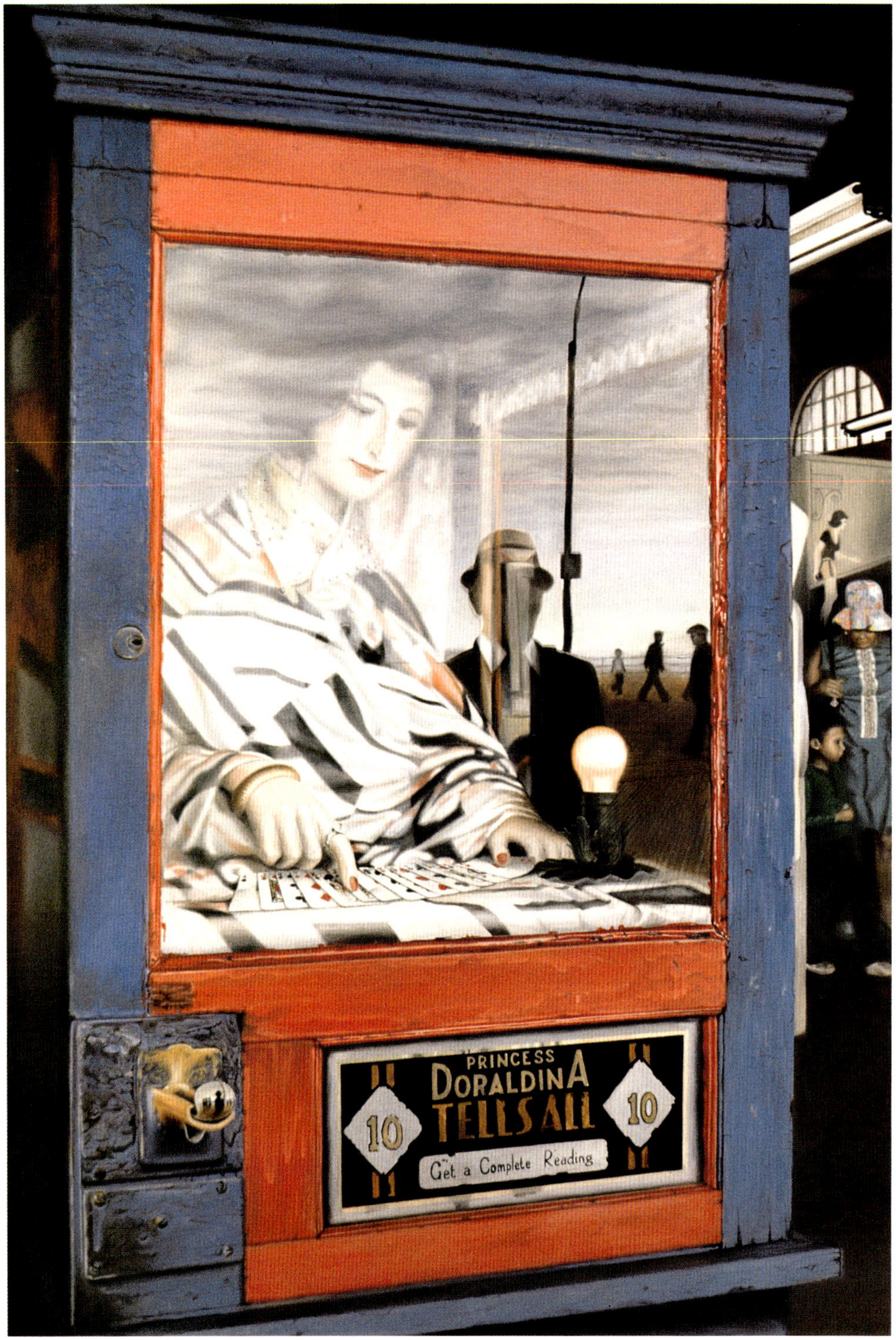

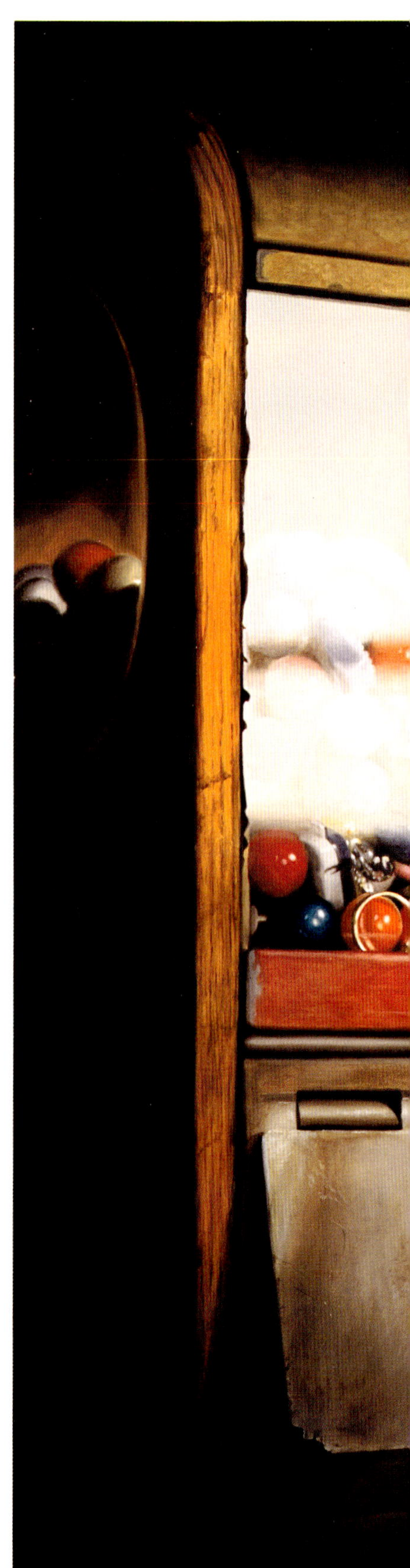

ABOVE: 67. *Fortune Teller*. 1974. Oil on canvas, 80 × 50″. Private collection

RIGHT: 68. *"Thank You," Gumball V*. 1974. Oil on canvas, 72 × 90″. Collection Jerome Nerman, Kansas

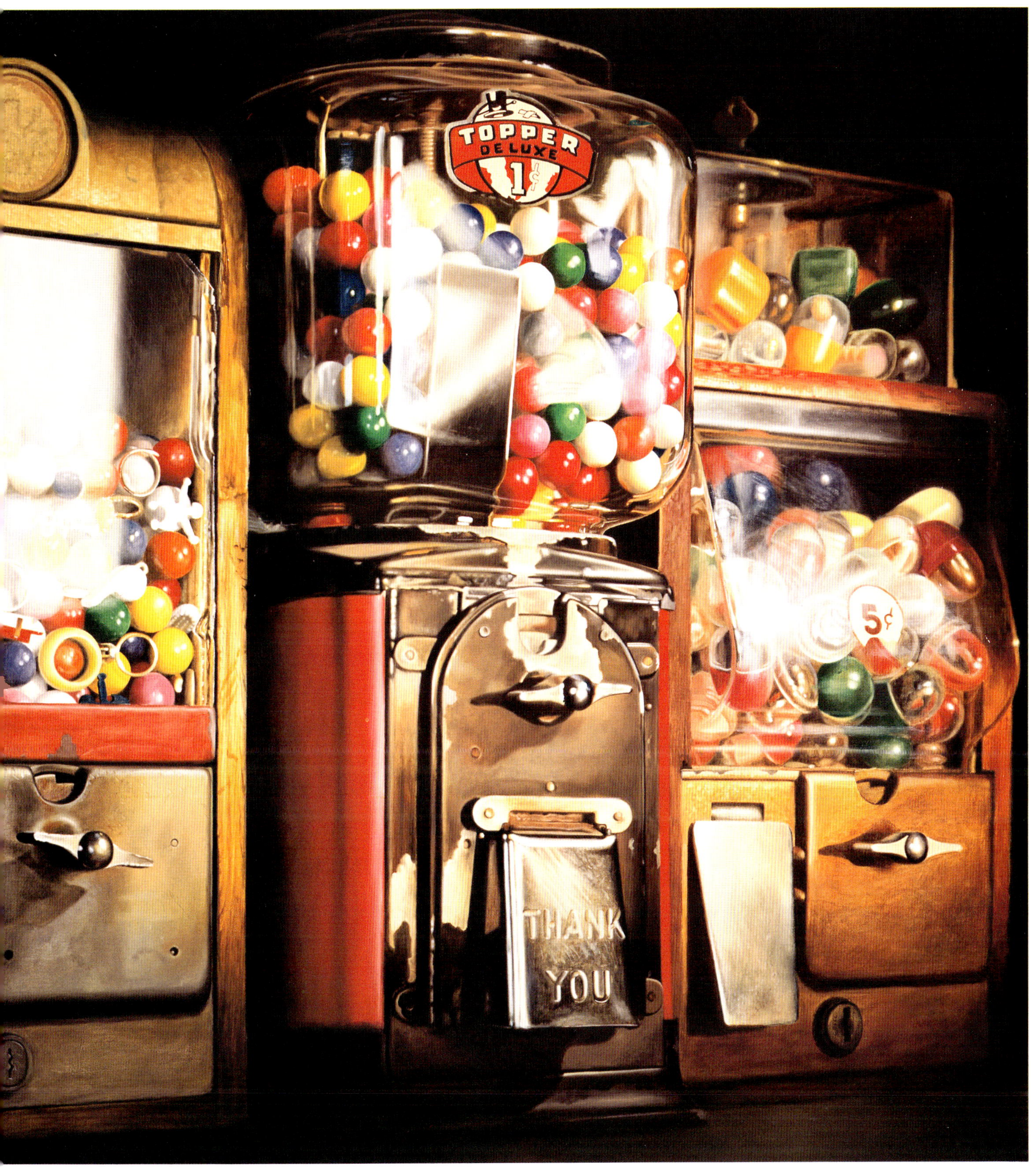
TOPPER
DE LUXE
1¢
5¢
THANK
YOU

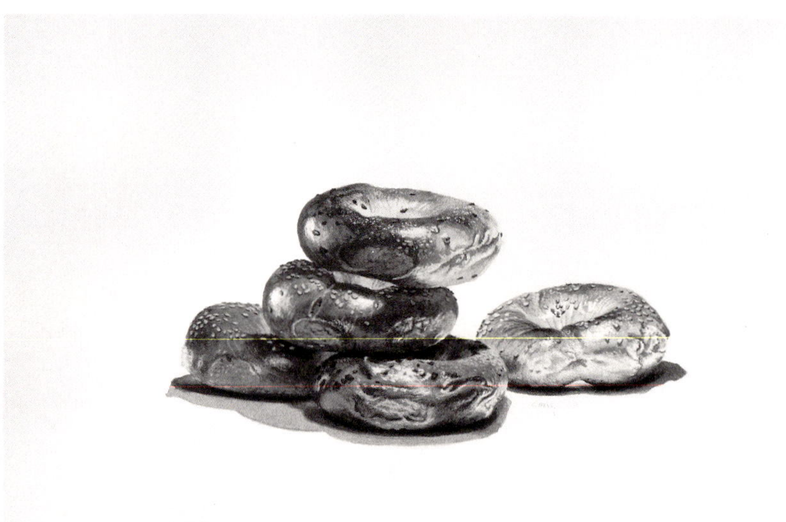

70. *Bagels*. 1974. Watercolor on paper, 12 × 17″. Collection Martin I. Harman, New York

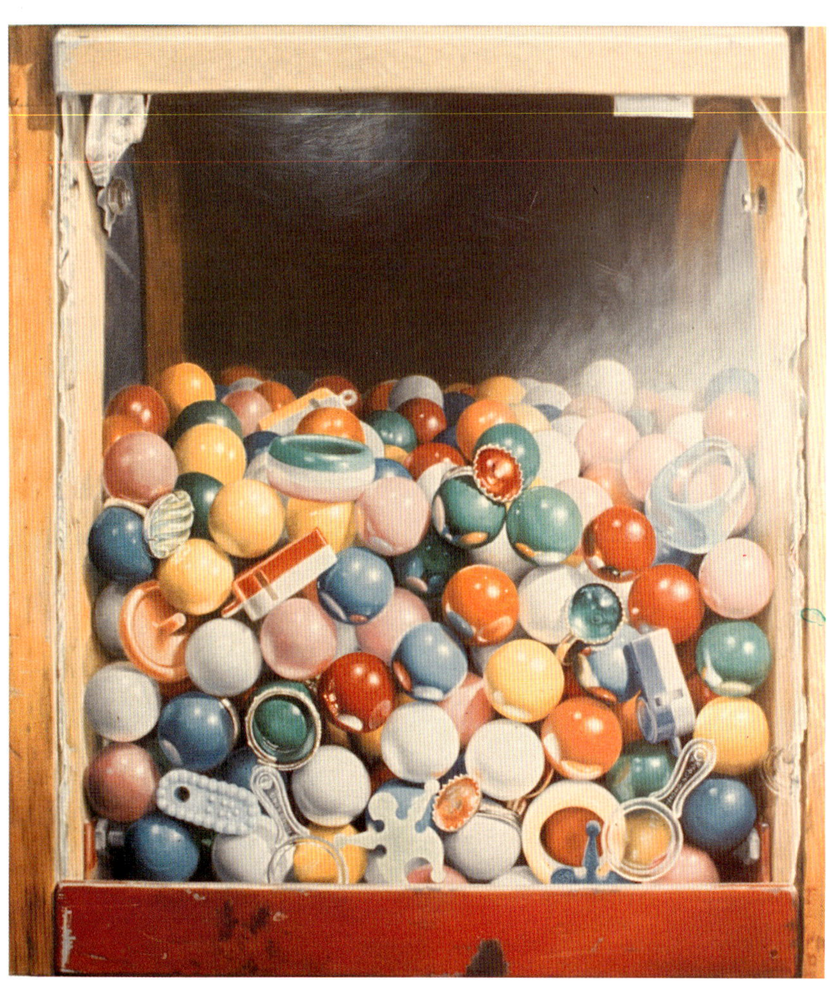

69. *Gumball VI*. 1974. Oil on canvas, 54 × 50″. Collection Richard Belger, Missouri

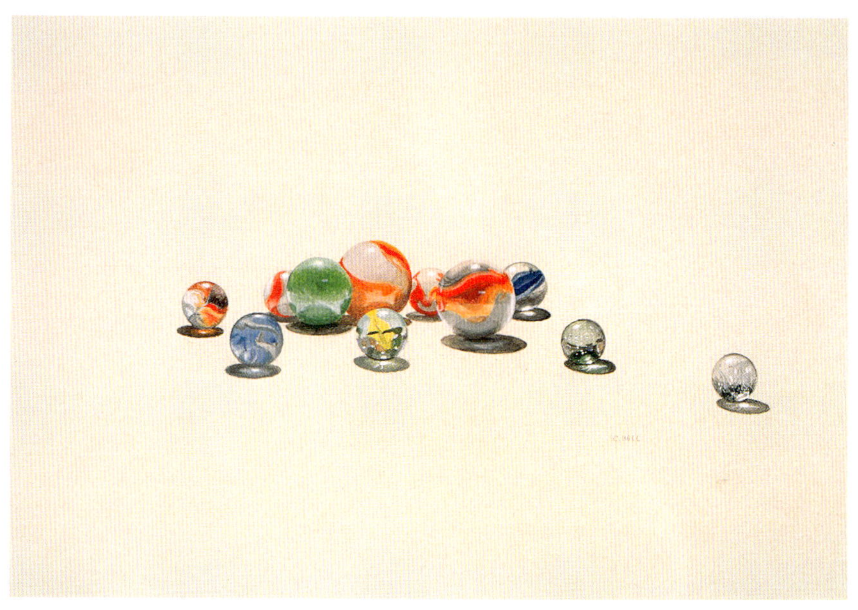

71. *Marbles*. 1974. Watercolor on paper, 9¼ × 12¾″. PieperPower Companies, Inc., Wisconsin

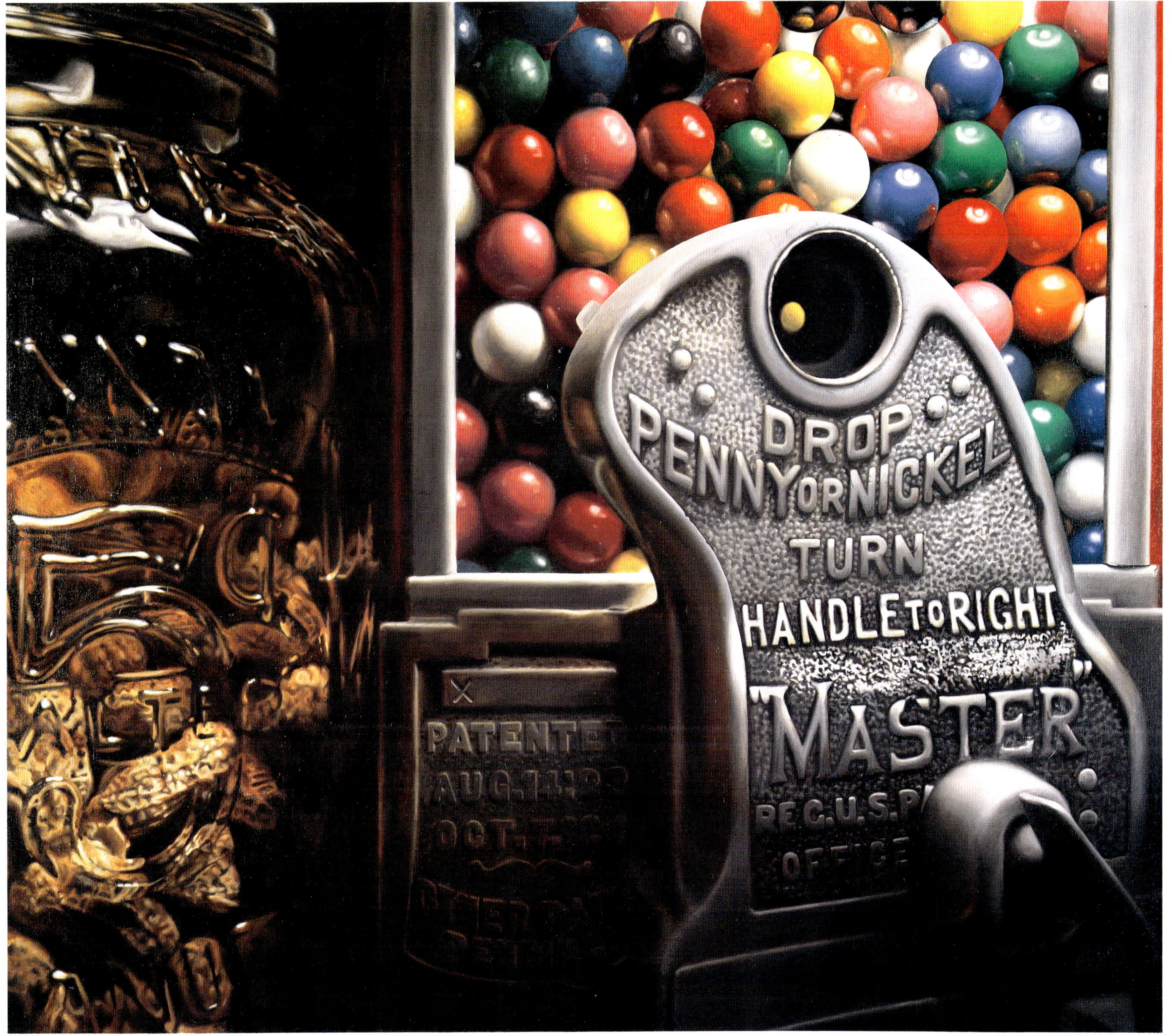

72. *Gumball VII*. 1975. Oil on canvas, 60 × 70″. Louis K. Meisel Gallery, New York

RIGHT: 73. *Gumball VIII*. 1975. Oil on canvas, 48 × 48″. Collection Richard Chestnov and Harvey Gold, New York

BELOW: 74. *Gumball IX*. 1975. Oil on canvas, 54 × 66″. Collection Mr. and Mrs. W. Jaeger, New York

OPPOSITE: 75. *"Sugar Daddy," Gumball X*. 1975. Oil on canvas, 66 × 66″. Solomon R. Guggenheim Museum, New York

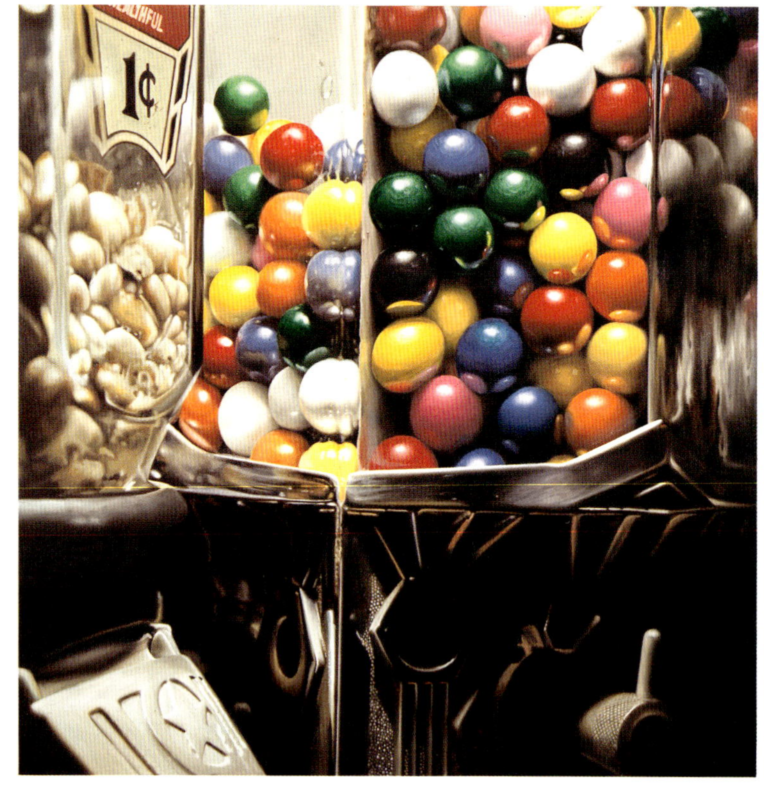

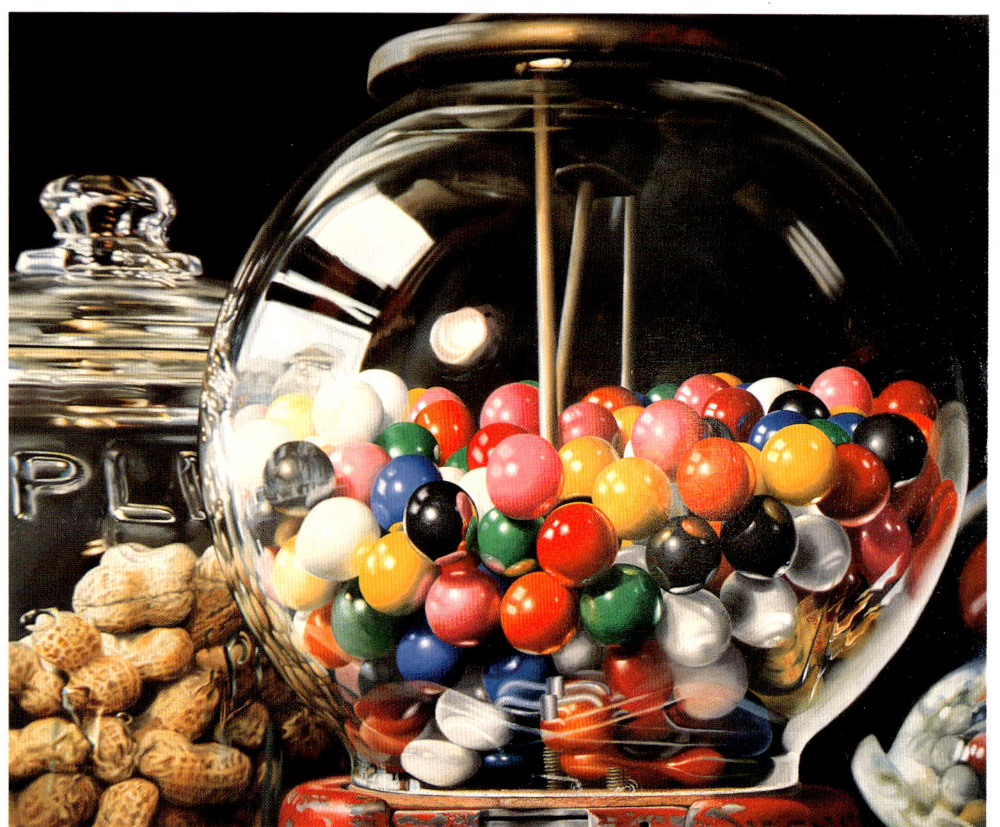

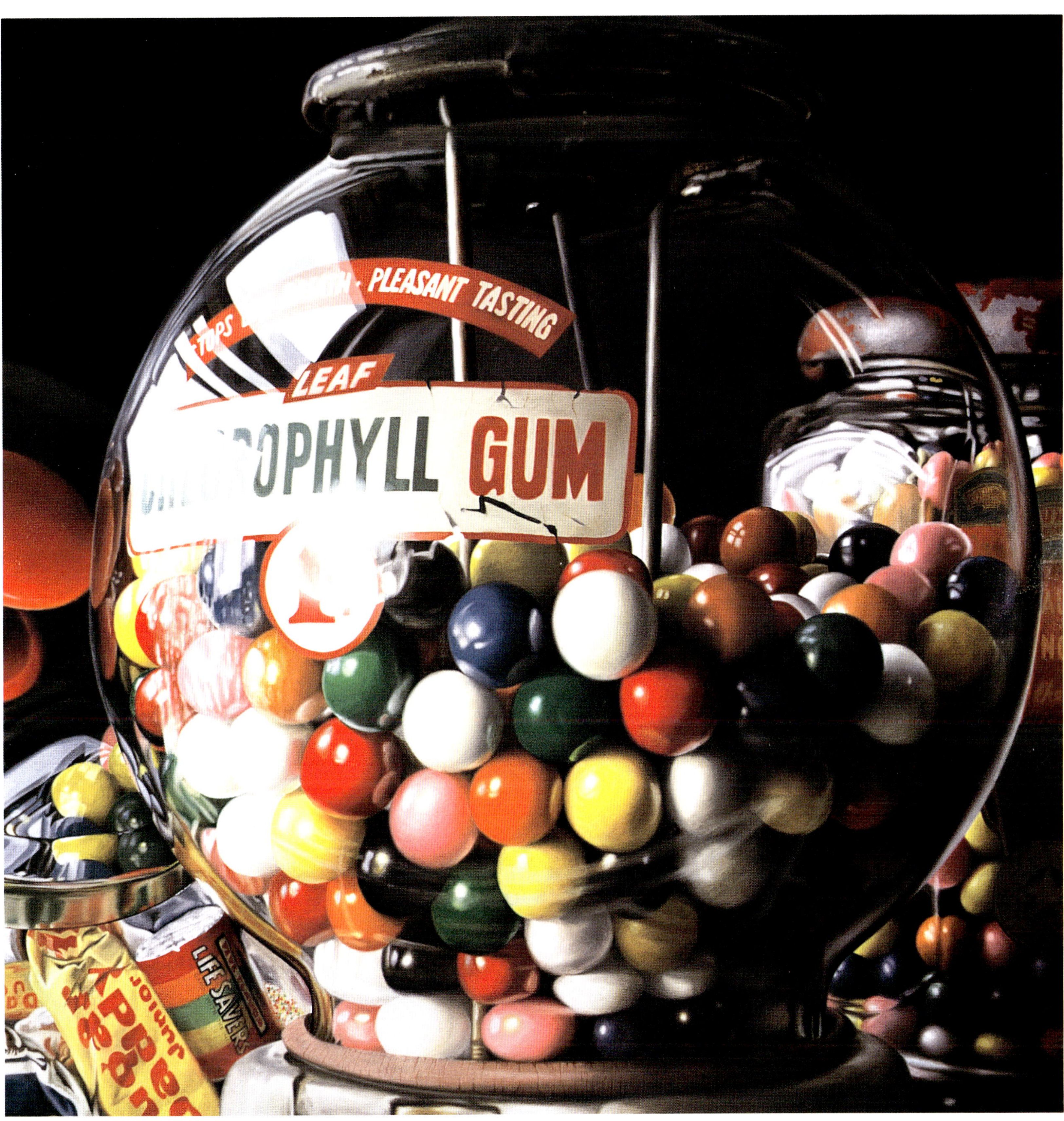
PLEASANT TASTING
LEAF
OPHYLL GUM
LIFE SAVERS

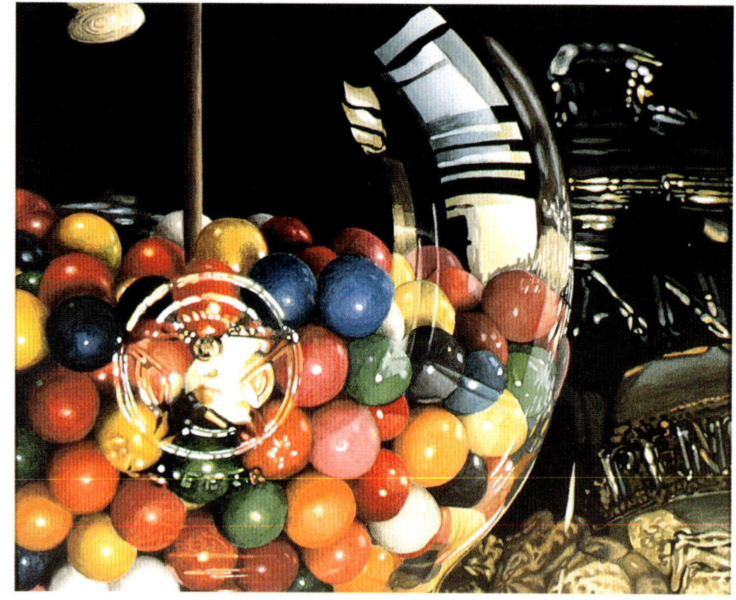

LEFT: 76. *Gumball Watercolor No. 1*. 1975. Watercolor on paper, 12 × 15″. Collection Louis K. and Susan Pear Meisel, New York

BELOW: 77. *"5 Cent Special," Gumball XII*. 1976. Oil on canvas, 72 × 72″. Private collection

OPPOSITE: 78. *Gumball XI*. 1976. Oil on canvas, 84 × 60″. Private collection, Paris

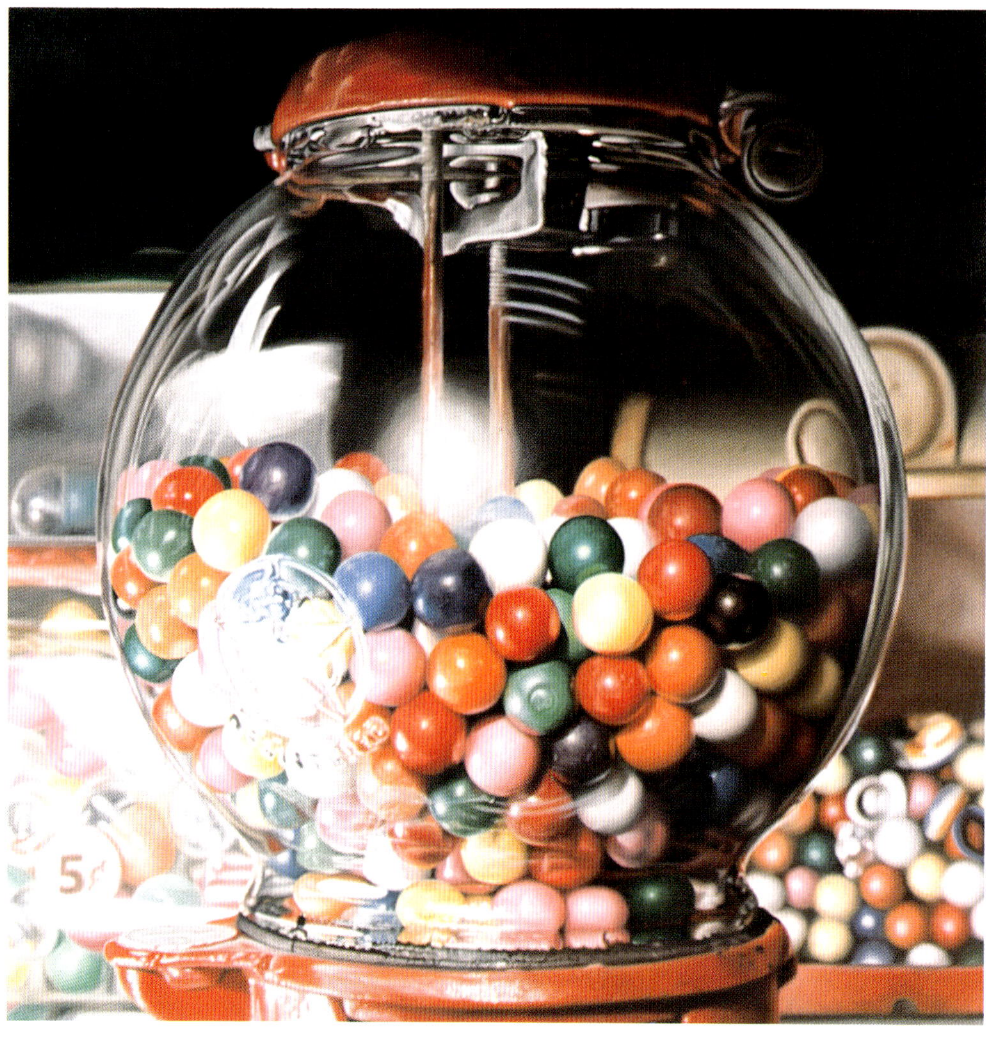

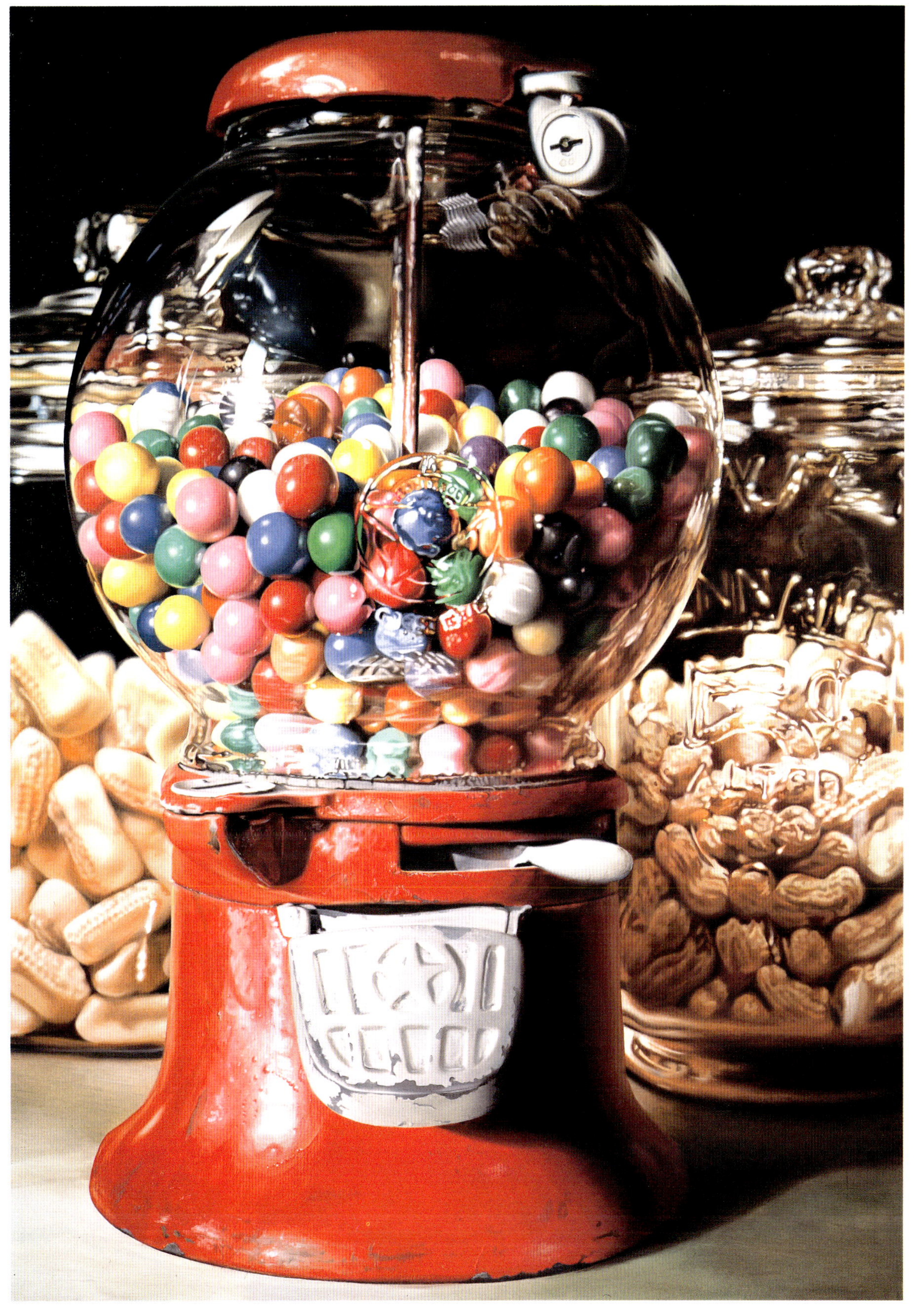

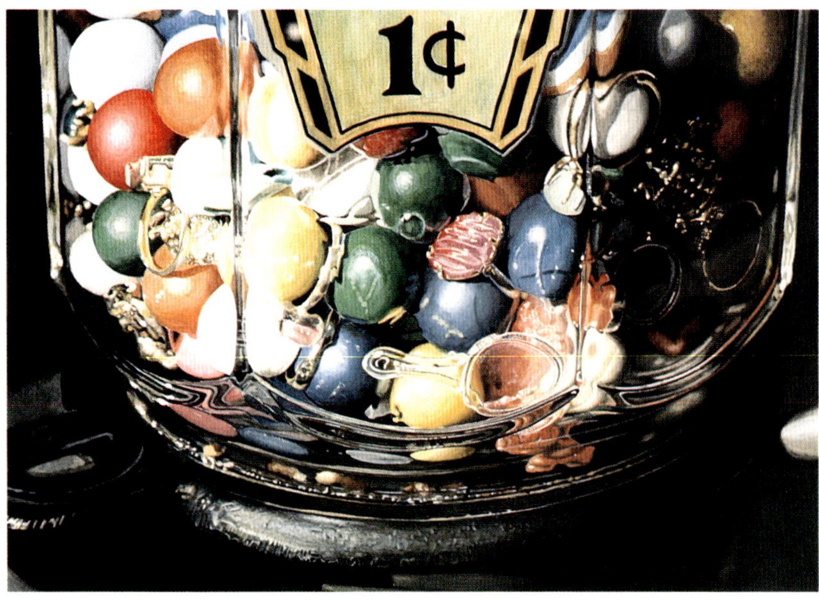

79. *Gumball Watercolor No. 2*. 1976. Watercolor on paper, 16 × 22½″. Private collection, New York

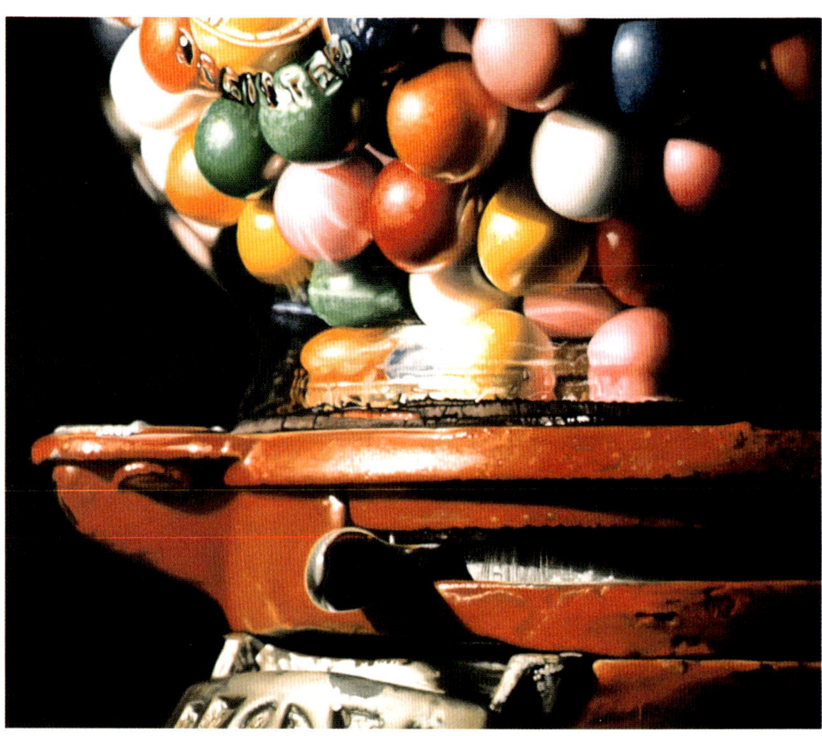

80. *Gumball Fragment No. 1*. 1976. Oil on canvas, 34 × 40″. Collection Stanton Rosenberg, M.D., Kansas

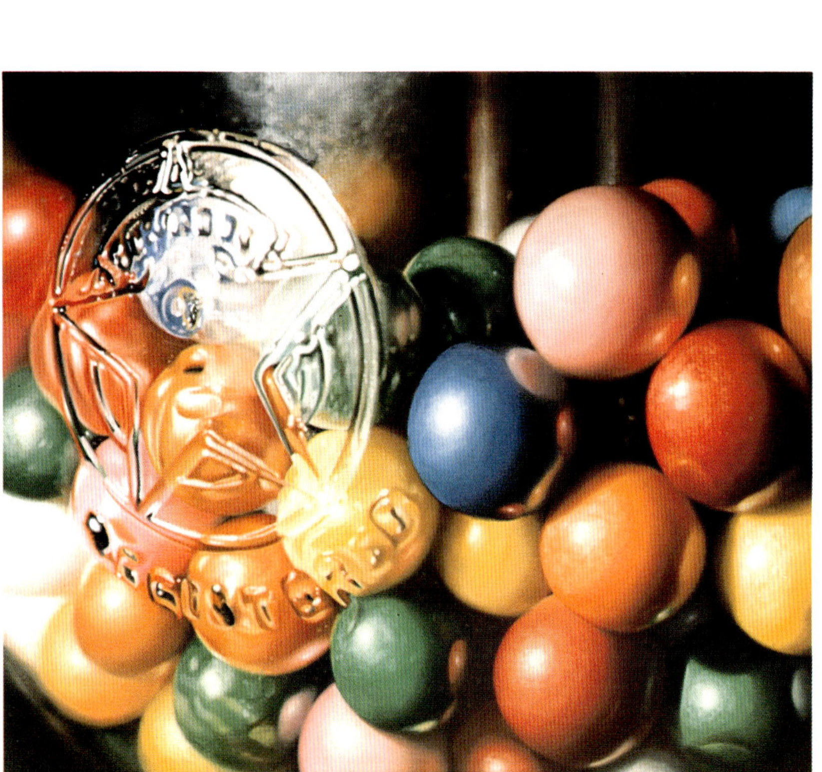

81. *Gumball Fragment No. 2*. 1976. Oil on canvas, 30 × 36″. Private collection

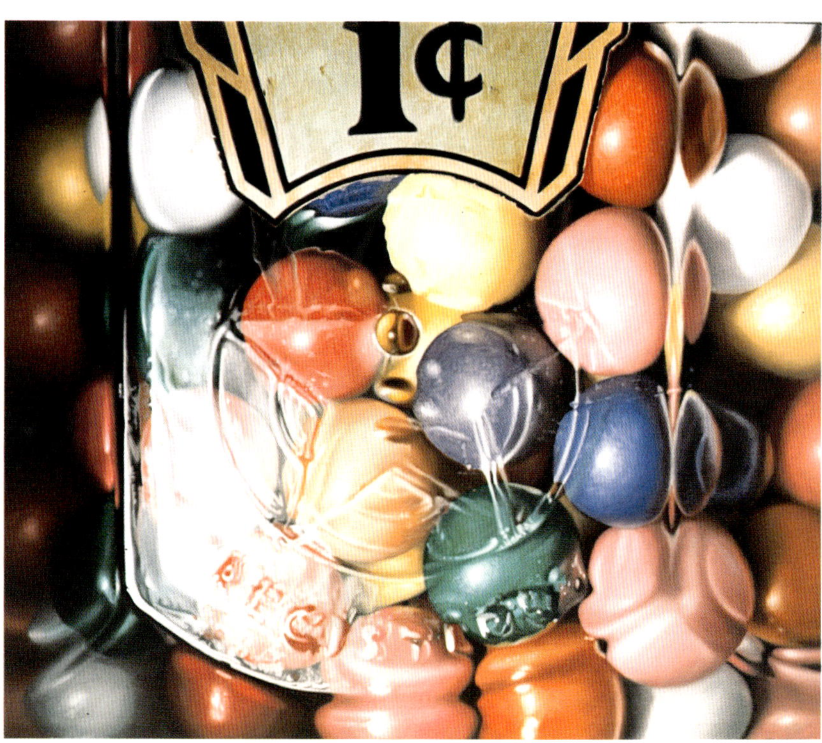

82. *"One Cent," Gumball Fragment No. 3*. 1976. Oil on canvas, 34 × 40″. Collection Ms. Carmel Roth, New York

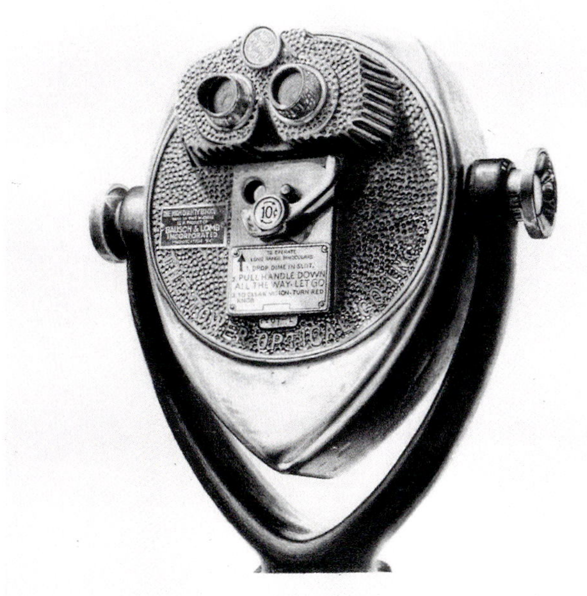

83. *Scenic Overlook*. 1976. Graphite on paper, 17 × 17″. Collection Louis K. and Susan Pear Meisel, New York

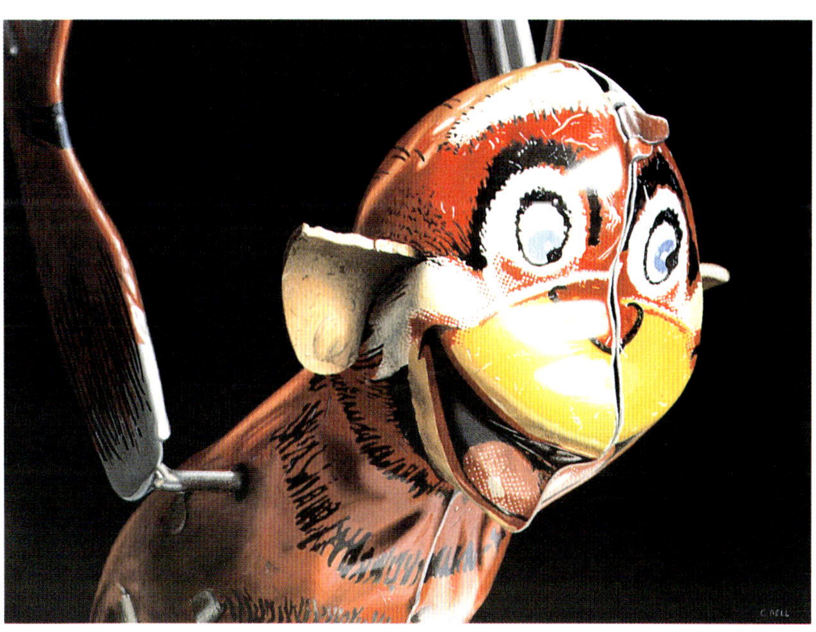

84. *Toy Portrait Series I*. 1978. Acrylic on illustration board, 15 × 19″. Private collection

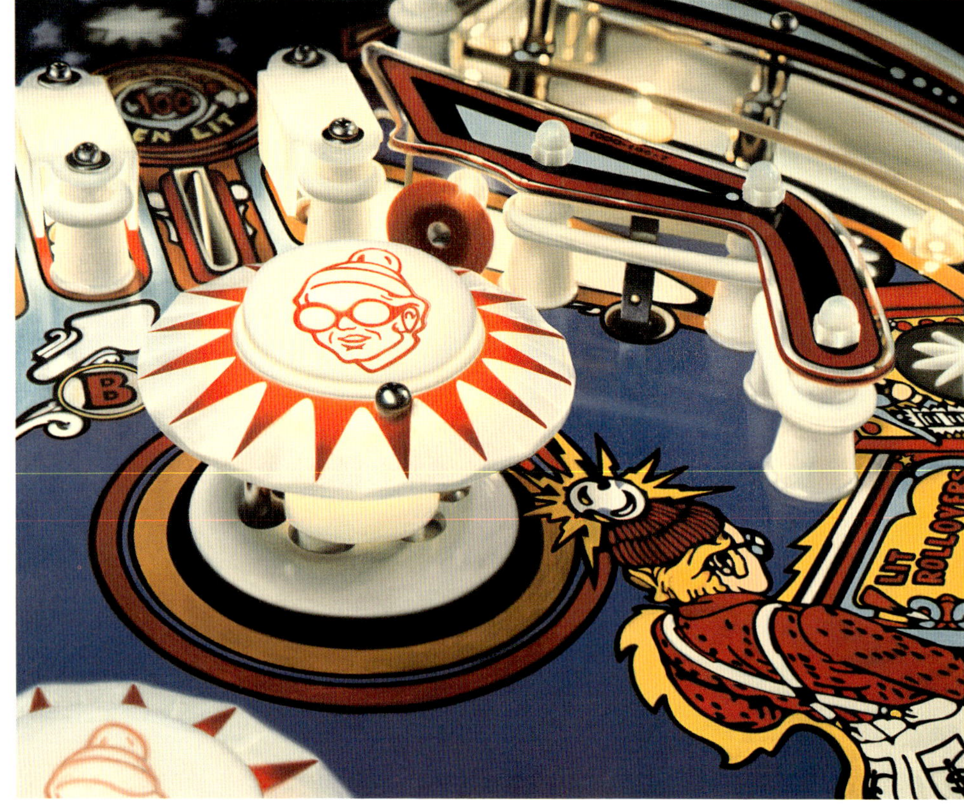

85. *The Wizard*. 1977. Oil on canvas, 54 × 66″. Collection Mr. and Mrs. Barry Hirschfeld, Colorado

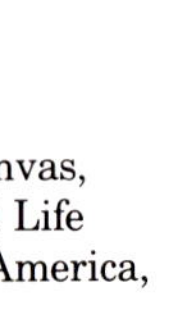

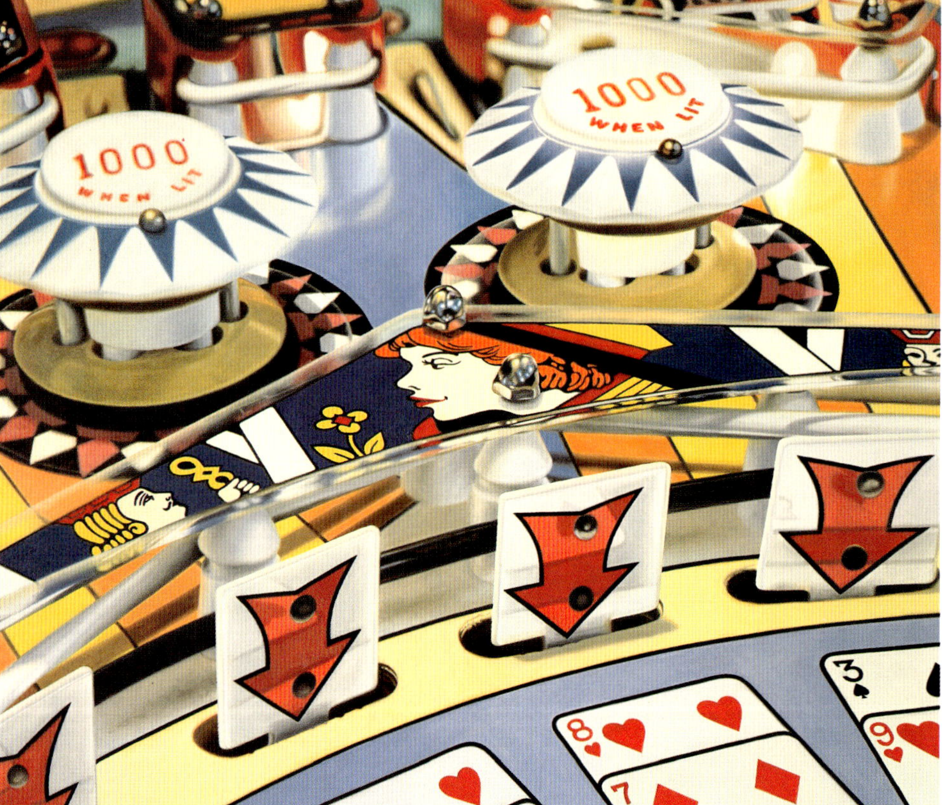

86. *Gin*. 1977. Oil on canvas, 60 × 72″. The Prudential Life Insurance Company of America, New Jersey

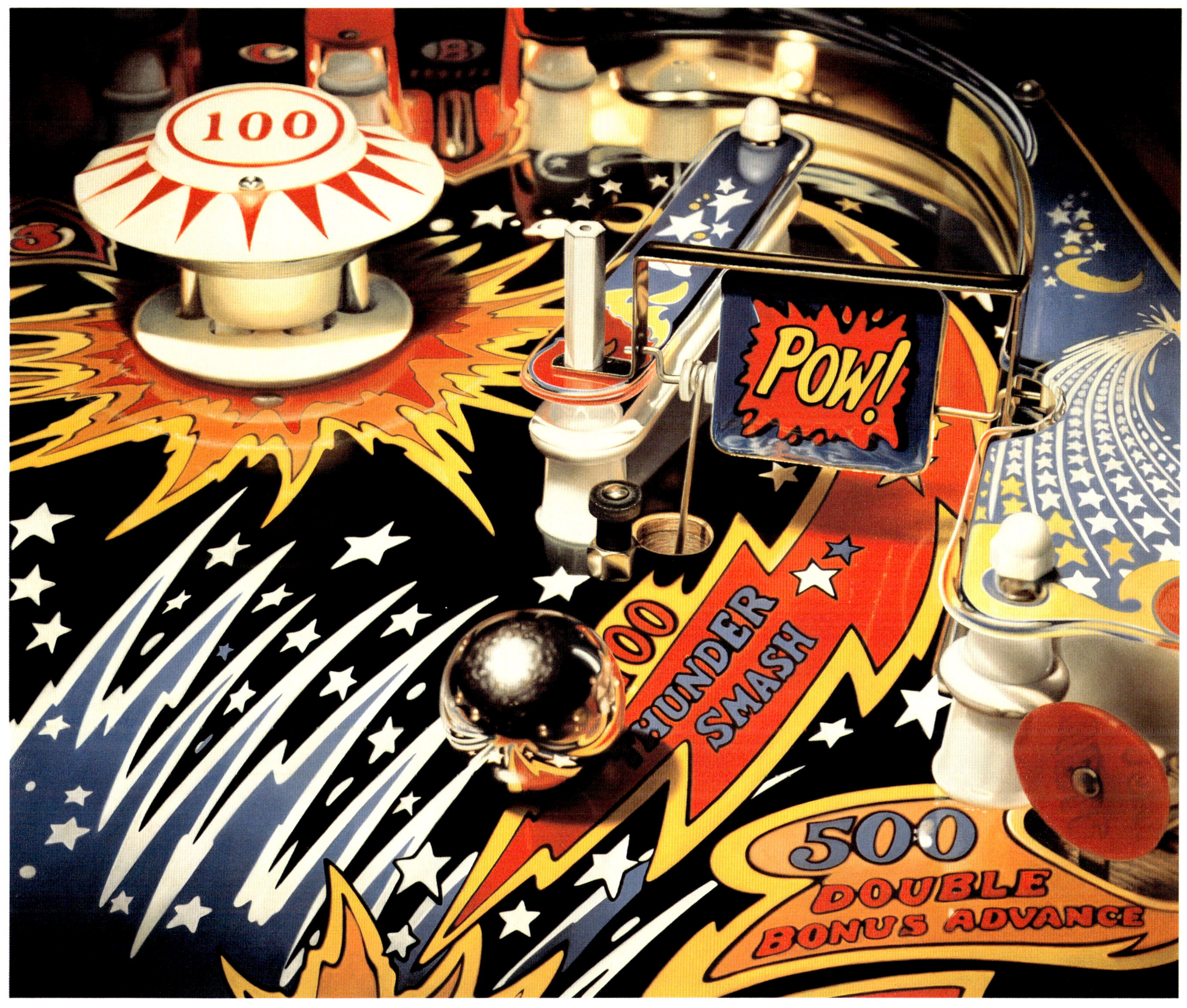

87. *Fire Ball 500 No. 1*. 1977. Oil on canvas, 54 × 66″. Private collection

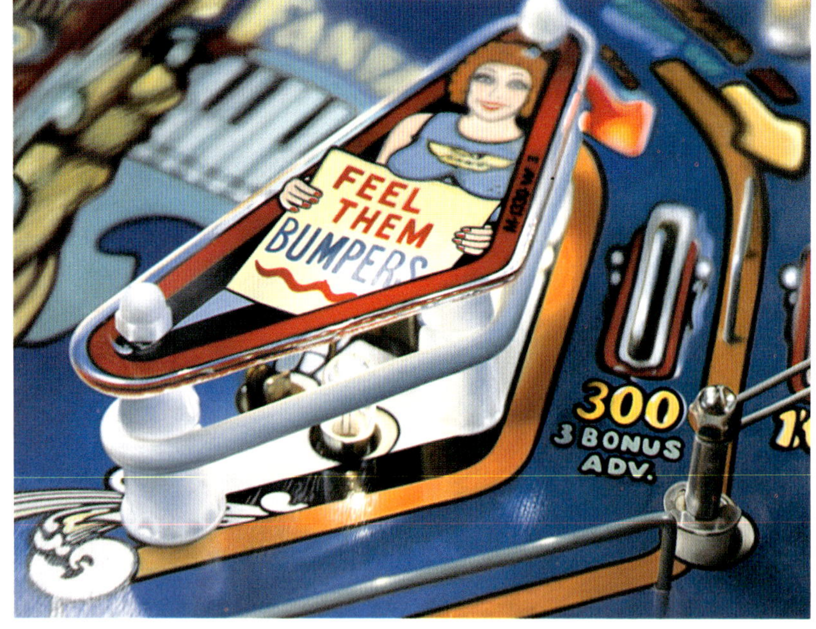

LEFT: 88. *Feel Them Bumpers*. 1977. Oil on canvas, 44 × 58″. Louis K. Meisel Gallery, New York

BELOW: 89. *Double Advance*. 1977. Oil on canvas, 48 × 60″. Private collection

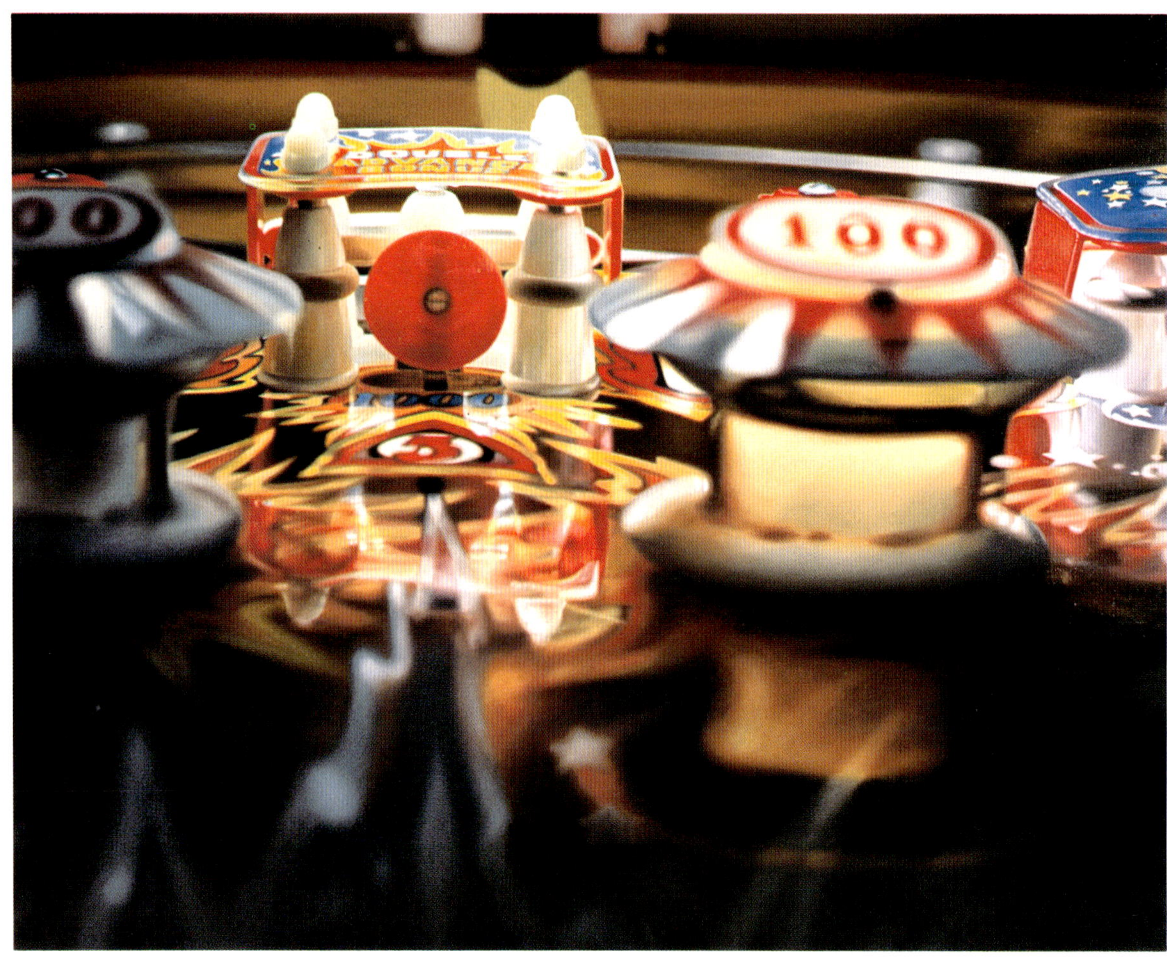

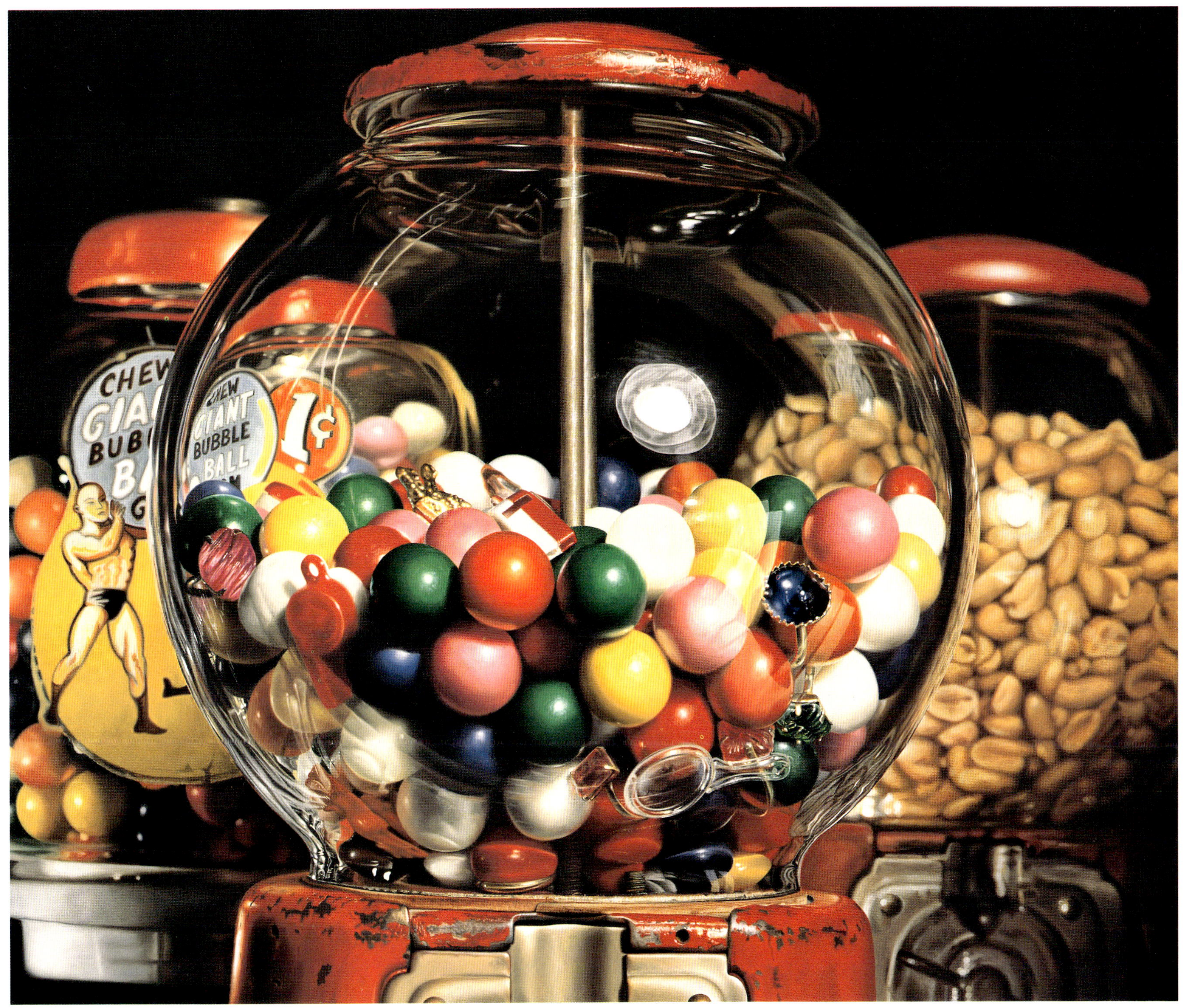

90. *The Ultimate Gumball*. 1978. Oil on canvas, 54¼ × 66″. Collection Joan and Barrie Damson, Connecticut

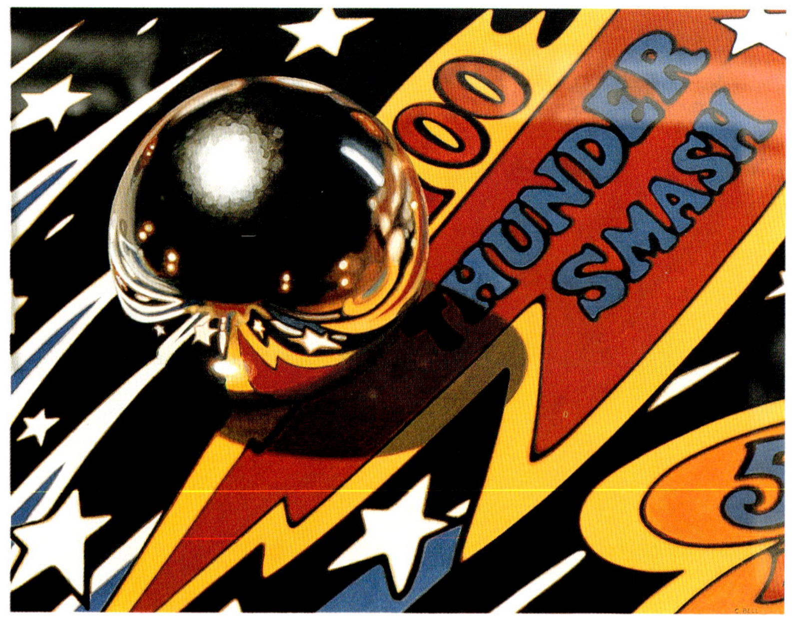

91. *Thunder Smash Fragment*. 1978. Watercolor on illustration board, 16 × 20″. Collection Louis K. and Susan Pear Meisel, New York

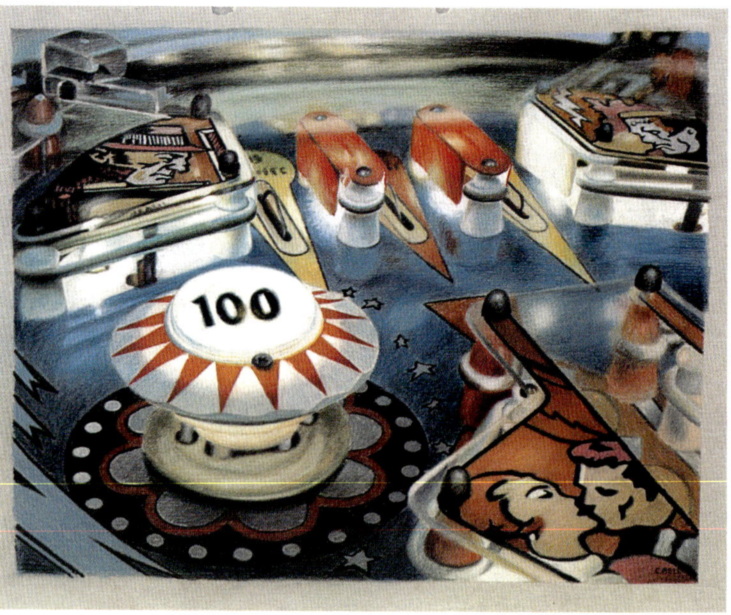

92. *Pinball No. 1*. 1976. Pastel on paper, 19 × 24″. Private collection

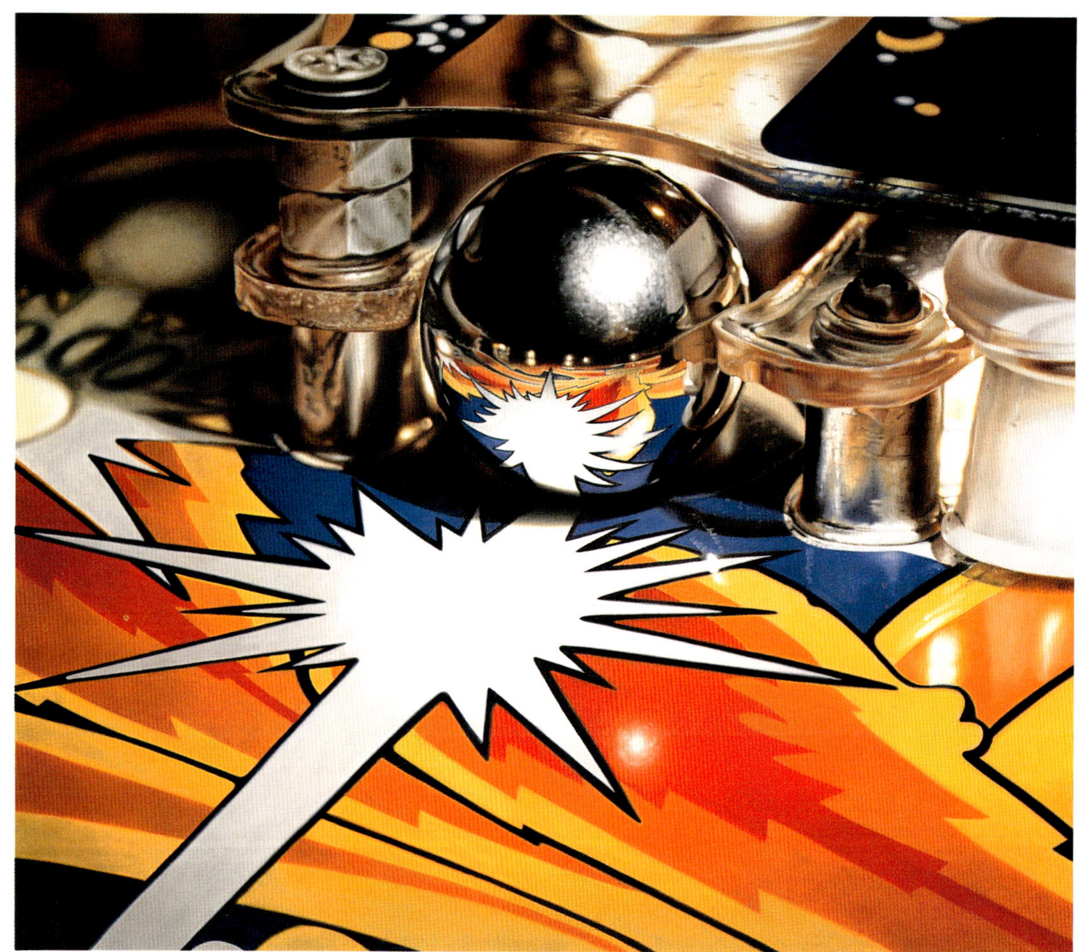

93. *Captive Messenger*. 1979. Oil on canvas, 36 × 42″. Private collection

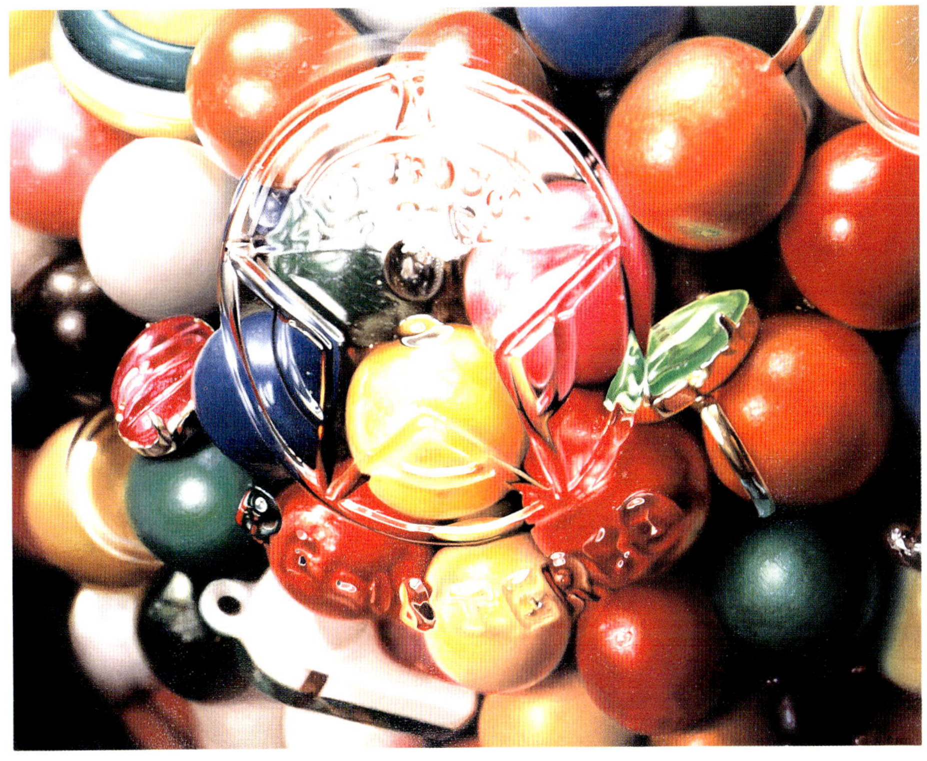

94. *Gumball Section A.* 1980. Oil on canvas, 32 × 40″. Private collection, New Jersey

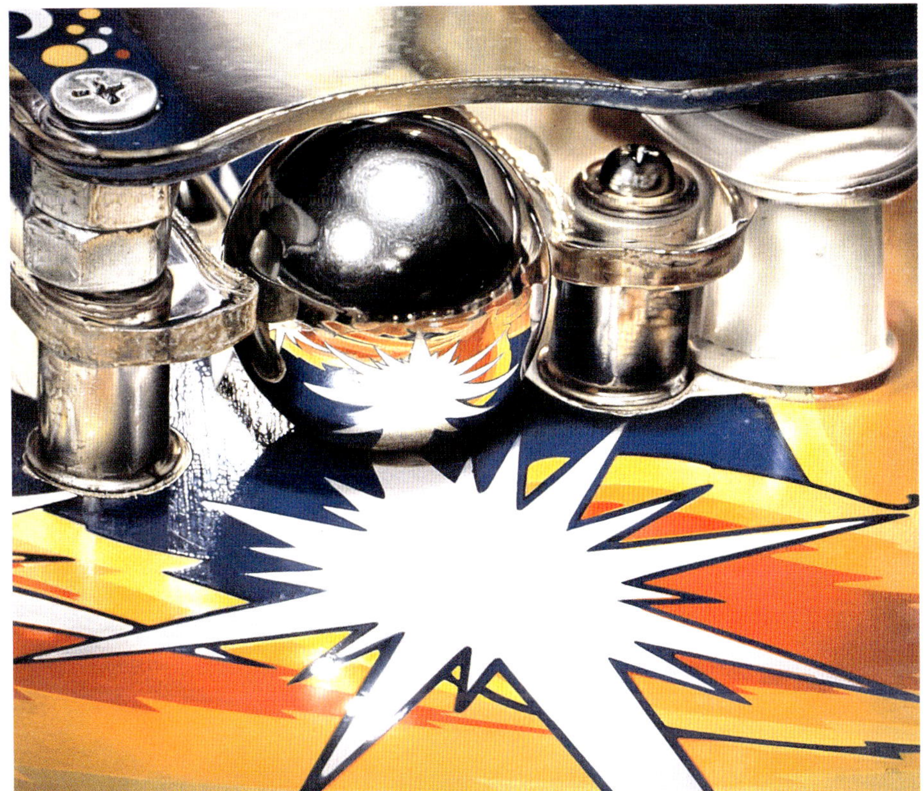

95. *Captive Messenger No. 2.* 1980. Oil on canvas, 34 × 40″. Private collection

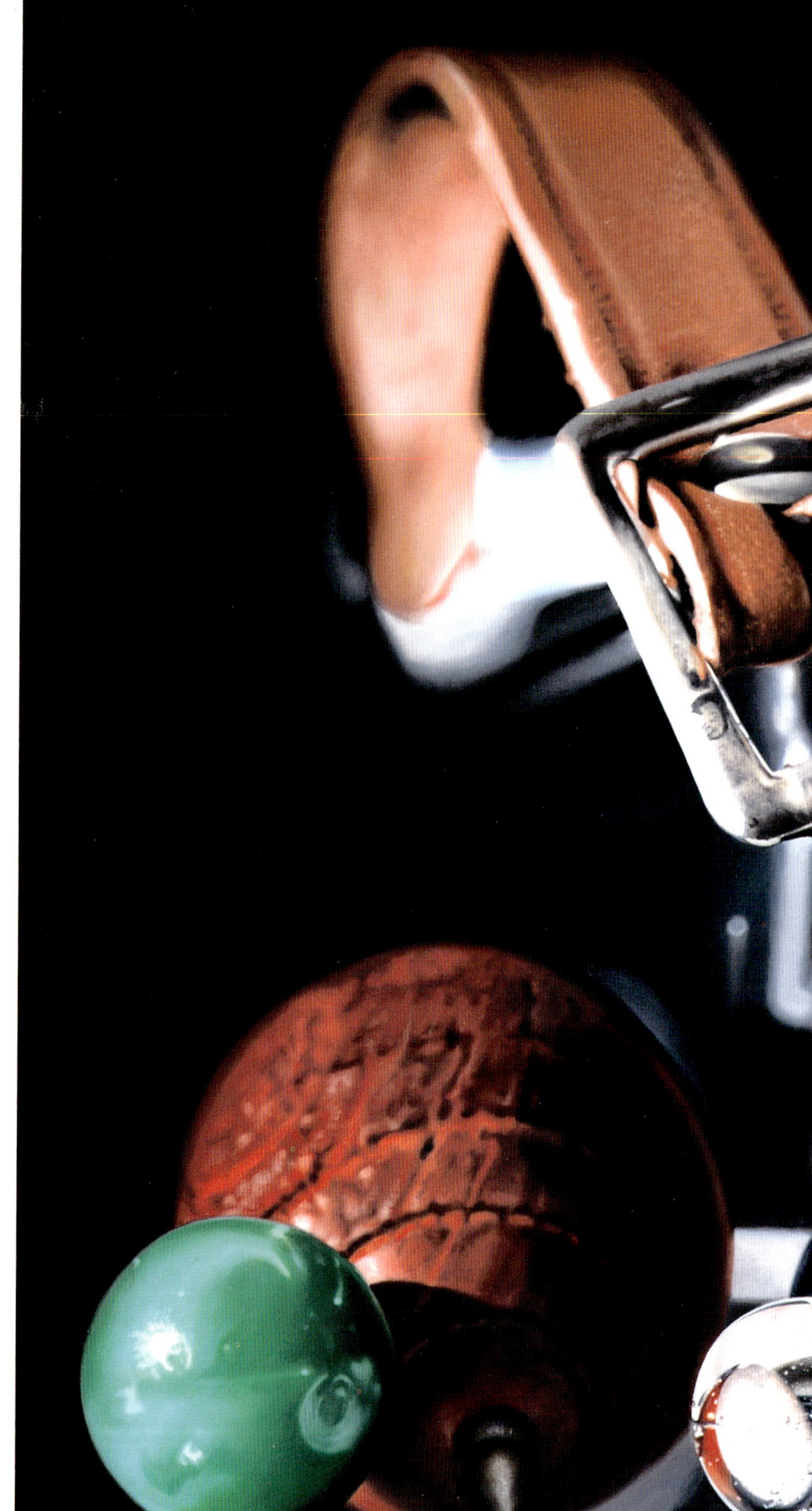

96. *"Chicago" Pat. No. 1,910,193*. 1980. Oil on canvas, 52 × 84″. Collection Jack and Harriet Stievelman, New York

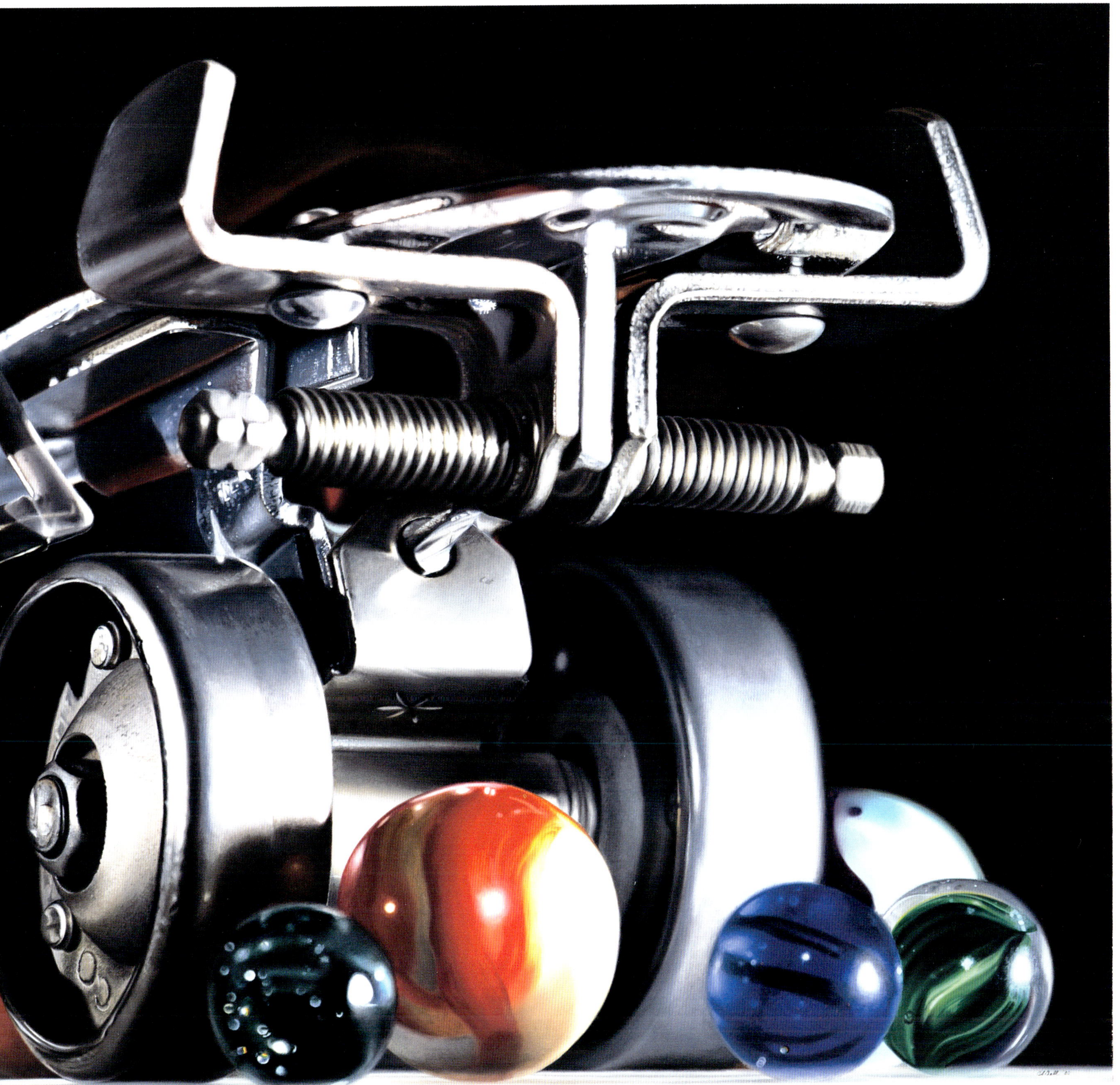

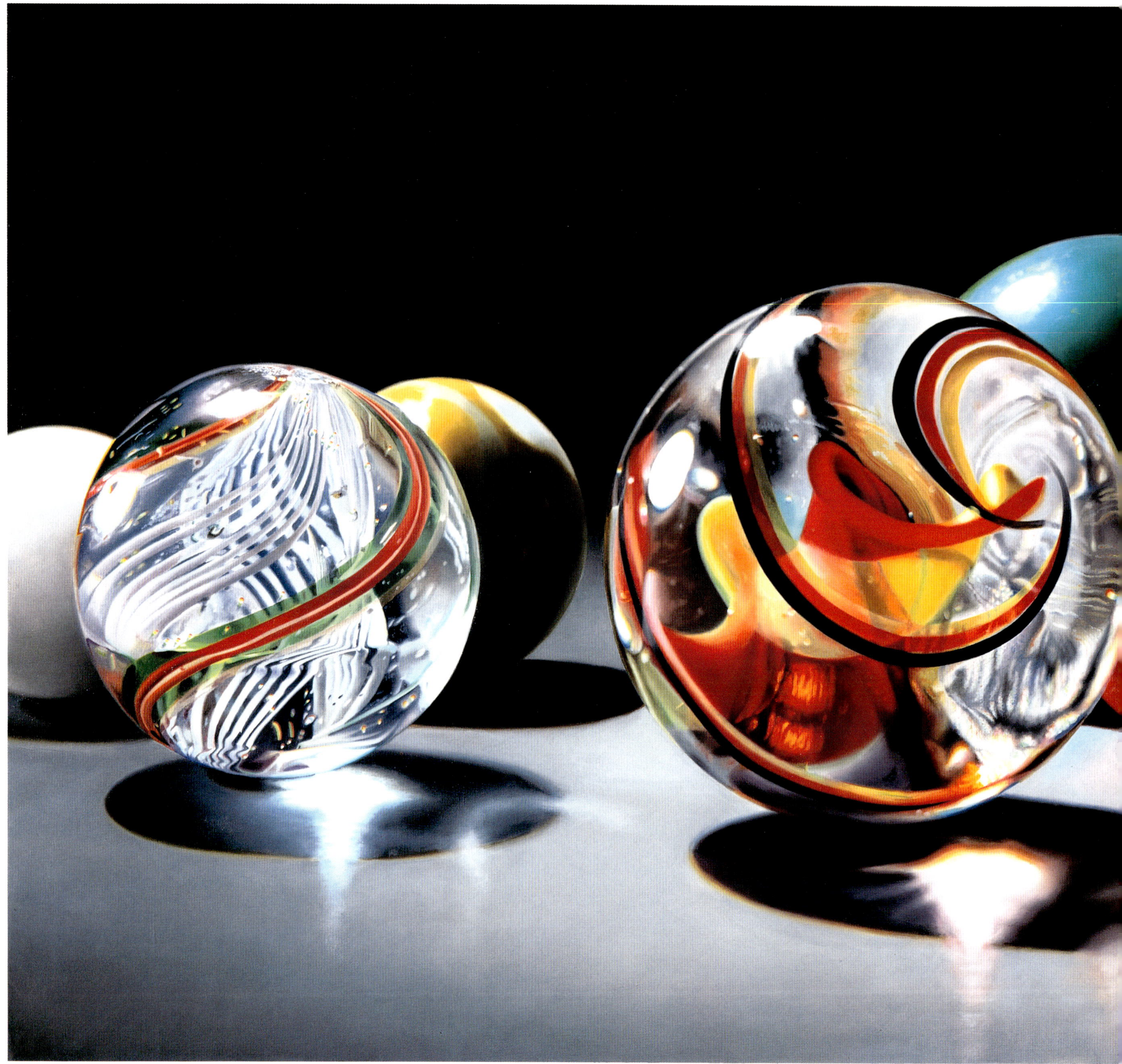

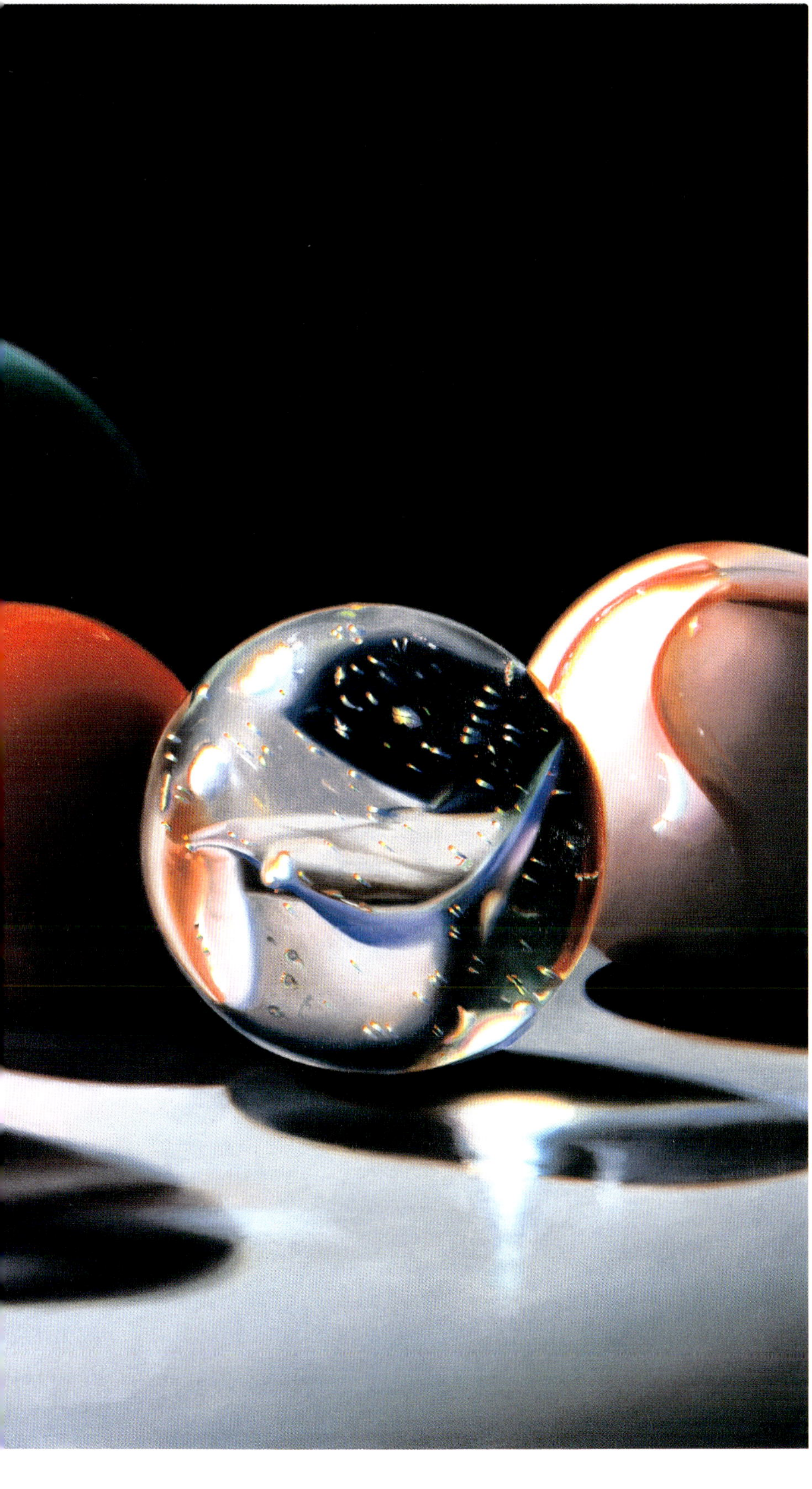

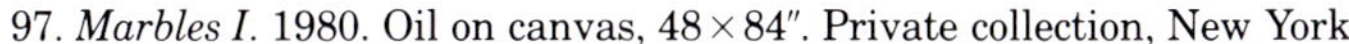

97. *Marbles I*. 1980. Oil on canvas, 48 × 84″. Private collection, New York

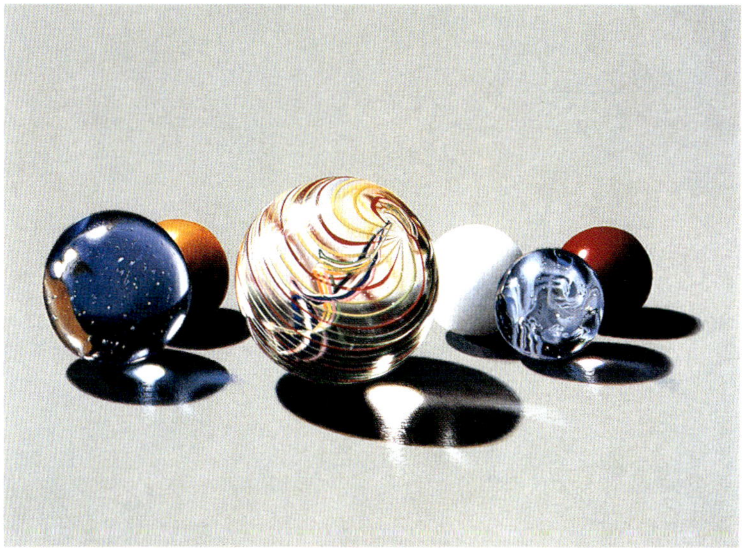

98. *Marbles*. 1980. Gouache on paper, 19½ × 27½″. Collection Mr. and Mrs. W. Jaeger, New York

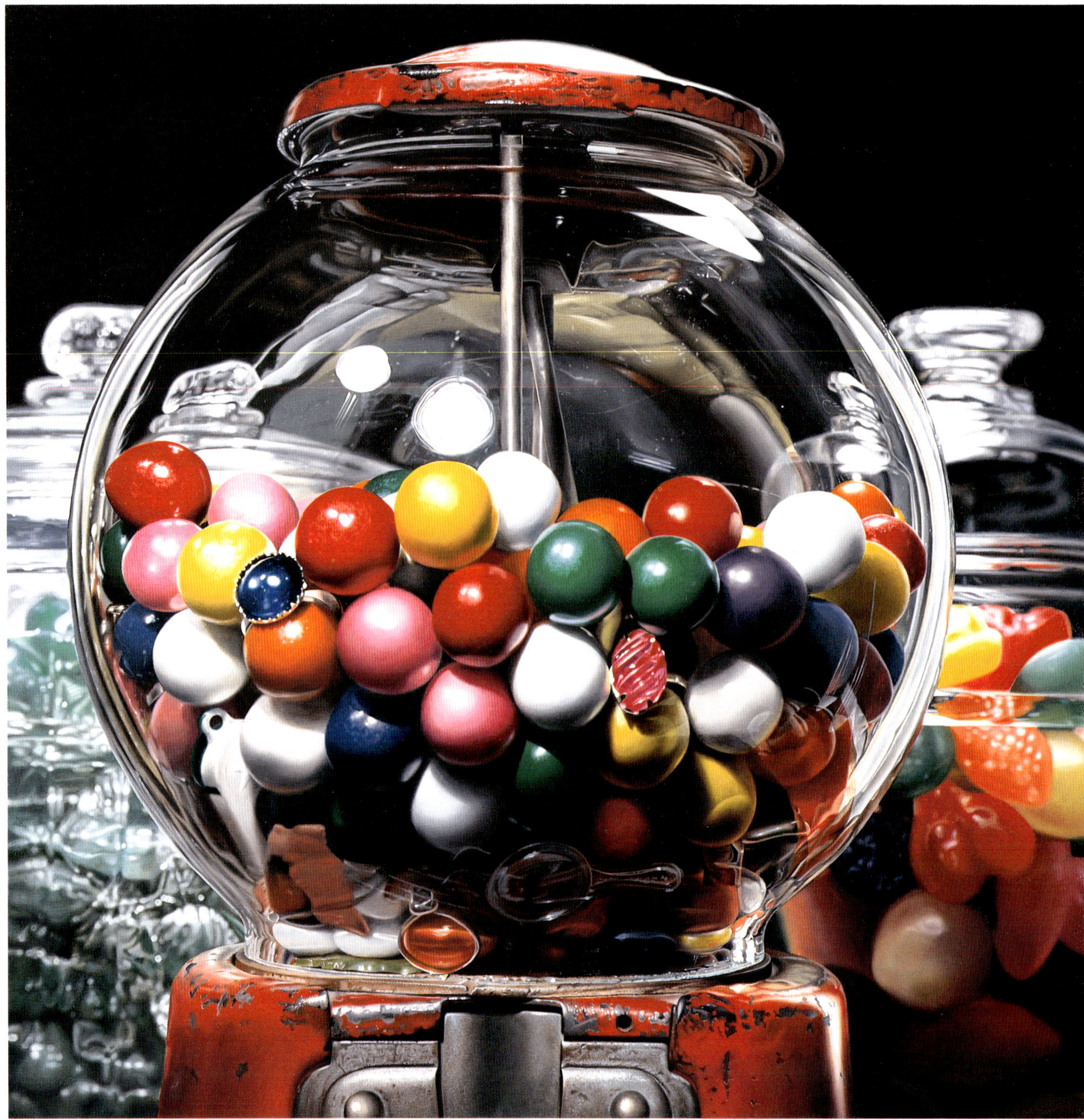

99. *Gumball XIV*. 1980. Oil on canvas, 66 × 66″. Collection Bruce R. Lewin, New York

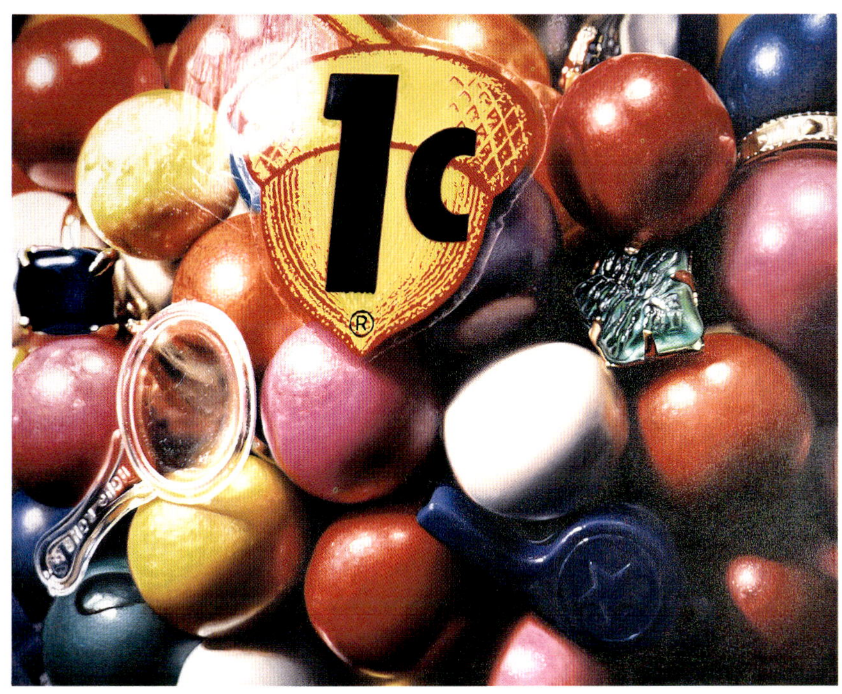

100. *1 Cent Win the Ring*. 1981. Oil on canvas, 32 × 40″. Private collection, New York

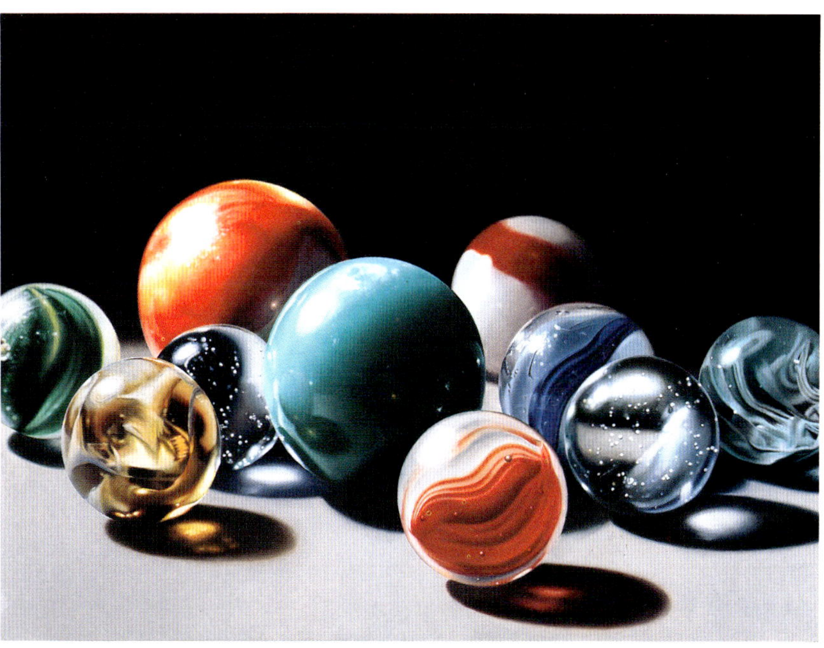

101. *Marbles II*. 1981. Oil on board, 29½ × 39¾″. Collection Mr. and Mrs. W. Jaeger, New York

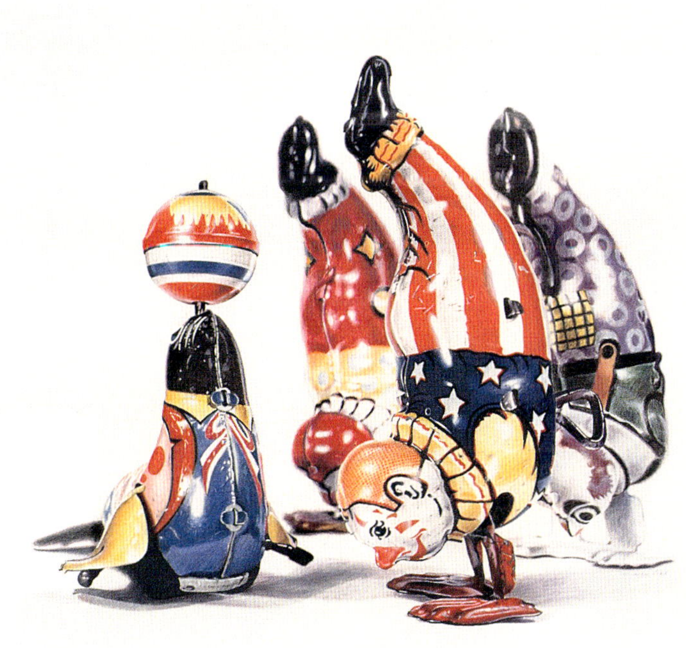

102. Study for *Troupe* (Clowns and Seal). 1981. Colored pencil on paper, 20 × 23″. Collection Louis K. and Susan Pear Meisel, New York

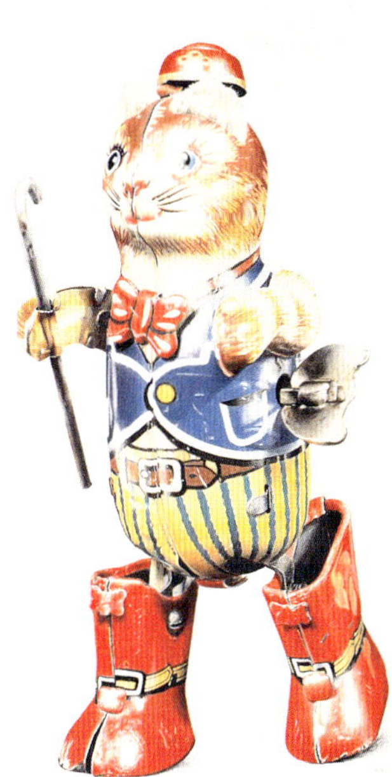

103. *Puss in Boots (Cat Toy)*. 1981. Colored pencil on paper, 30 × 22¼″. Collection Gilbert and Judith Shapiro, New York

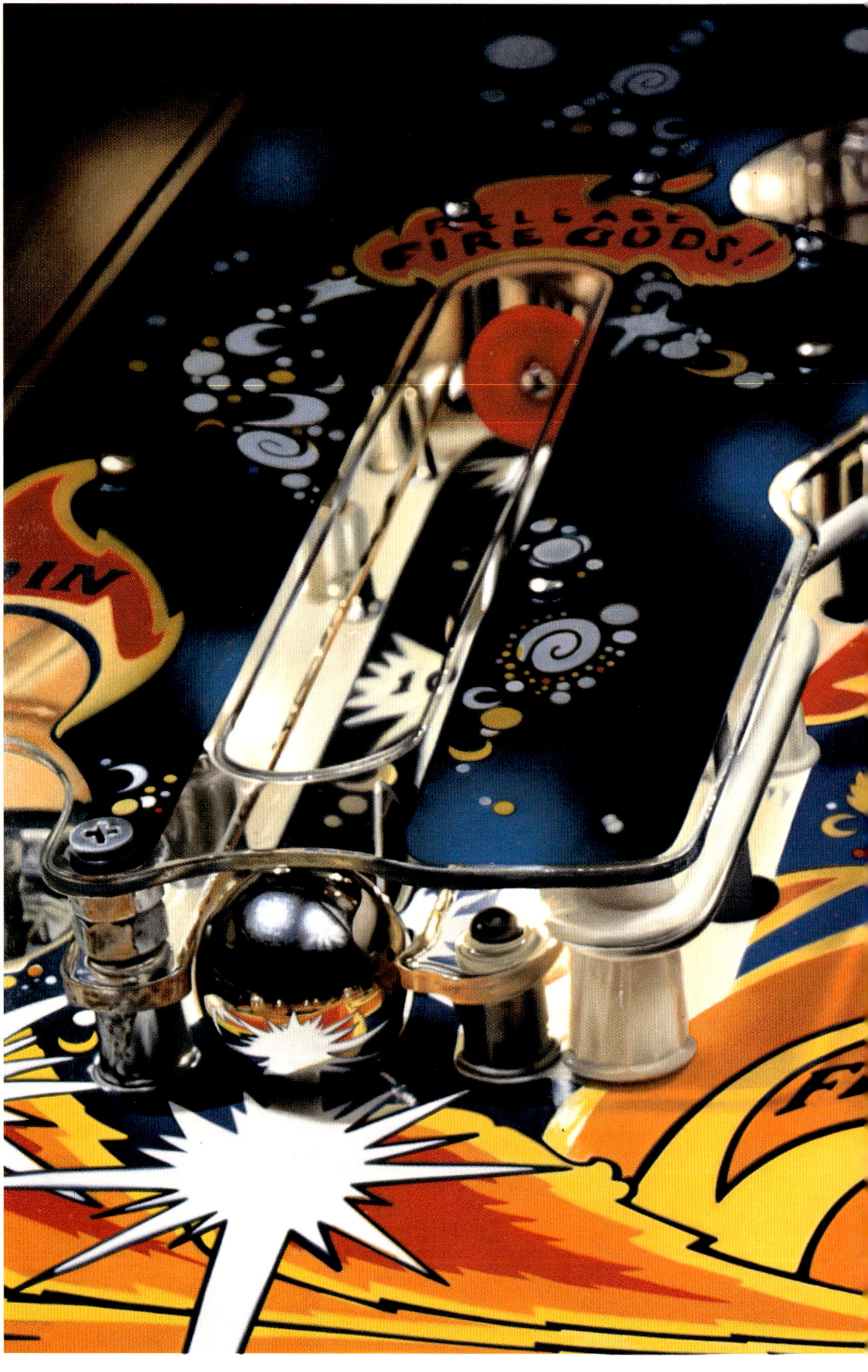

104. *100 Points When Lit.* 1981. Oil on canvas, 60 × 108″. Private collection, New York

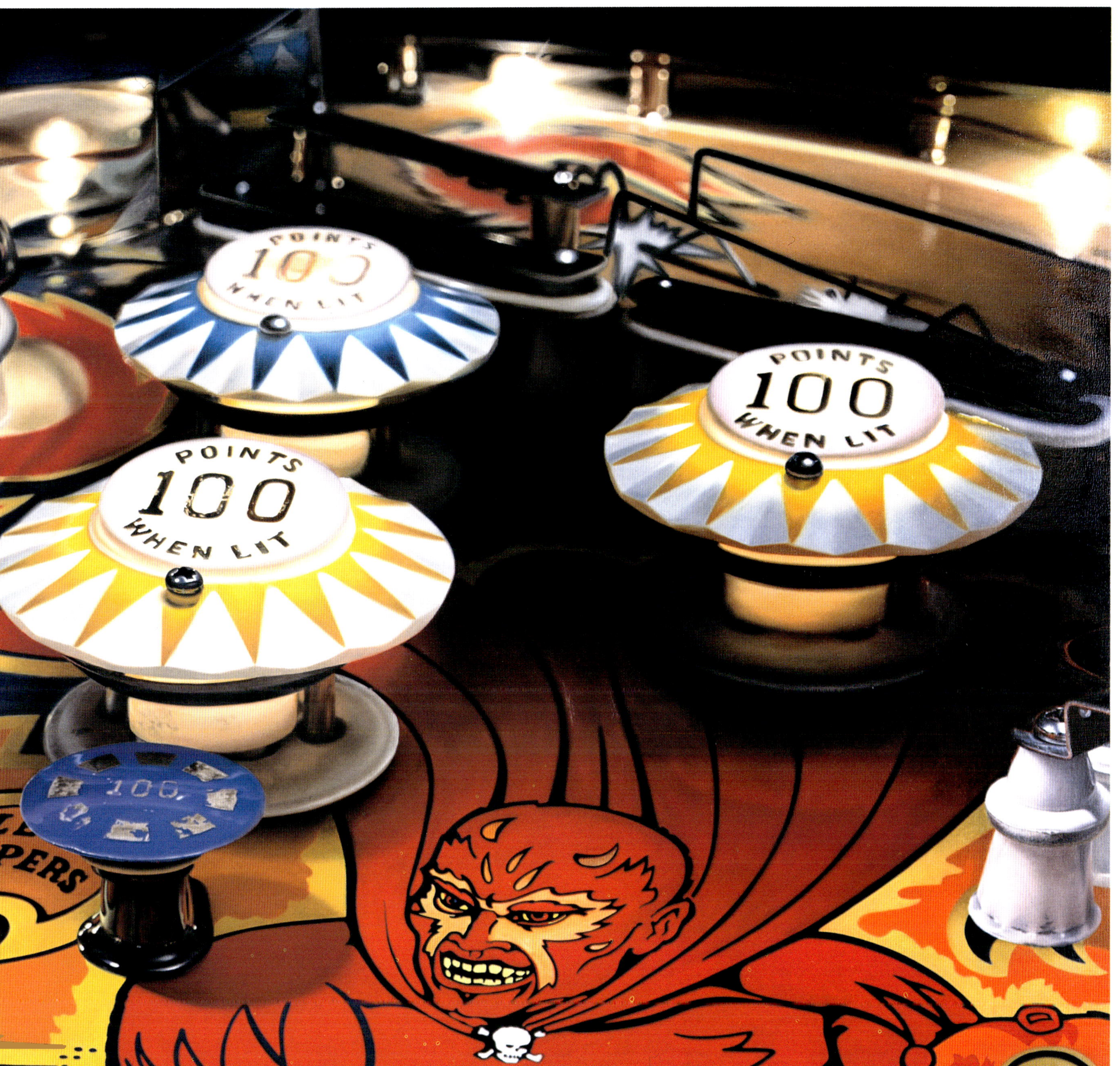
POINTS
100
WHEN LIT
POINTS
100
WHEN LIT

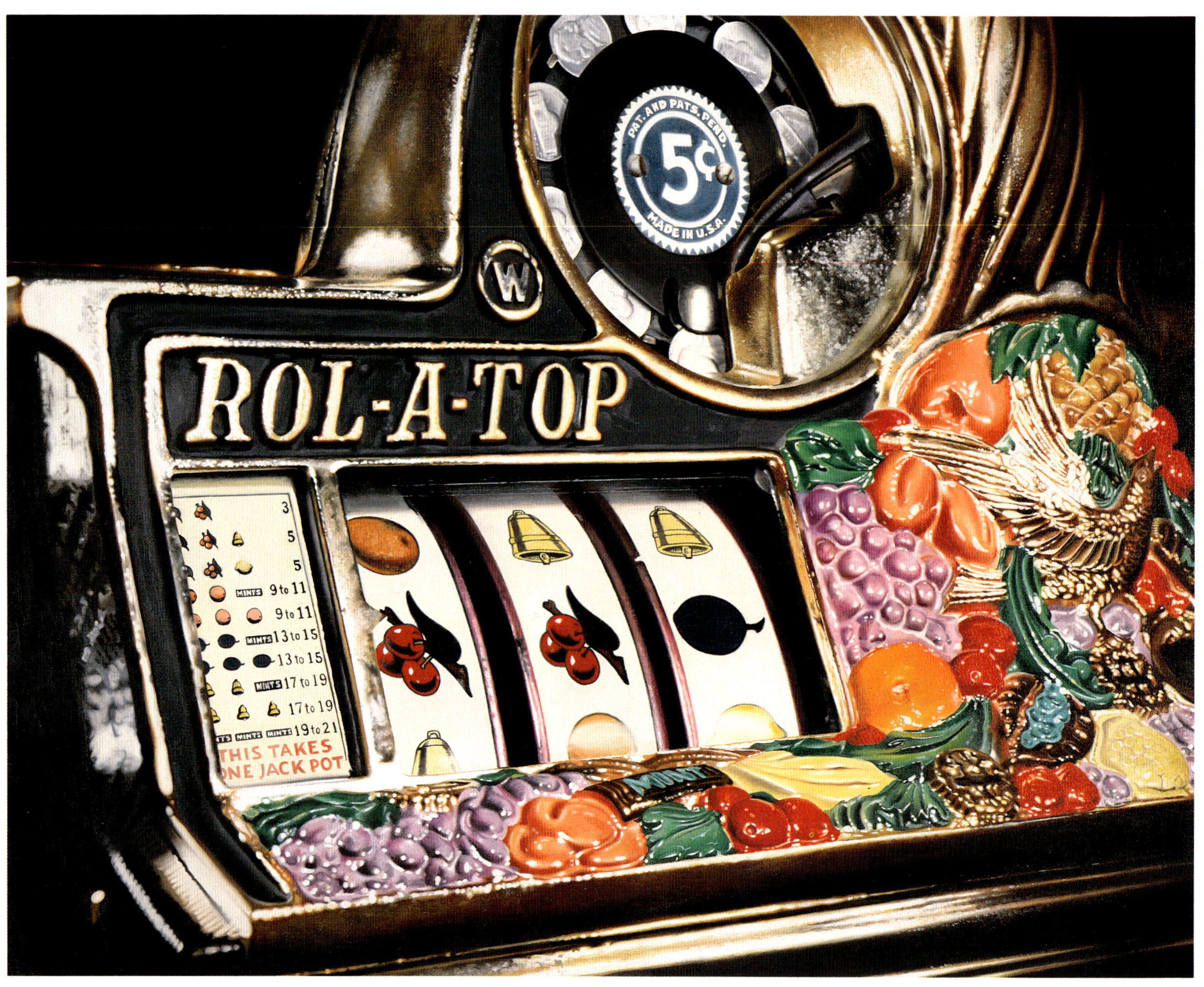

105. *Rol-A-Top.* 1981. Oil on canvas, 32½ × 40″. Private collection

OPPOSITE, ABOVE LEFT: 106. *5 Marbles and 465 West Broadway IV.* 1981. Oil on canvas, 32 × 42″. Private collection, New York

OPPOSITE, ABOVE RIGHT: 107. *"Solitaire Blue," Marbles VI.* 1982. Oil on canvas, 42 × 36″. Private collection, New Jersey

OPPOSITE, BELOW: 108. *Marbles V.* 1982. Oil on canvas, 48 × 84½″. Private collection, Switzerland

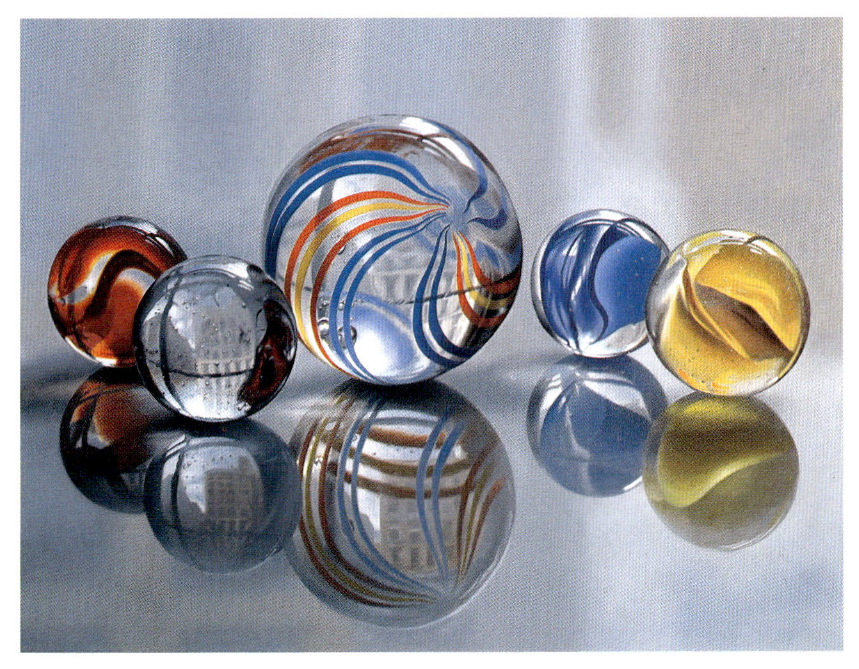

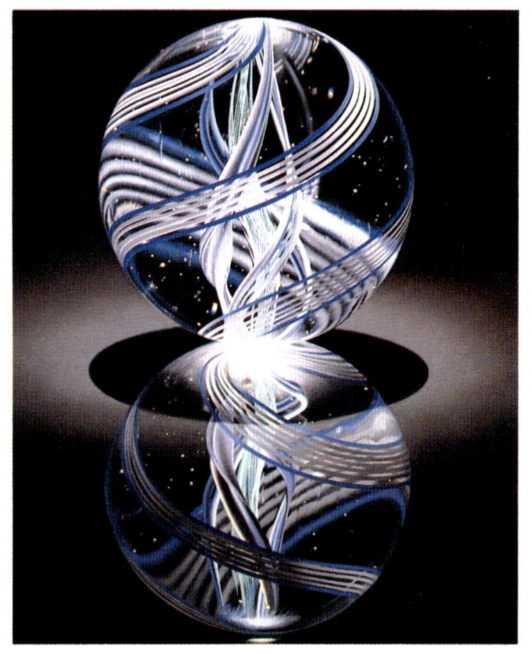

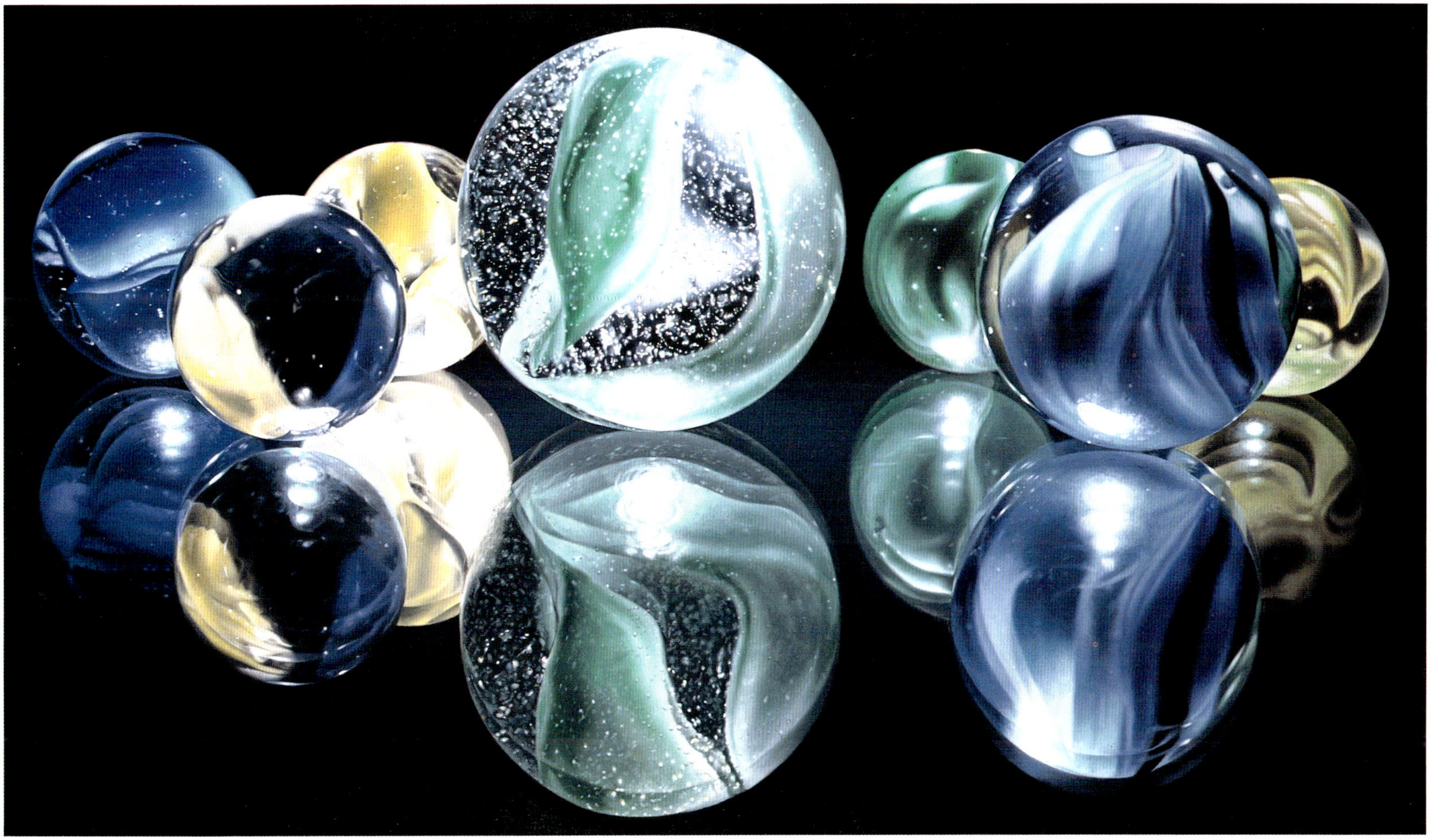

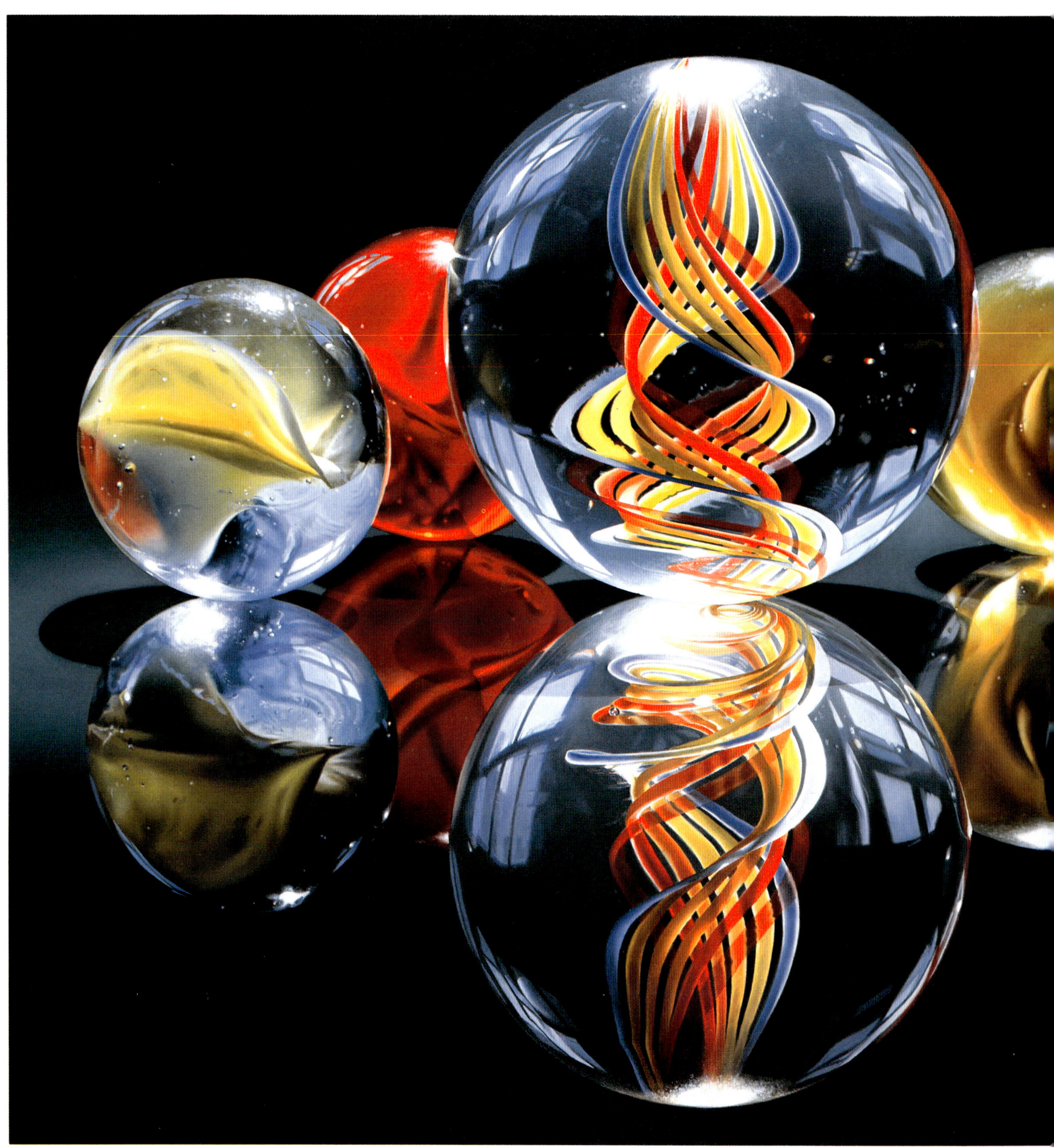

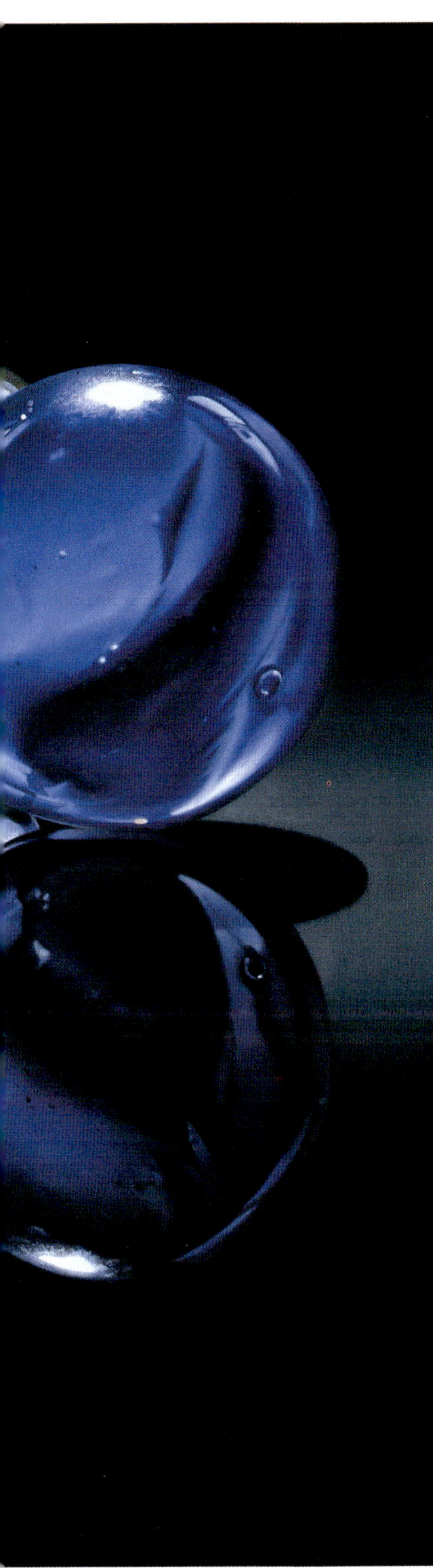

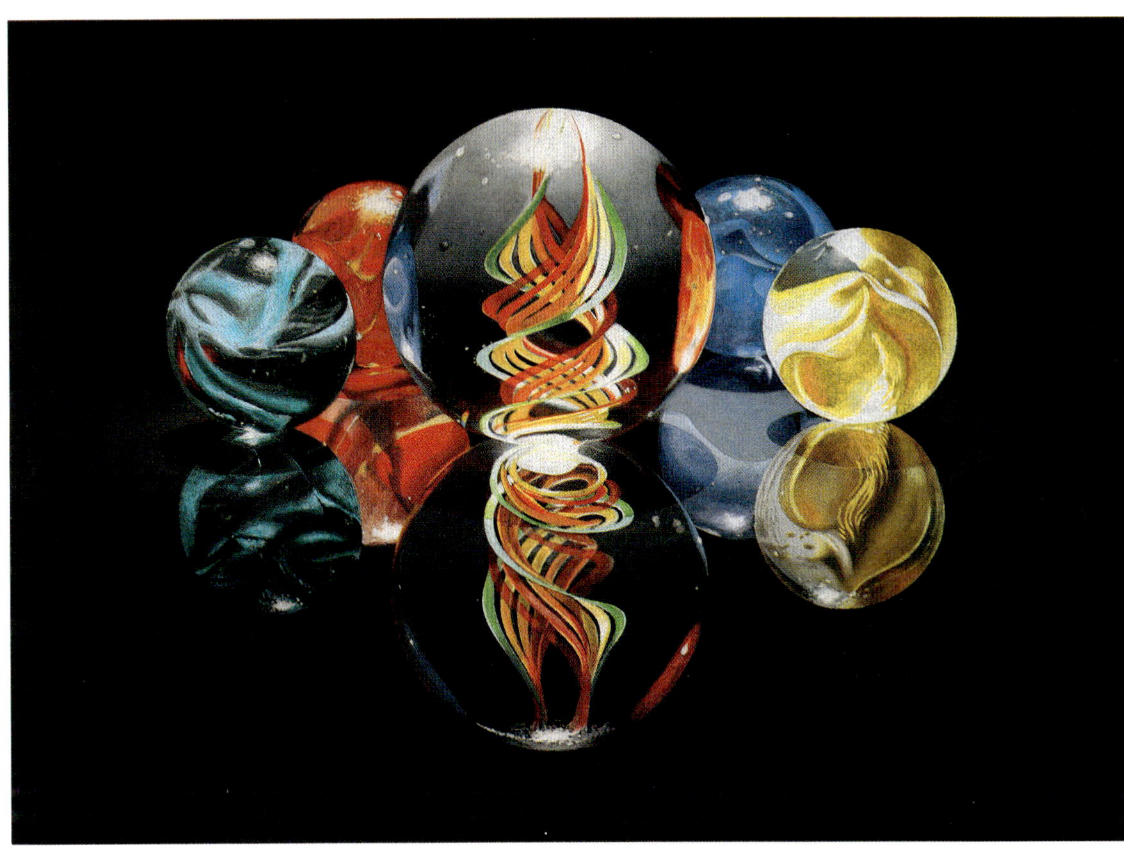

110. *Marbles*. 1982. Pastel on black paper, 21 × 29½″. Collection Louis K. and Susan Pear Meisel, New York

109. *Marbles VII*. 1982. Oil on canvas, 60 × 78¼″. Collection Zoe and Joel Dictrow, New York

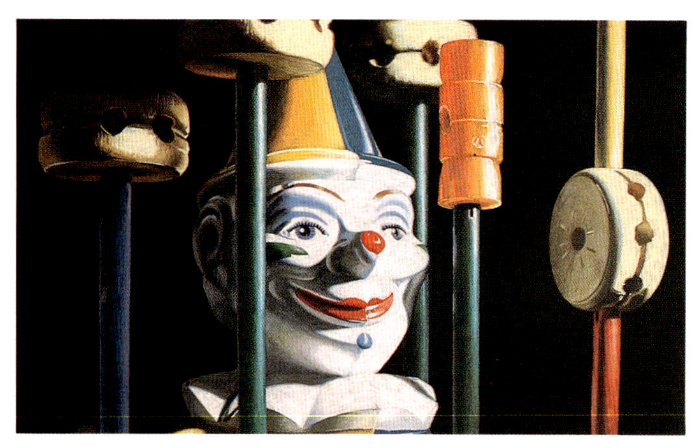

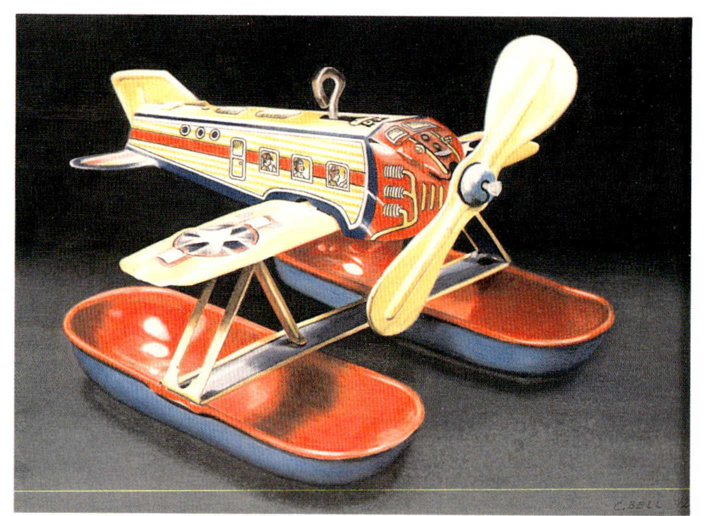

C. BELL

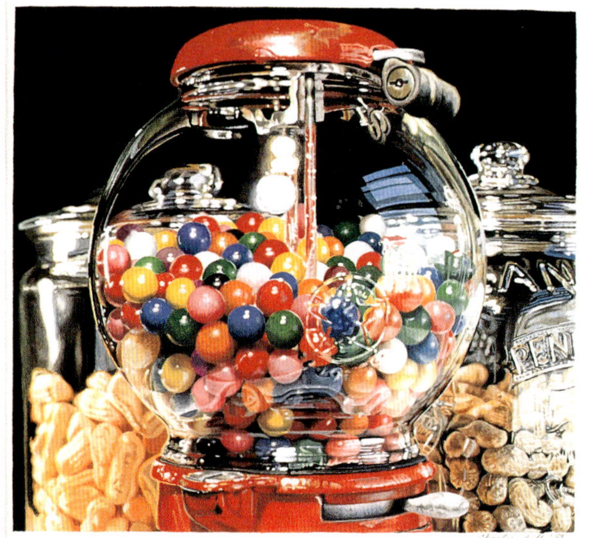

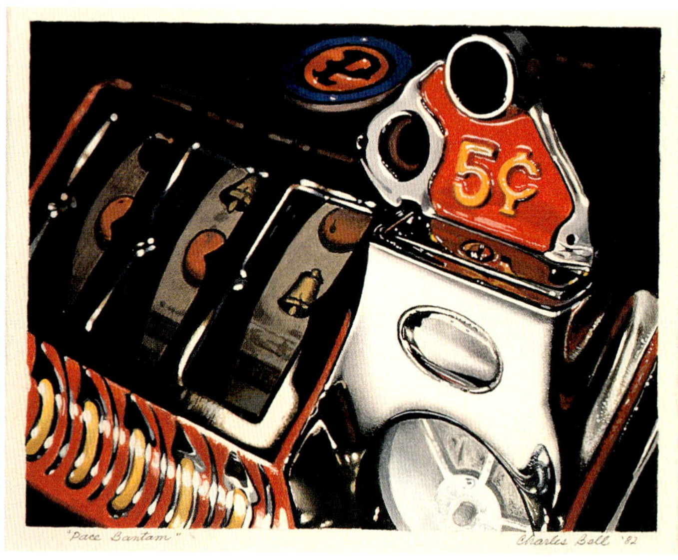

5¢
"Pace Bantam"
Charles Bell '82

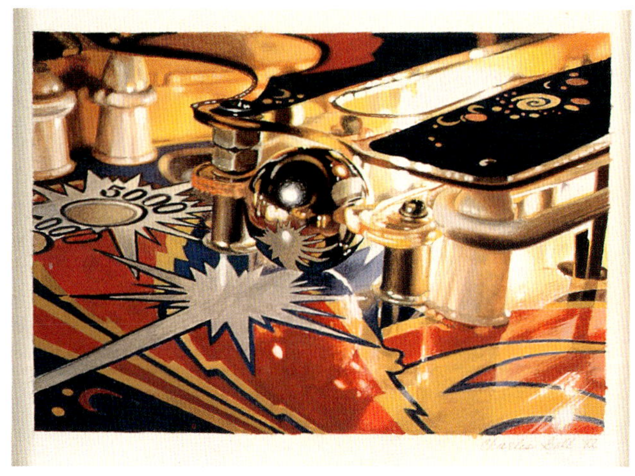

5000

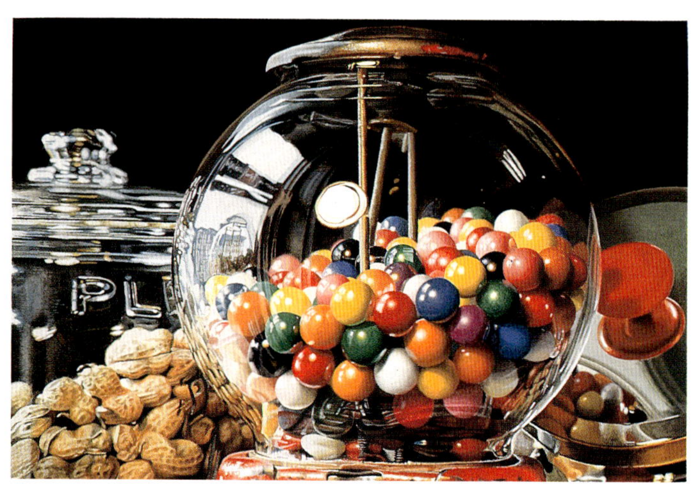

OPPOSITE, ABOVE LEFT: 111. *Tinker Toys and Clown*. 1982. Colored pencil on black paper, 16 × 26″. Private collection, New York

OPPOSITE, ABOVE RIGHT: 112. *Seaplane*. 1982. Colored pencil on paper, 8½ × 11½″. Collection Louis K. and Susan Pear Meisel, New York

OPPOSITE, CENTER LEFT: 113. *"Columbus Star," Gumball Watercolor No. 3*. 1982. Watercolor on paper, 10¾ × 12″. PieperPower Companies, Inc., Wisconsin

OPPOSITE, CENTER RIGHT: 114. *Pace Bantam*. 1982. Watercolor on paper, 7⅜ × 9⅜″. Collection Bruce Vinokour, California

OPPOSITE, BELOW LEFT: 115. *"Captive Messenger," Pinball Watercolor No. 2*. 1982. Watercolor on paper, 4¾ × 7″. Collection Pierre and Sylvie Mirabaud, Switzerland

OPPOSITE, BELOW RIGHT: 116. *Gumball Watercolor No. 4*. 1982. Watercolor on paper, 9½ × 14¼″. Private collection, New York

RIGHT: 117. *Red Rider*. 1982. Oil on canvas, 47 × 35″. Collection Dale C. and Alexandra Zetlin Jones, New York

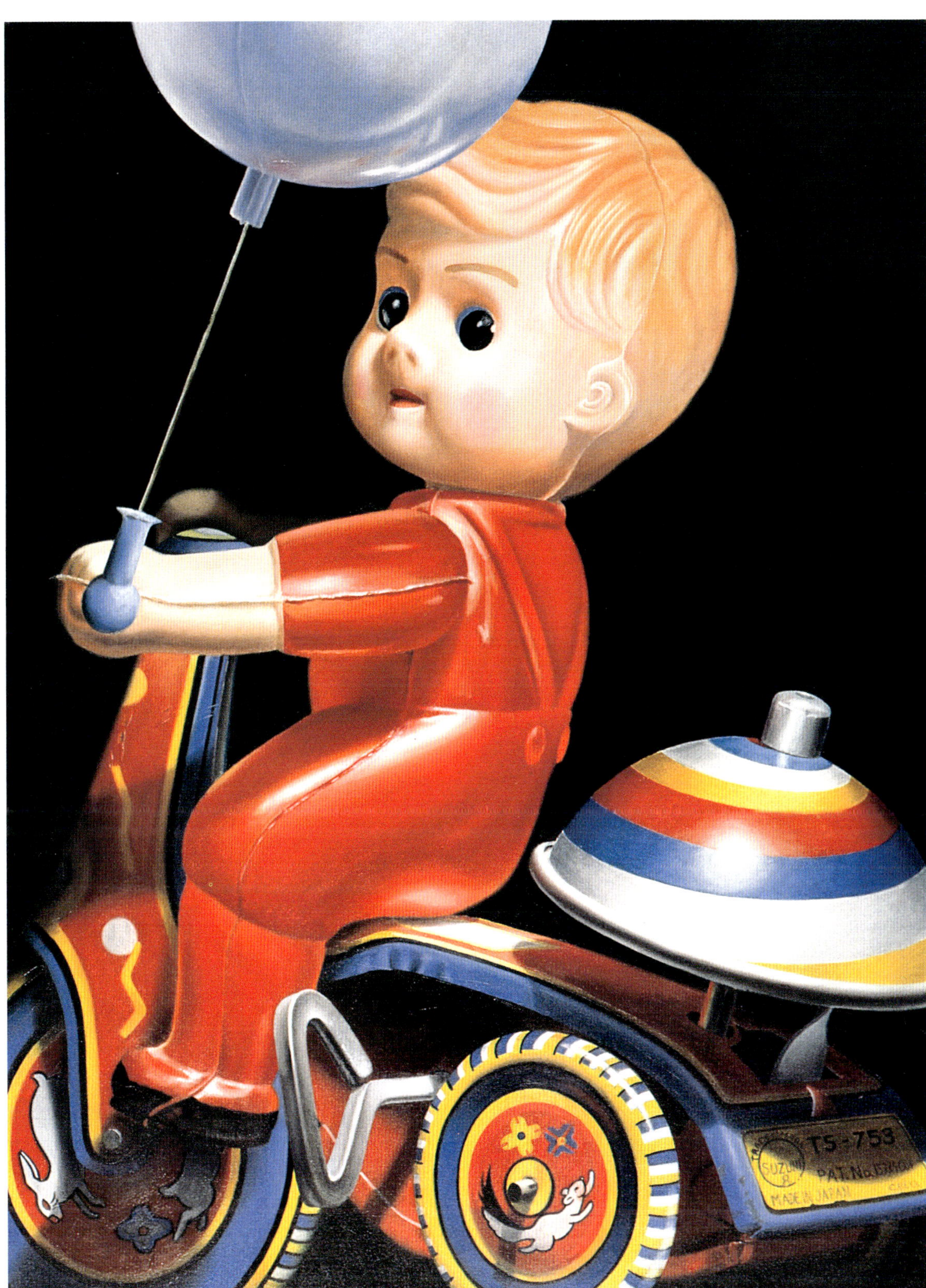

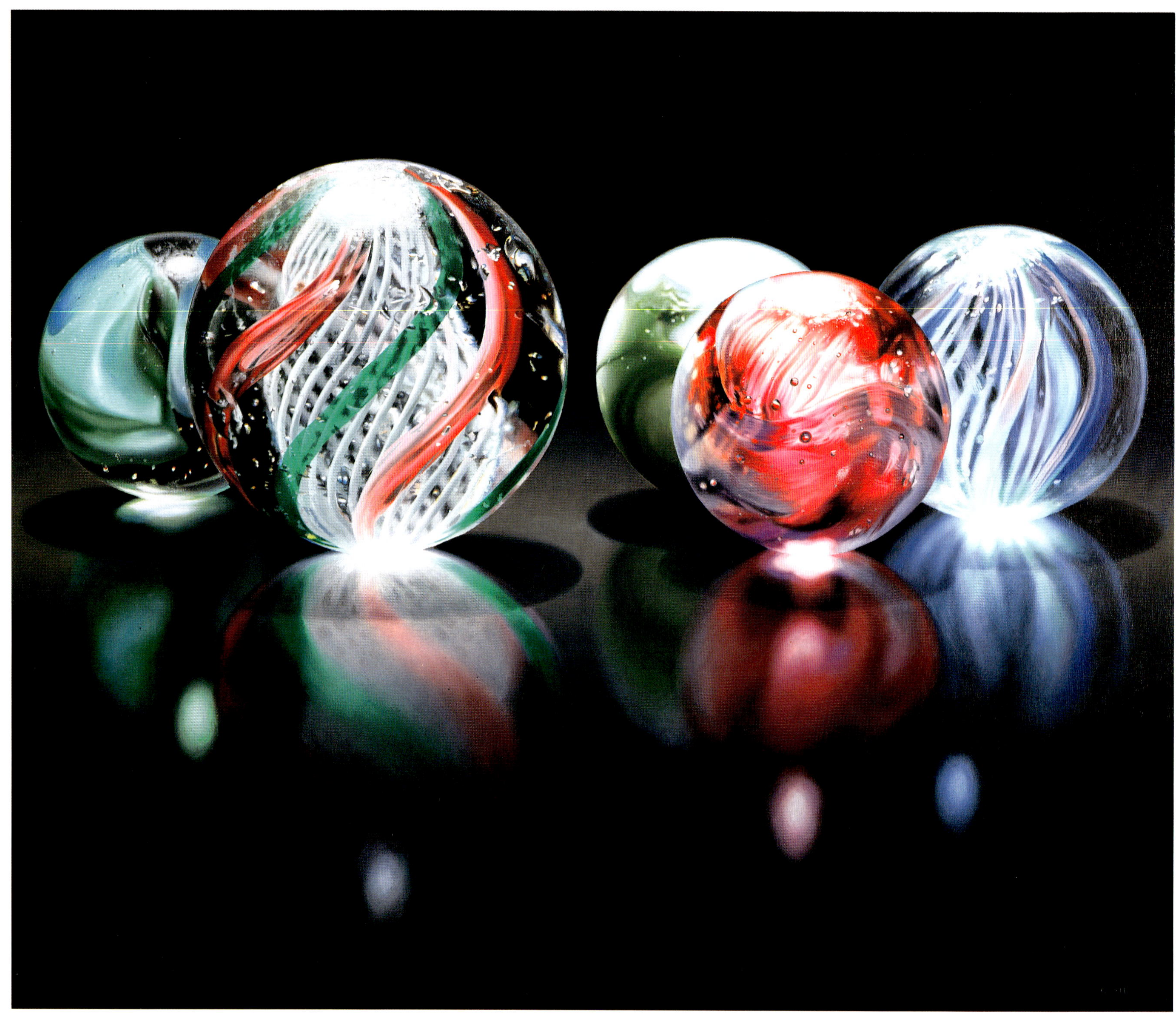

118. *Marbles VIII*. 1982. Oil on canvas, $54\frac{1}{2} \times 66\frac{1}{4}''$. Collection Jack and Harriet Stievelman, New York

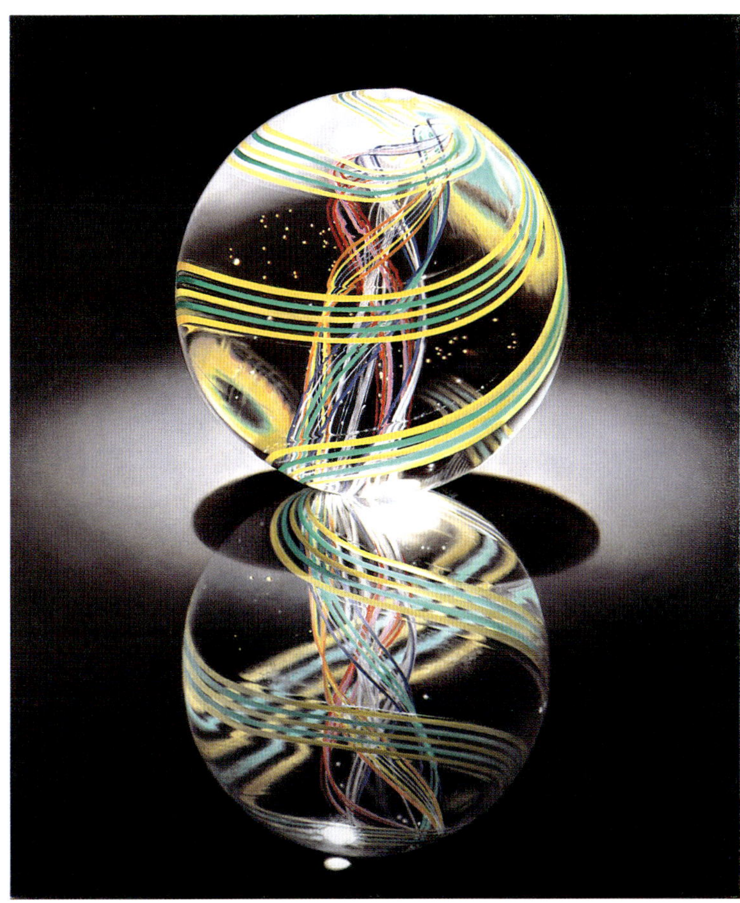

119. *Solitaire Yellow.* 1982. Oil on canvas, 42 × 36″. Private collection, California

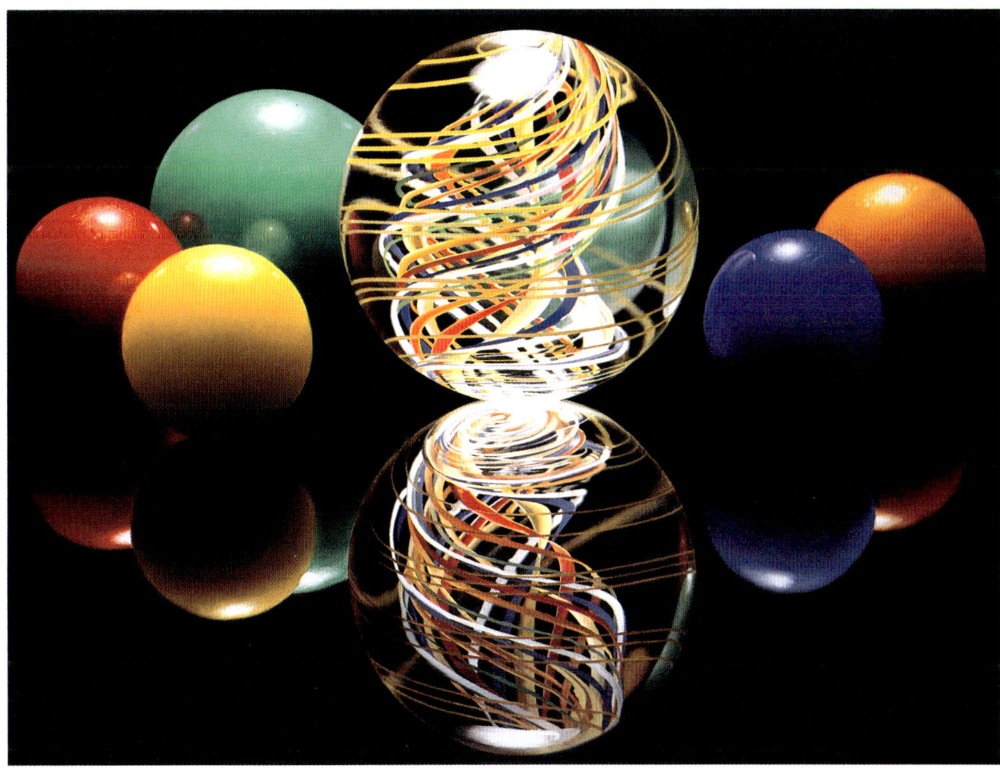

120. *Marbles IX.* 1982. Oil on canvas, 36 × 48″. Private collection, New York

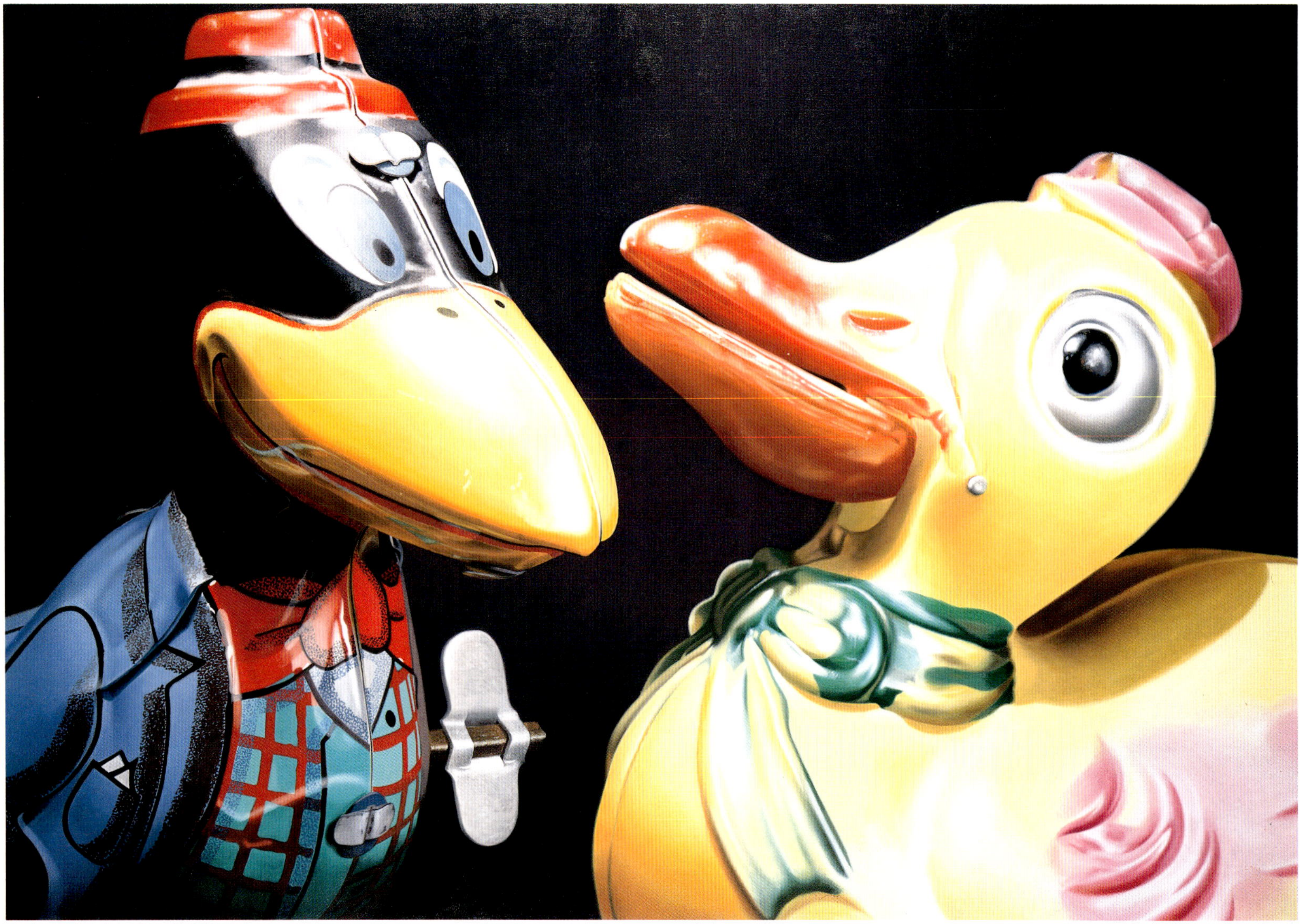

121. *The Critics.* 1982. Oil on canvas, 66 × 96¼″. Collection Donna and Neil Weisman, New Jersey

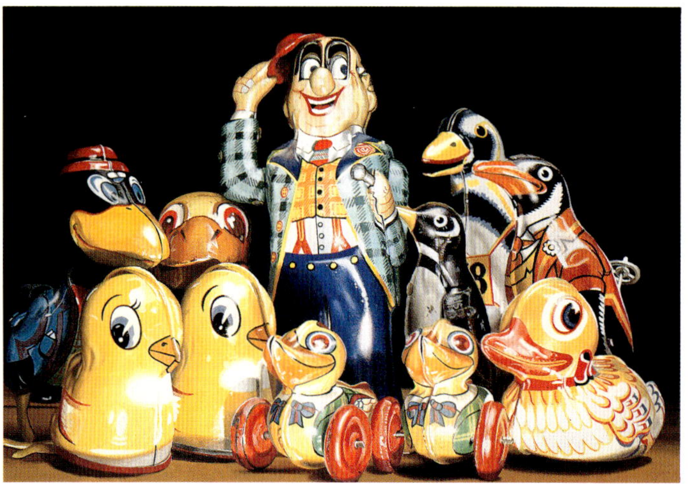

122. *Curtain Call.* 1982. Watercolor on paper, 9¼ × 14″. Collection Glenn C. Janss, Idaho

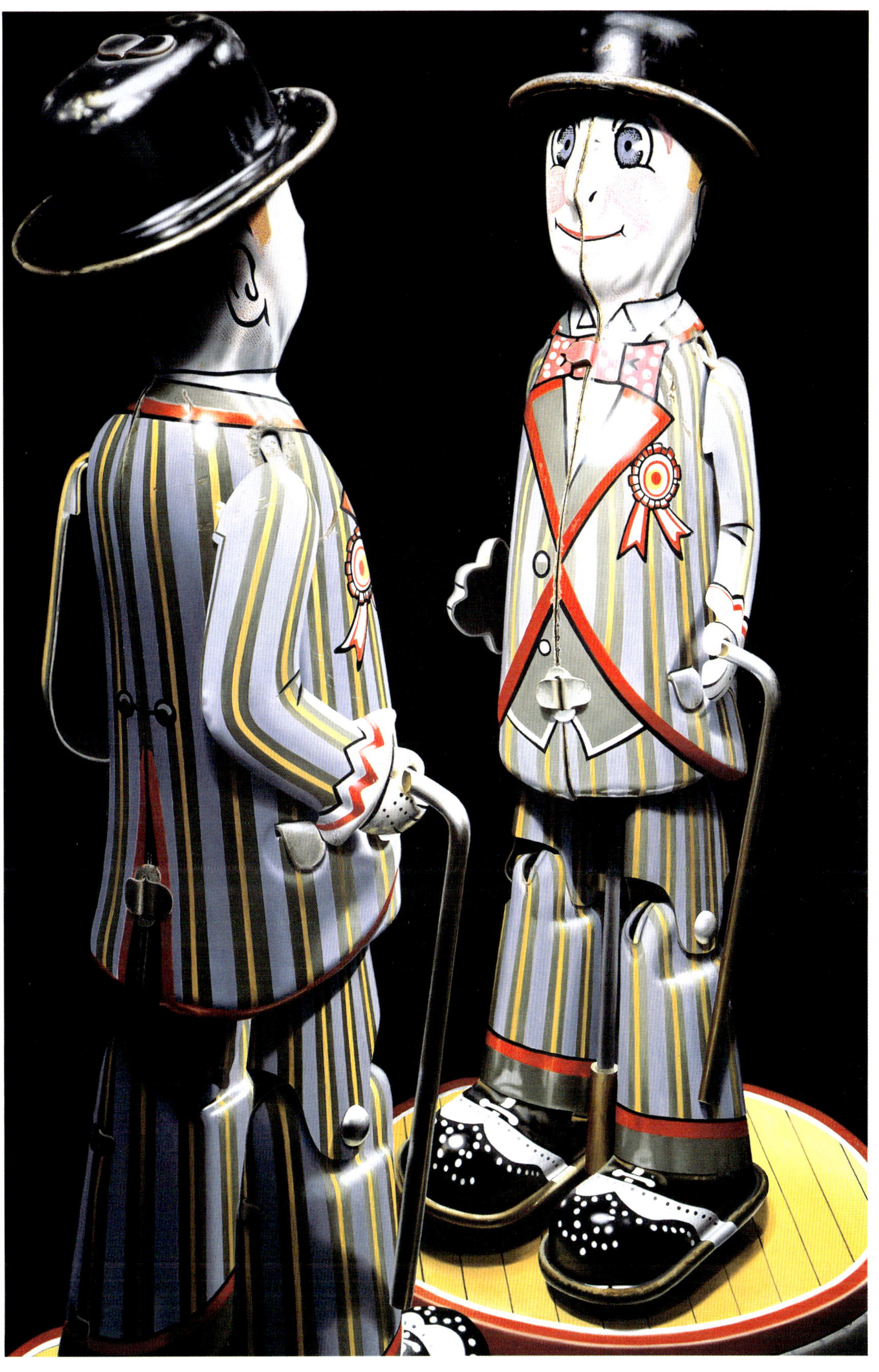

123. *Celebrity.* 1983. Oil on canvas, 72 × 48″. Collection Joan and Barrie Damson, Connecticut

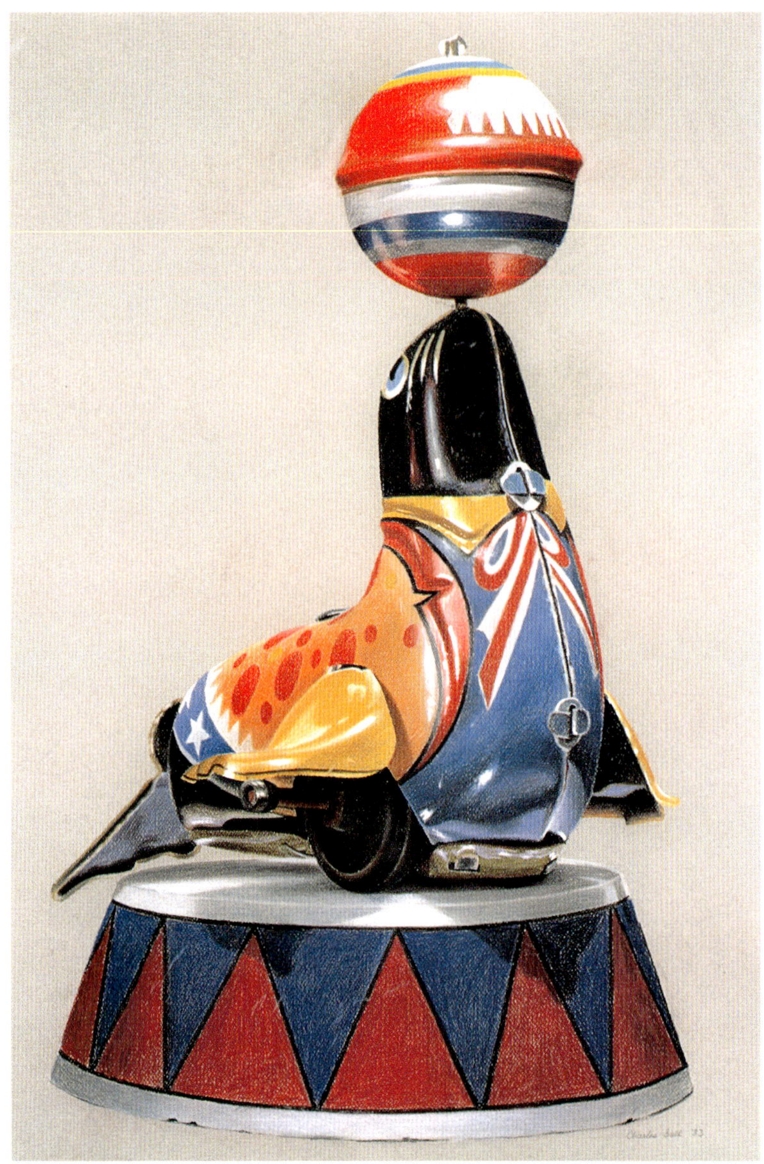

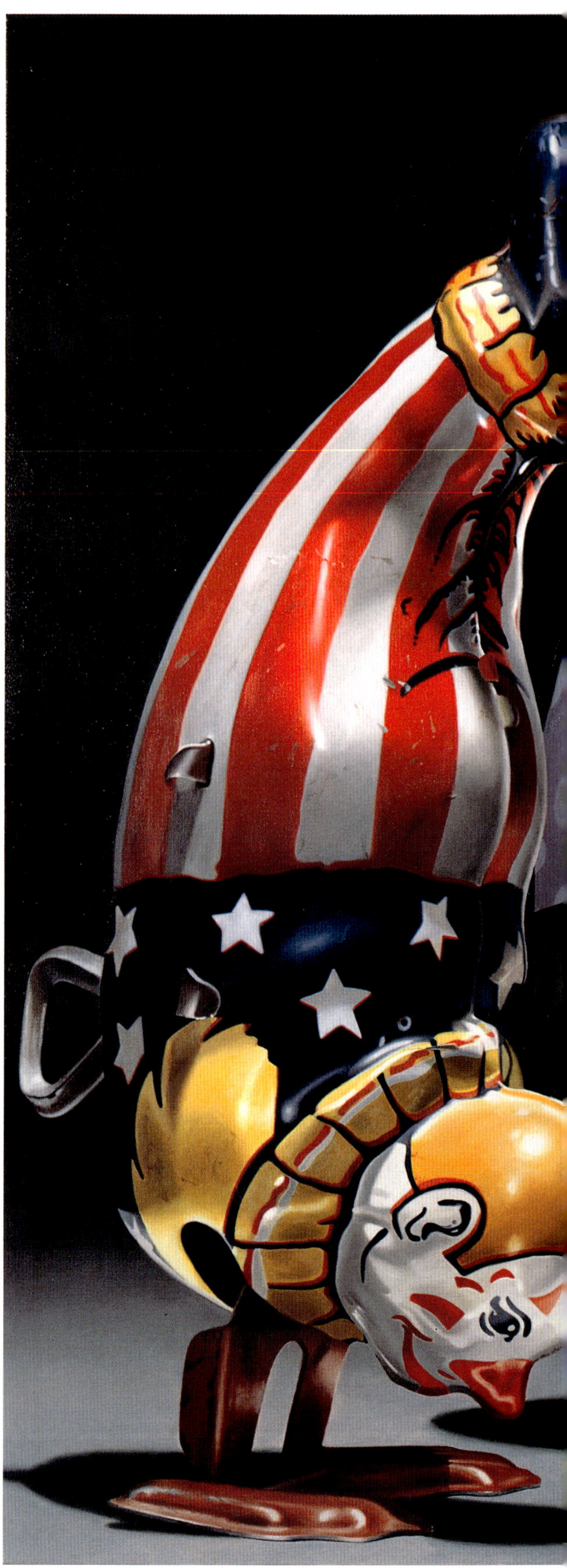

ABOVE: 124. *Trained Seal*. 1983. Colored pencil on paper, 39¼ × 27½″. Private collection, New York

RIGHT: 125. *Troupe*. 1983. Oil on canvas, 68 × 102″. Collection Gilbert and Judith Shapiro, New York

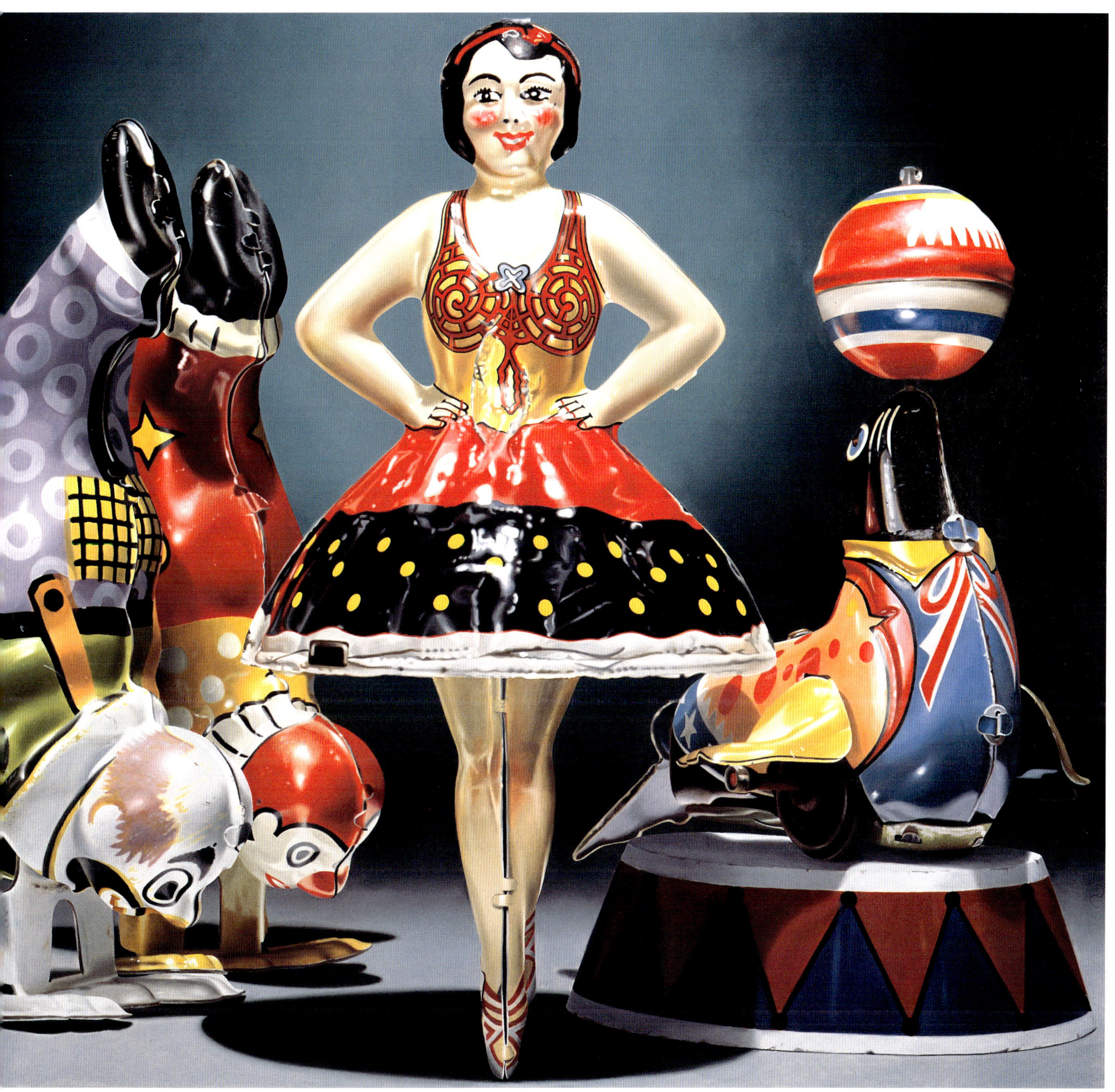

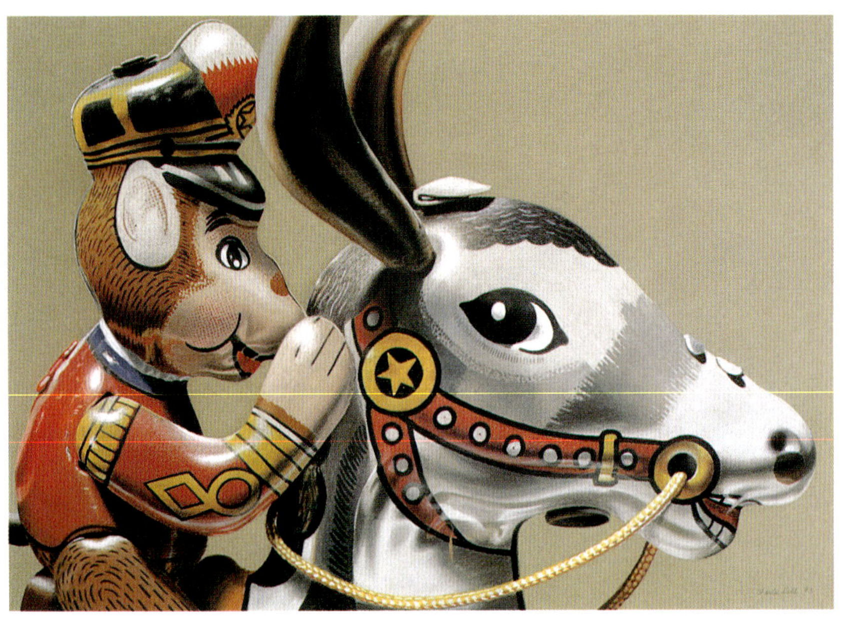

126. *The Secret.* 1983. Colored pencil on paper, 27¼ × 39¼″. Collection Barry and Susan Paley, New York

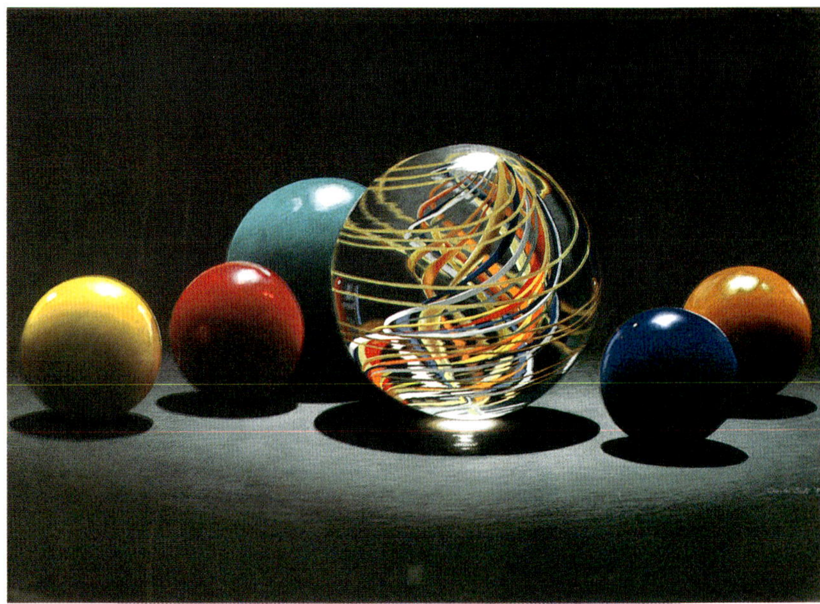

127. *Marbles X.* 1983. Pastel on paper, 27 × 38″. Collection Mark Schiff, New York

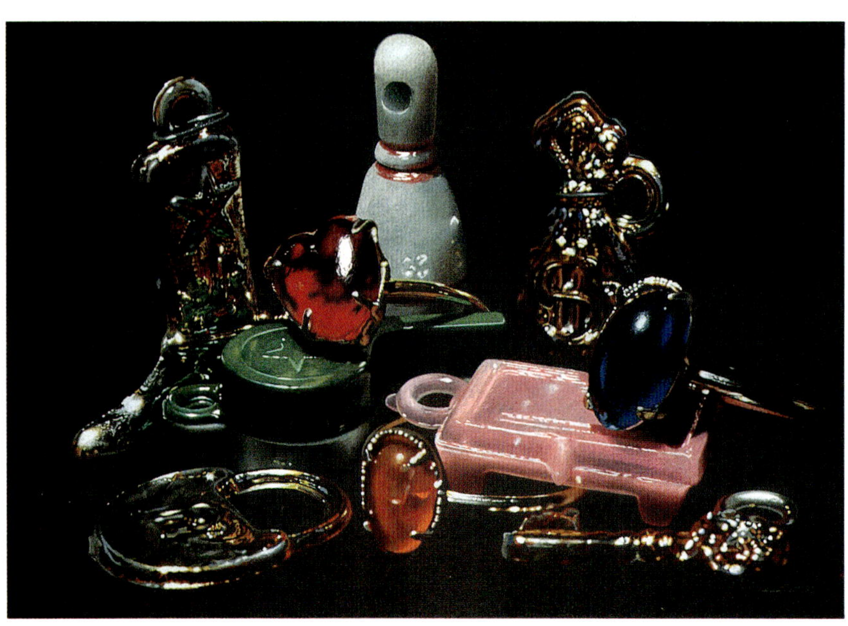

128. *Texas.* 1983. Colored pencil on black paper, 27½ × 39½″. Private collection, Texas

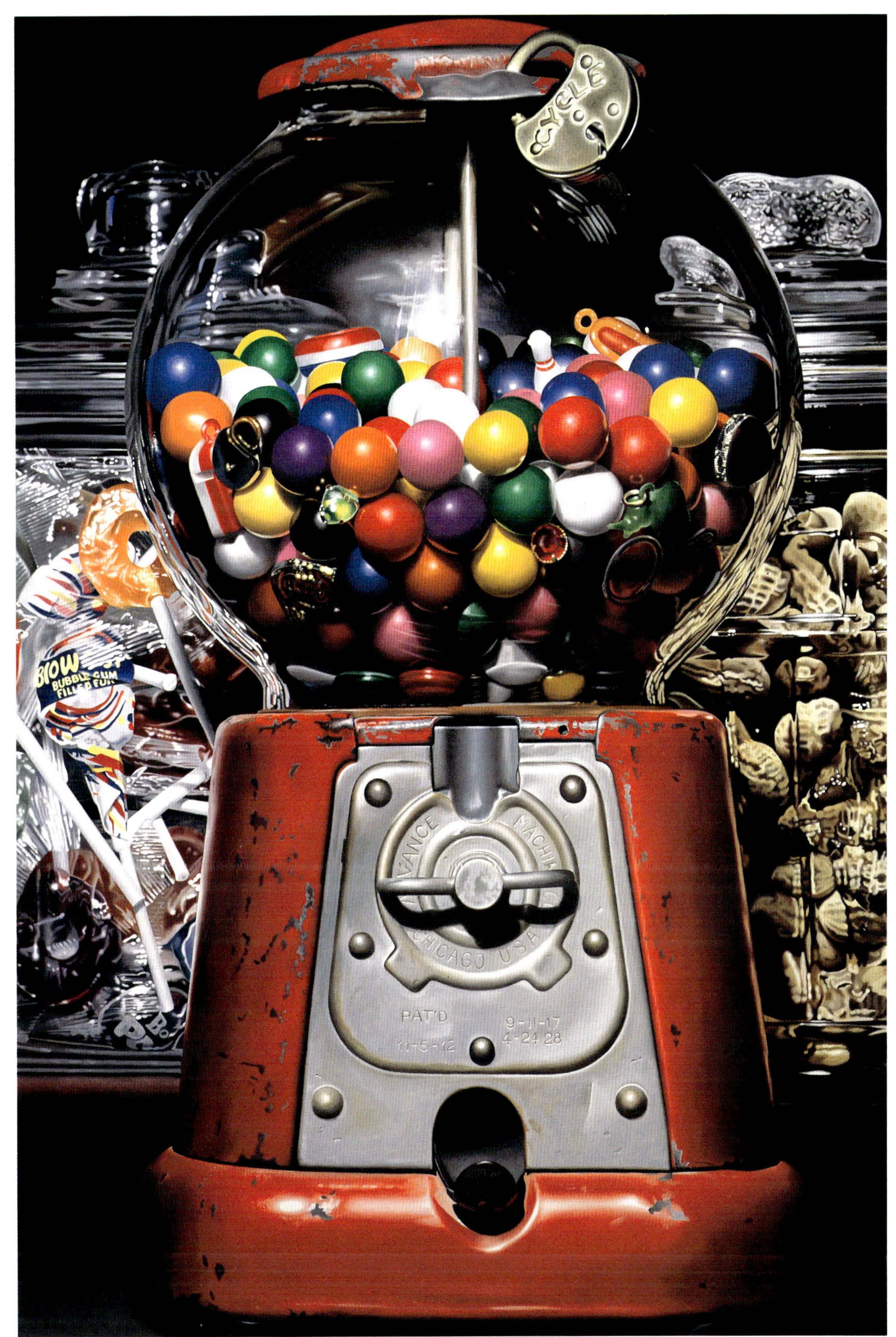

129. *Gumball XV*. 1983.
Oil on canvas, 89 × 61″.
Collection Jack and
Harriet Stievelman, New
York

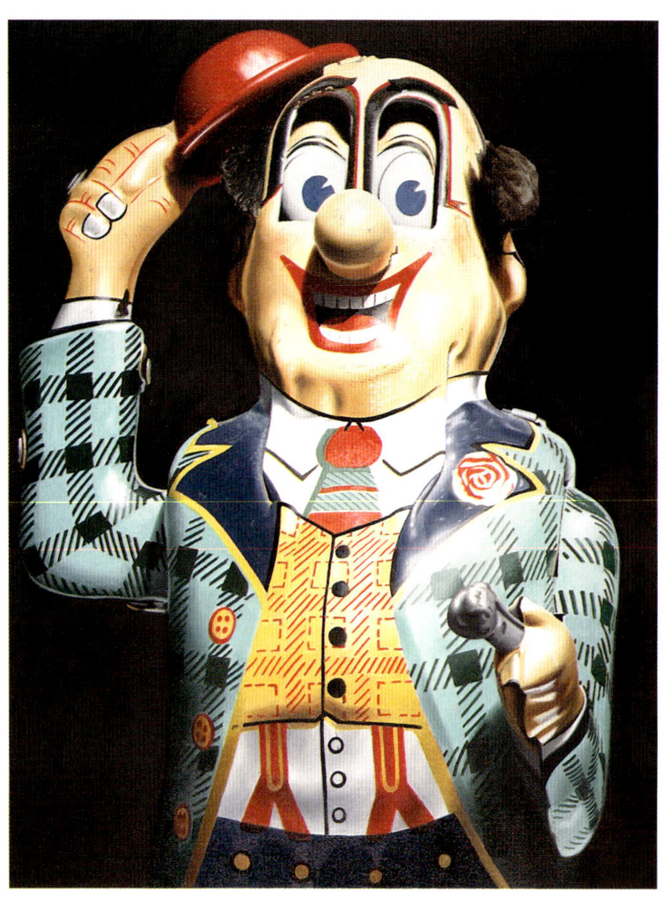

LEFT: 130. *Uncle Harry.* 1983. Oil on canvas, 28 × 22″. Collection Stan and Beverly Salsberg, Ontario

BELOW: 131. *The Optimist.* 1983. Oil on canvas, 36 × 48″. Private collection, Illinois

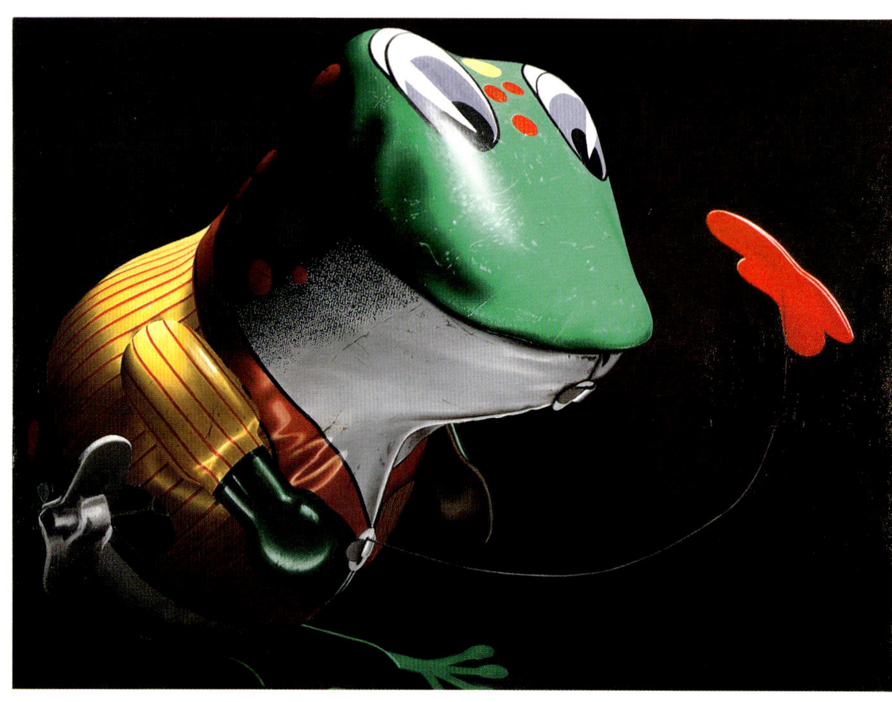

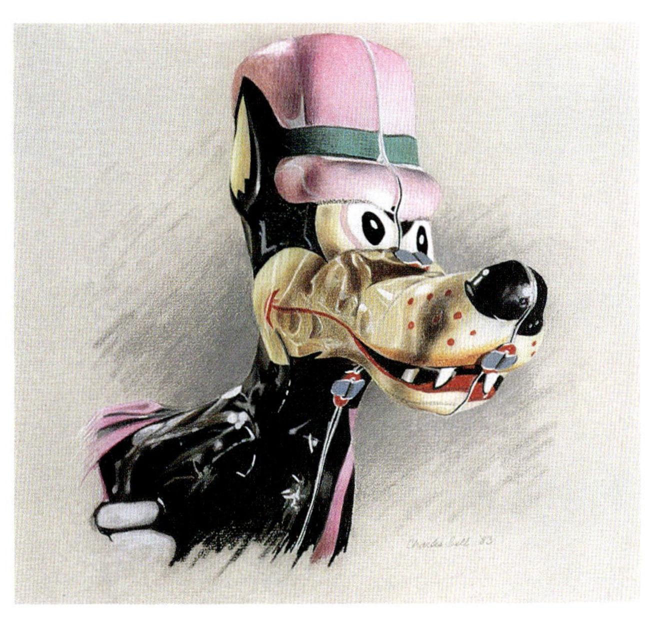

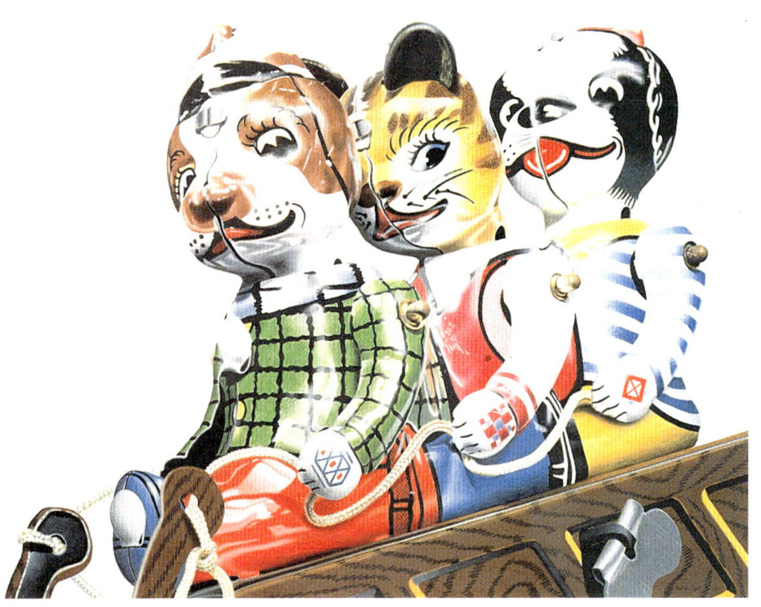

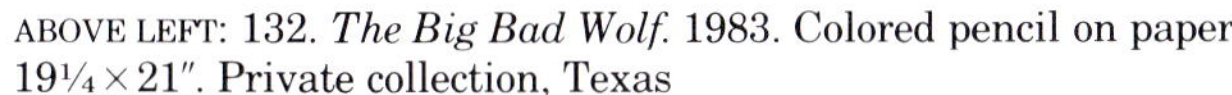

ABOVE LEFT: 132. *The Big Bad Wolf.* 1983. Colored pencil on paper, 19¼ × 21″. Private collection, Texas

ABOVE RIGHT: 133. *Snow Scene.* 1983. Colored pencil on paper, 27 × 37″. Private collection, California

BELOW: 134. *A Study for The Journey.* 1983. Colored pencil on paper, 31½ × 39½″. Private collection

RIGHT: 135. *Study (Roly-Poly).* 1983. Oil pastel on paper, 77 × 52″. Collection Copy Berg and Paul Nash, New York

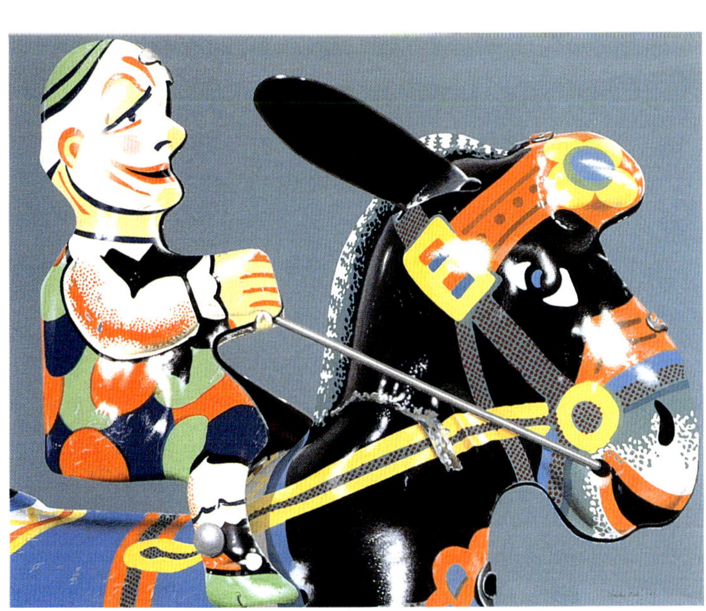

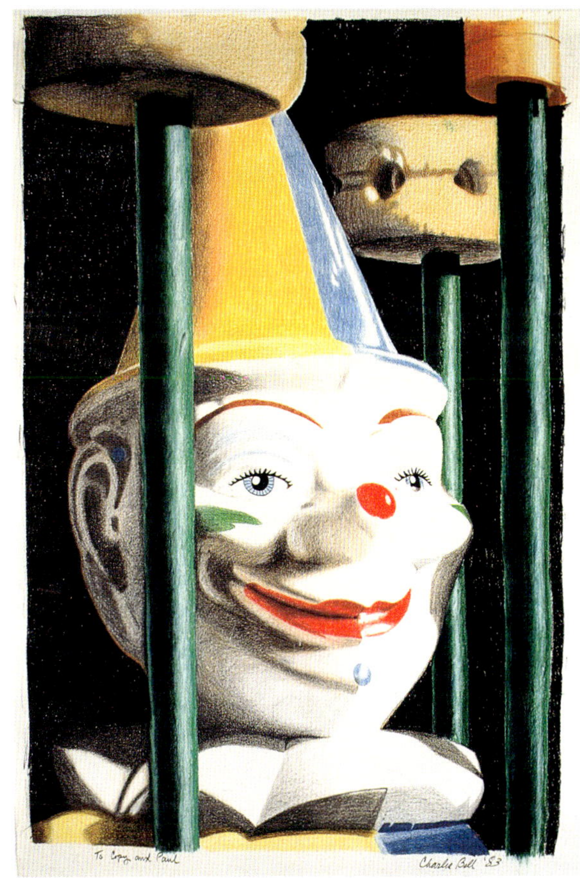

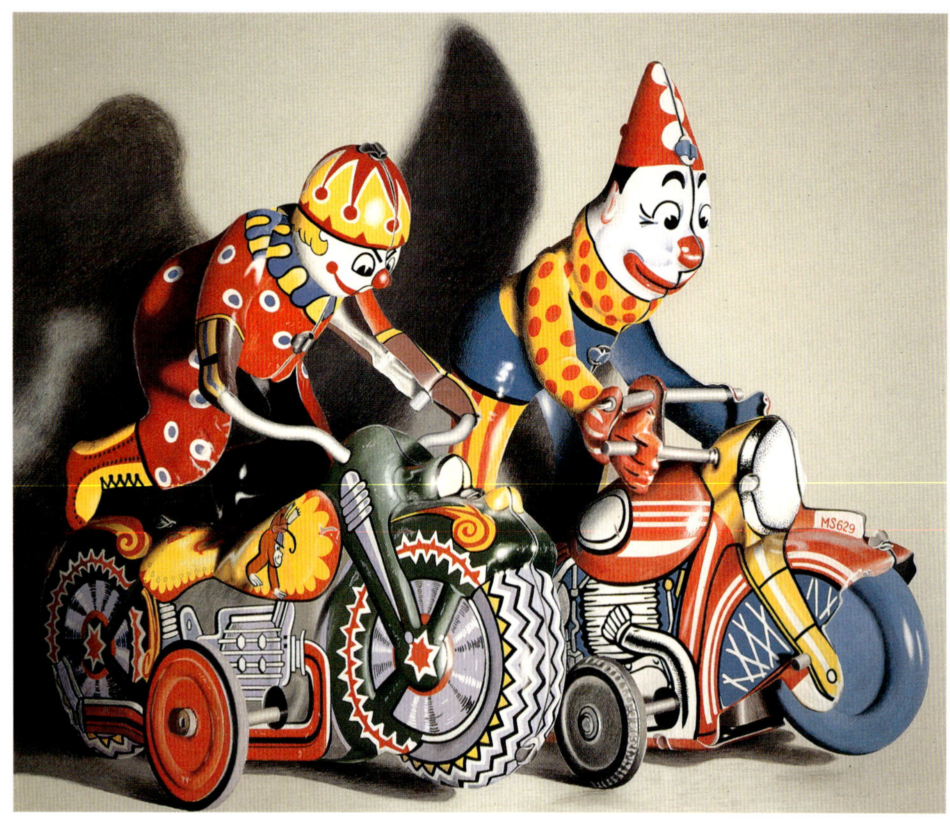

136. *Hot Pursuit*. 1984. Pastel and colored pencil on board, 40 × 50″. Private collection, New York

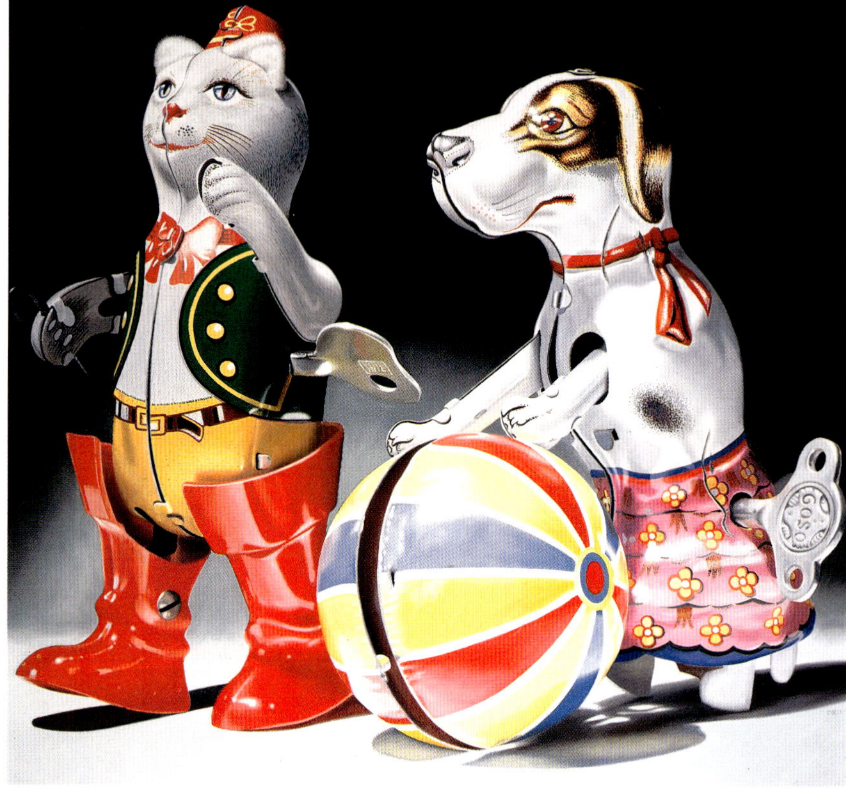

137. *Circus Act*. 1983. Oil on canvas, 58 × 64″. Private collection, New Jersey

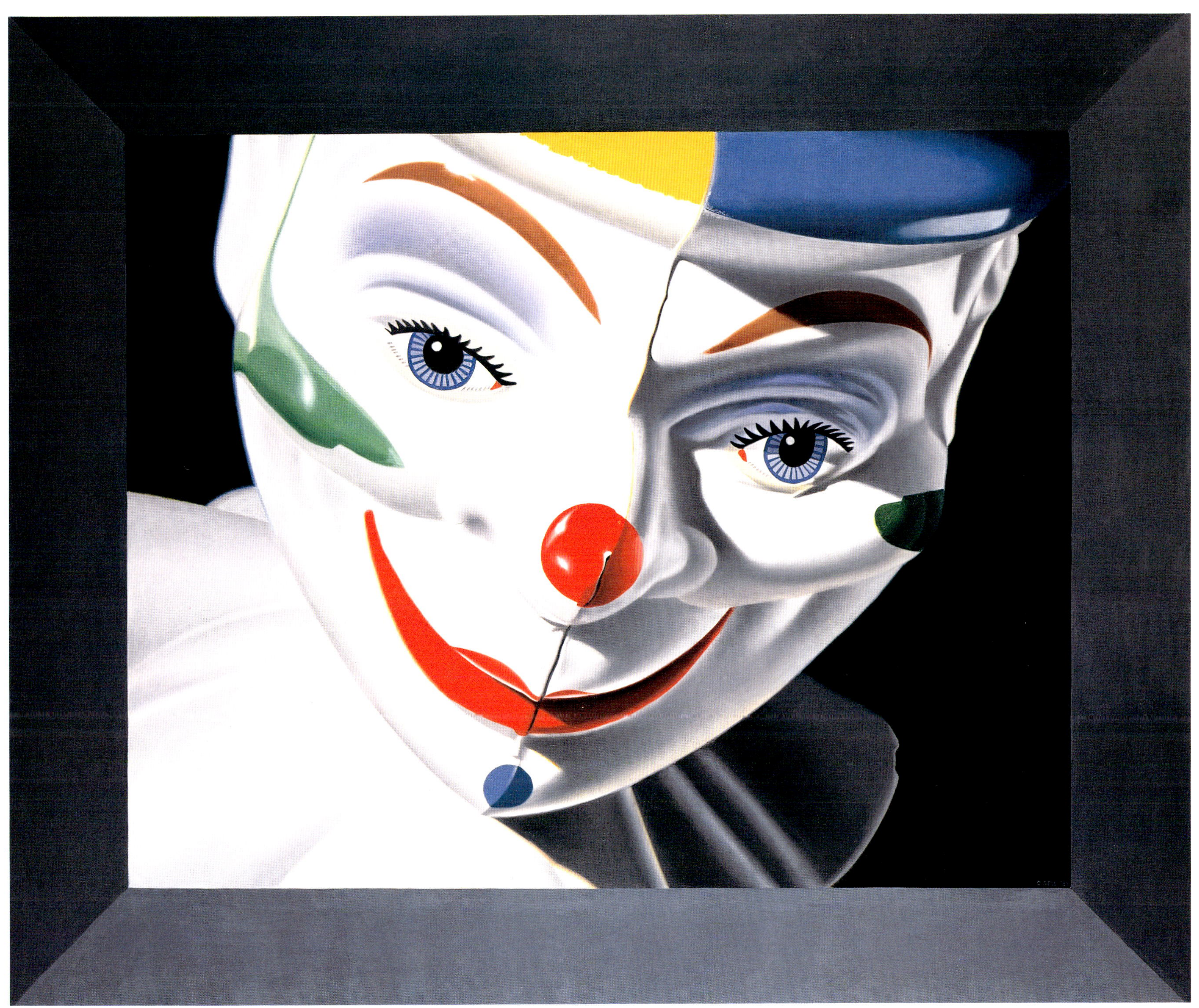

138. *Lullaby*. 1983. Oil on canvas, 64¼ × 78¼. Philbrook Museum of Art, Oklahoma. Gift of Arthur and Jeanne Cohen

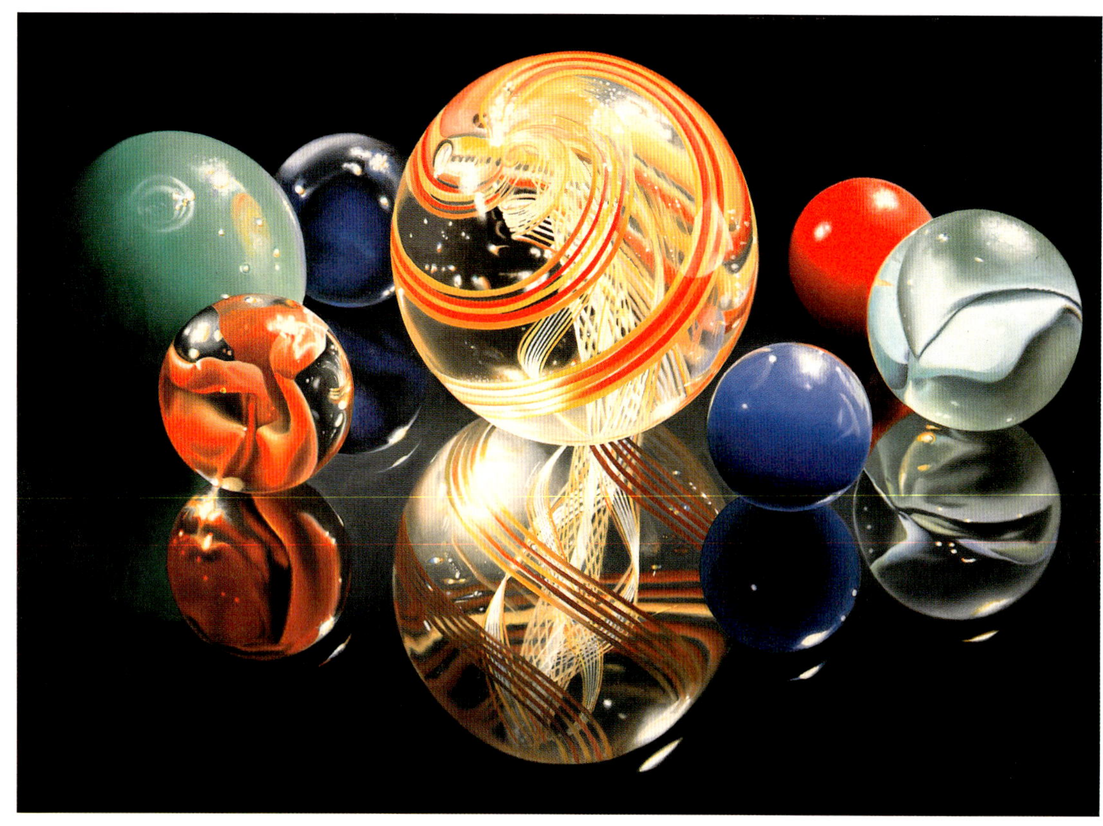

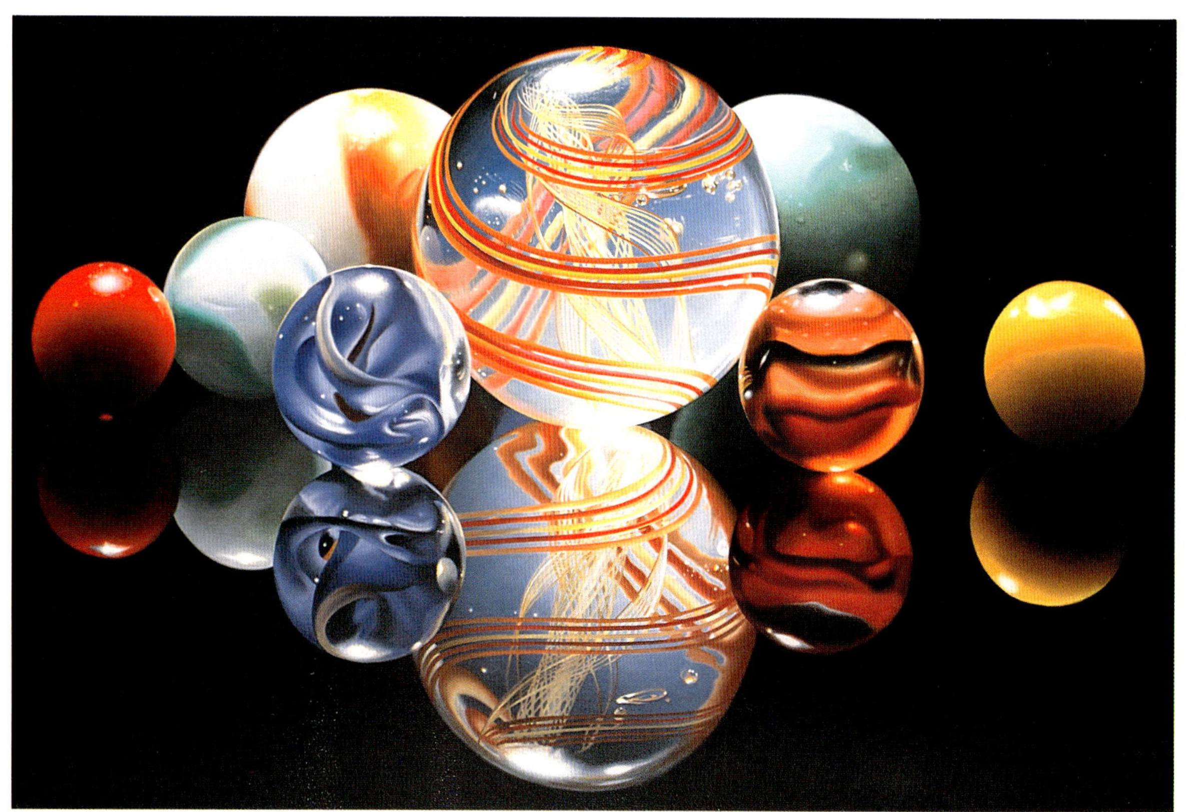

OPPOSITE ABOVE: 139. *Marbles XI*. 1984. Oil on canvas, 38 × 54″. Private collection, California

OPPOSITE BELOW: 140. *Marbles XIII*. 1984. Oil on canvas, 40 × 60″. Private collection, Pennsylvania

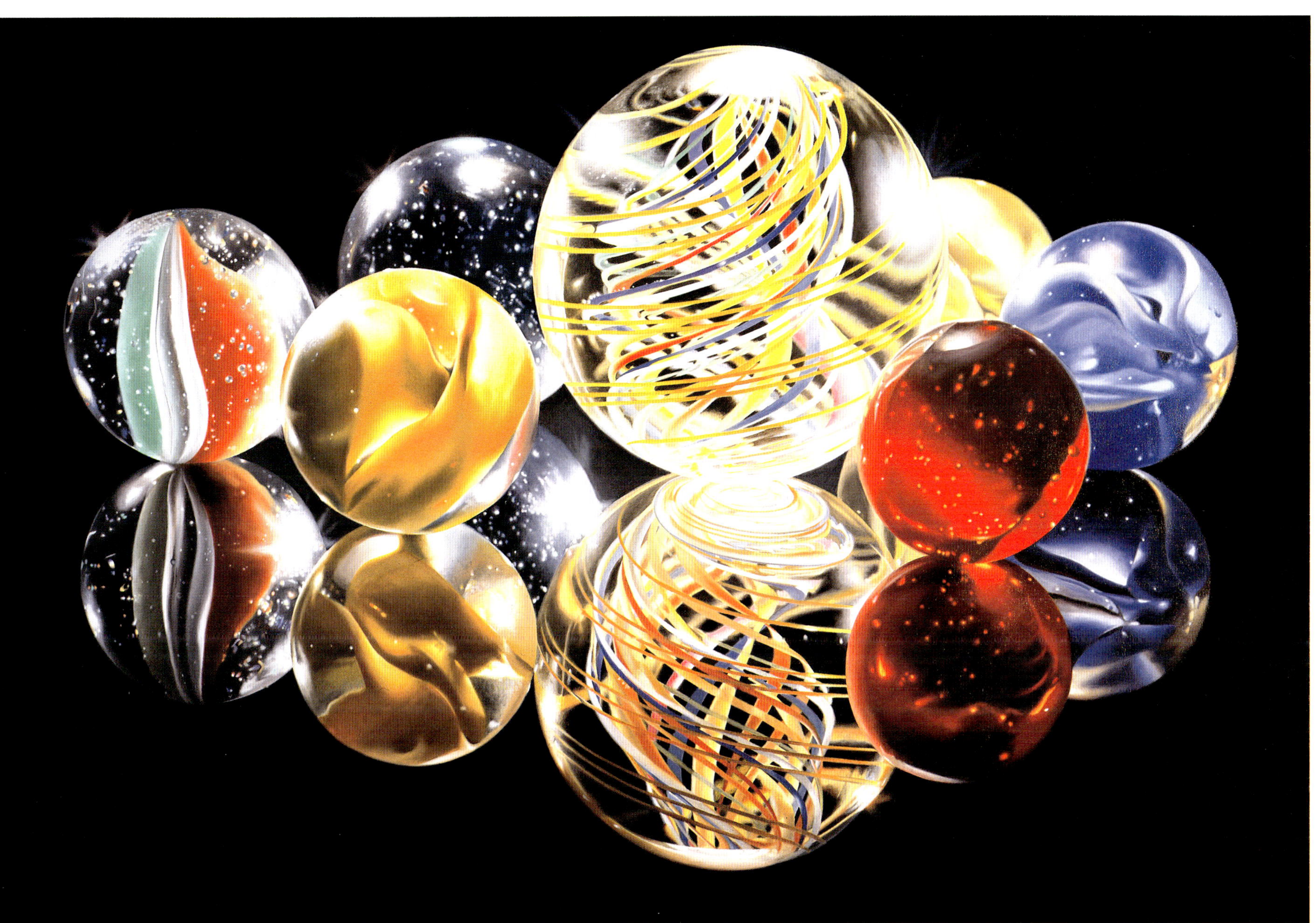

141. *Marbles XII*. 1984. Oil on canvas, 48 × 72″. Private collection, Florida

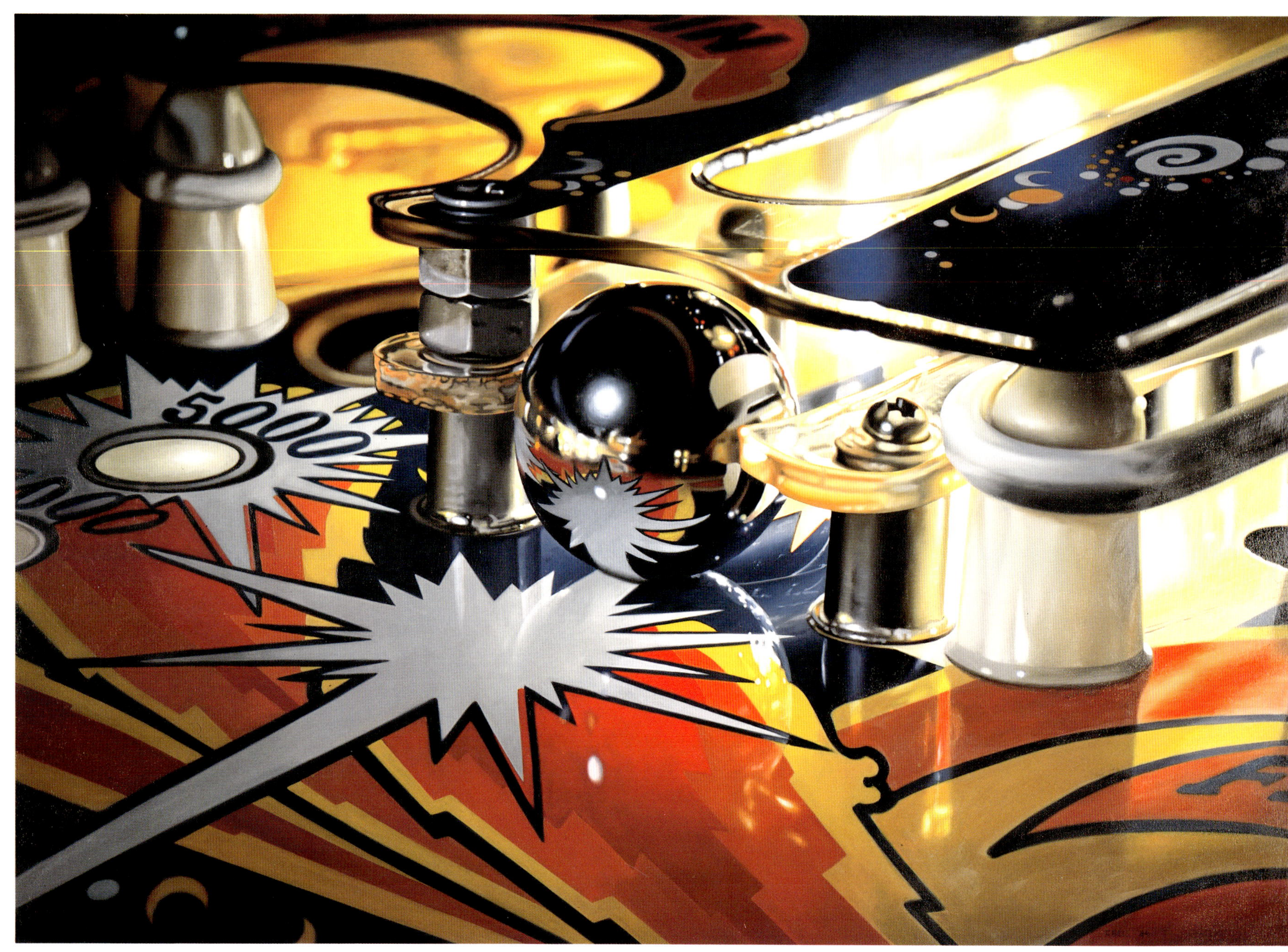

ABOVE: 142. *Night Fireball*. 1984. Oil on canvas, 60 × 84″. Collection Hope and Howard Stringer, Tennessee

OPPOSITE: 143. *Side Show*. 1984. Oil on canvas, 72 × 60″. Phoenix Art Museum, Arizona. Museum Purchase with Partial Funding by The Contemporary Forum

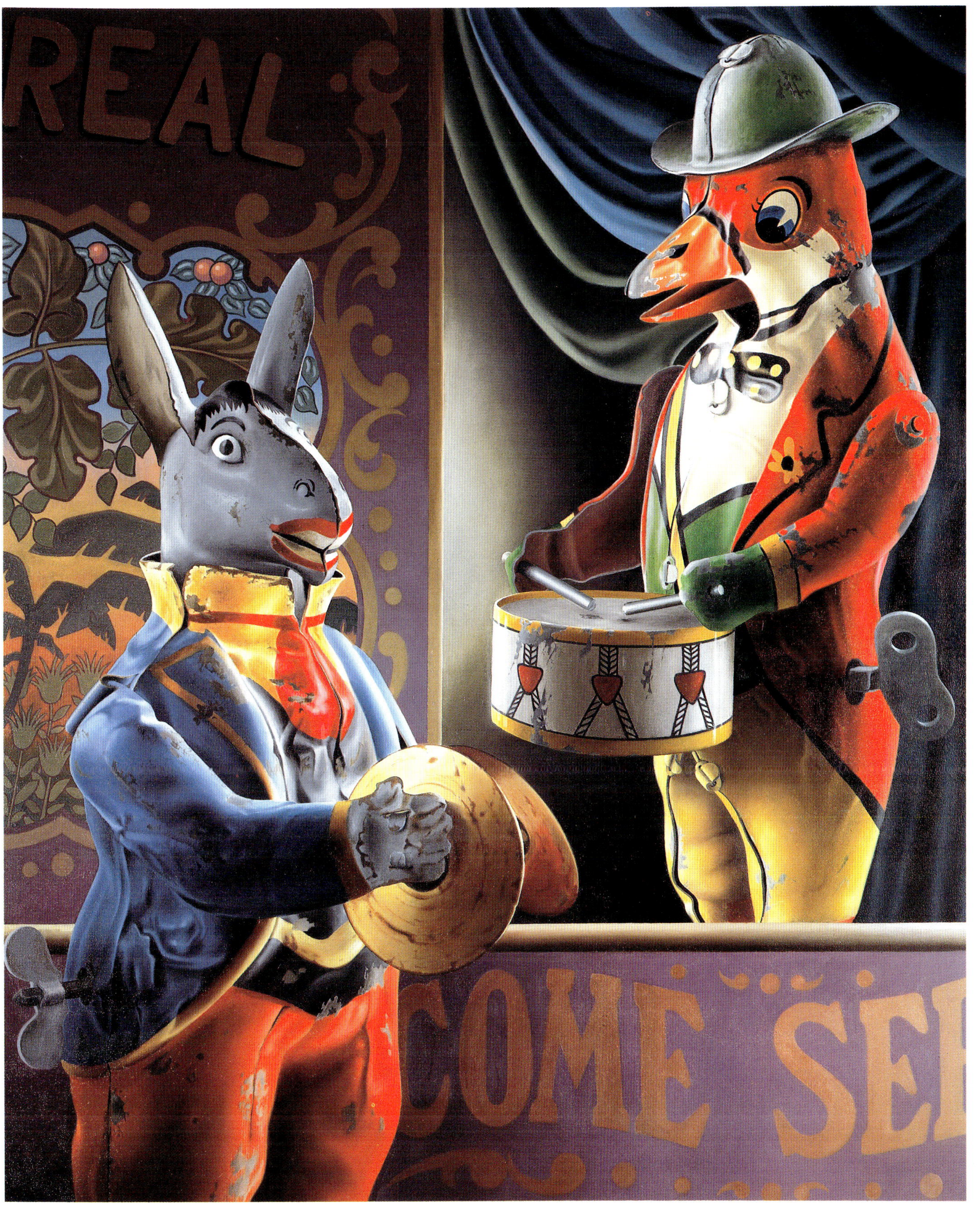
REAL
COME SE

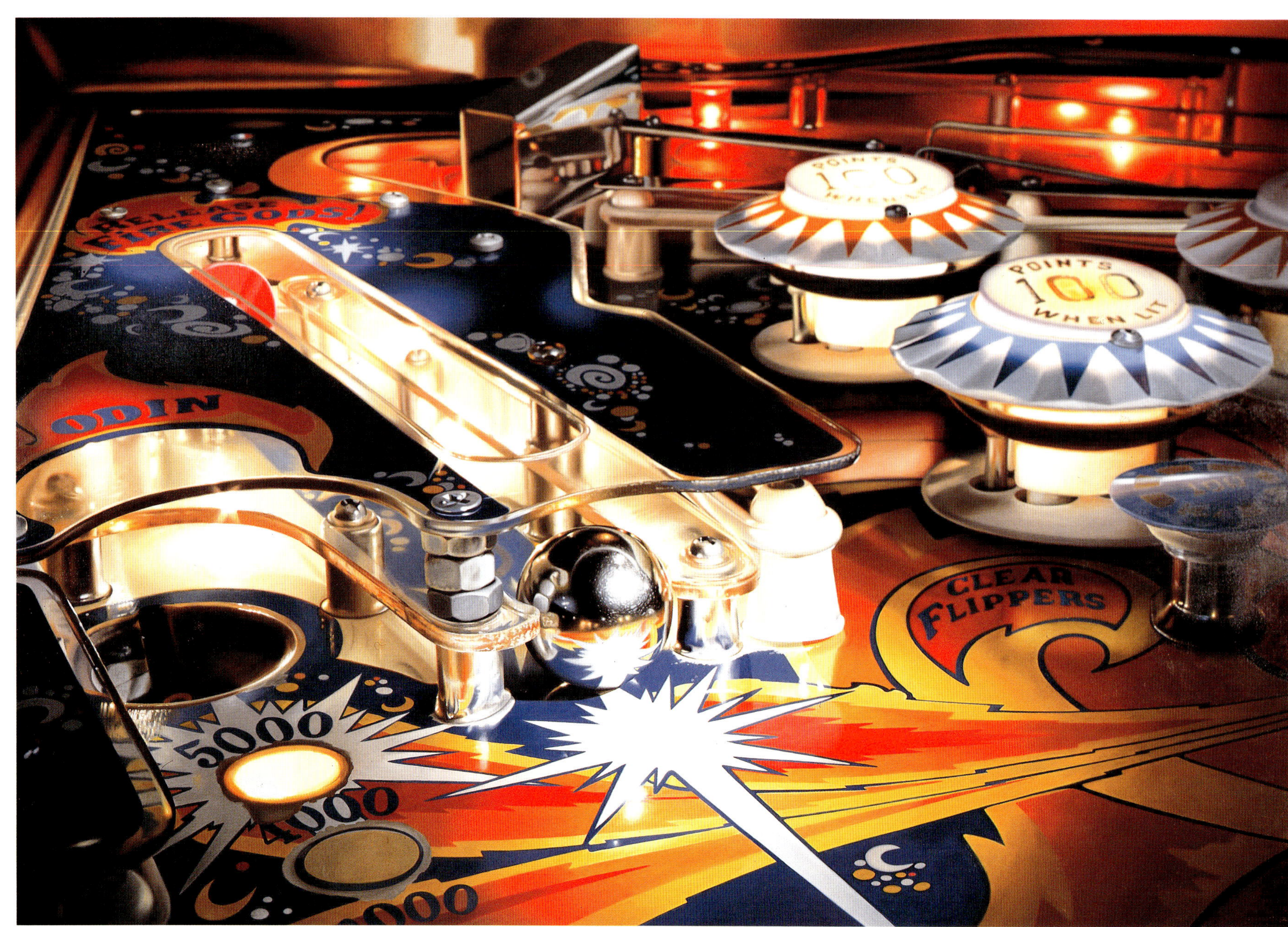

144. *Clear Flippers and Release Fire Gods.* 1984. Oil on canvas, 62 × 90″. Virlane Foundation, Louisiana

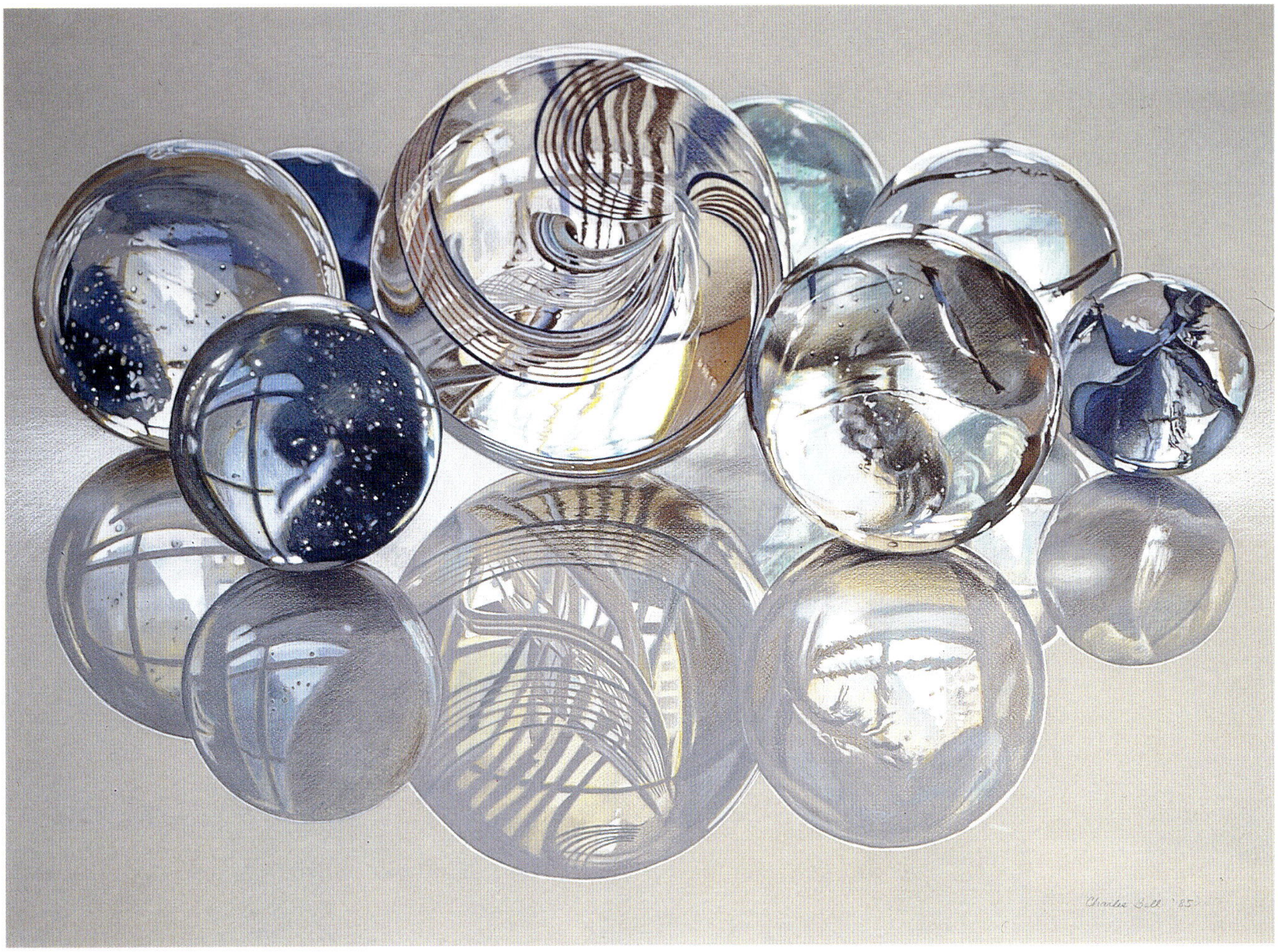

145. *"Glassies," Marbles XIV*. 1985. Colored pencil on gray paper, 27½ × 39⅜″. Private collection, Texas

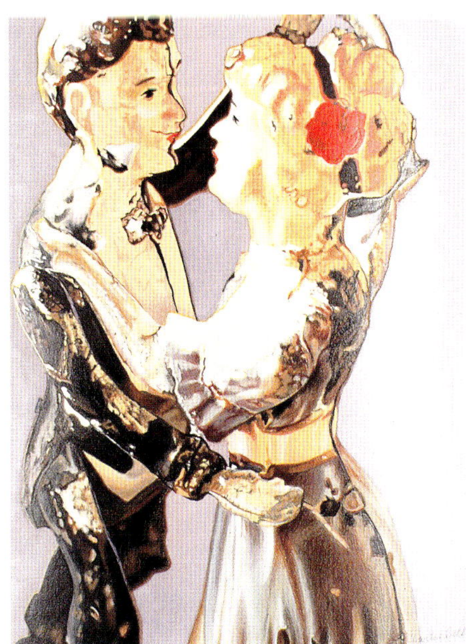

146. *Valentine*. 1984. Oil on board, c. 10 × 7″. Private collection

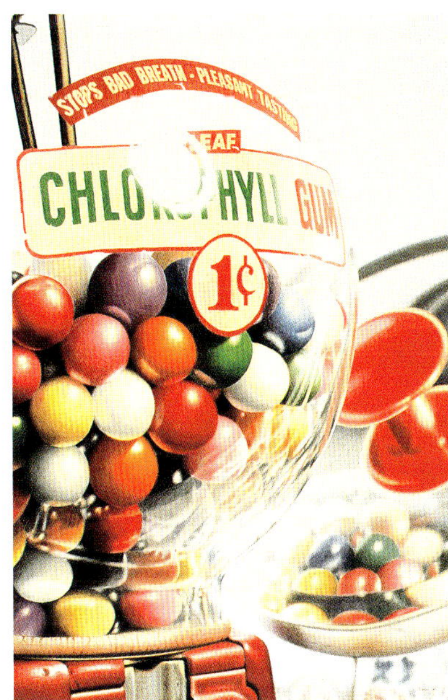

147. *"Pleasant Tasting," Gumball XVI*. 1985. Colored pencil on board, 56½ × 39½″. Akron Art Museum, Ohio

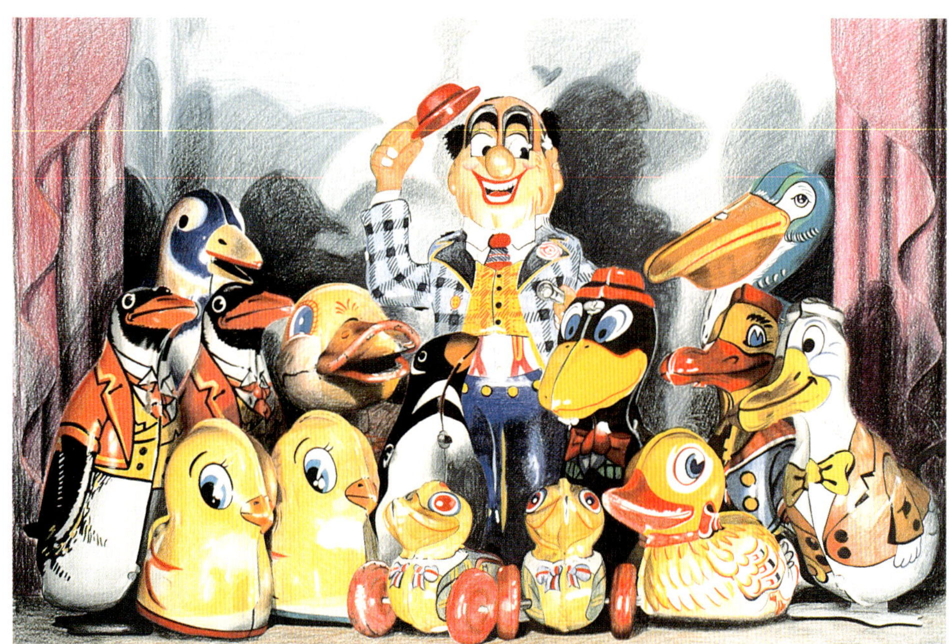

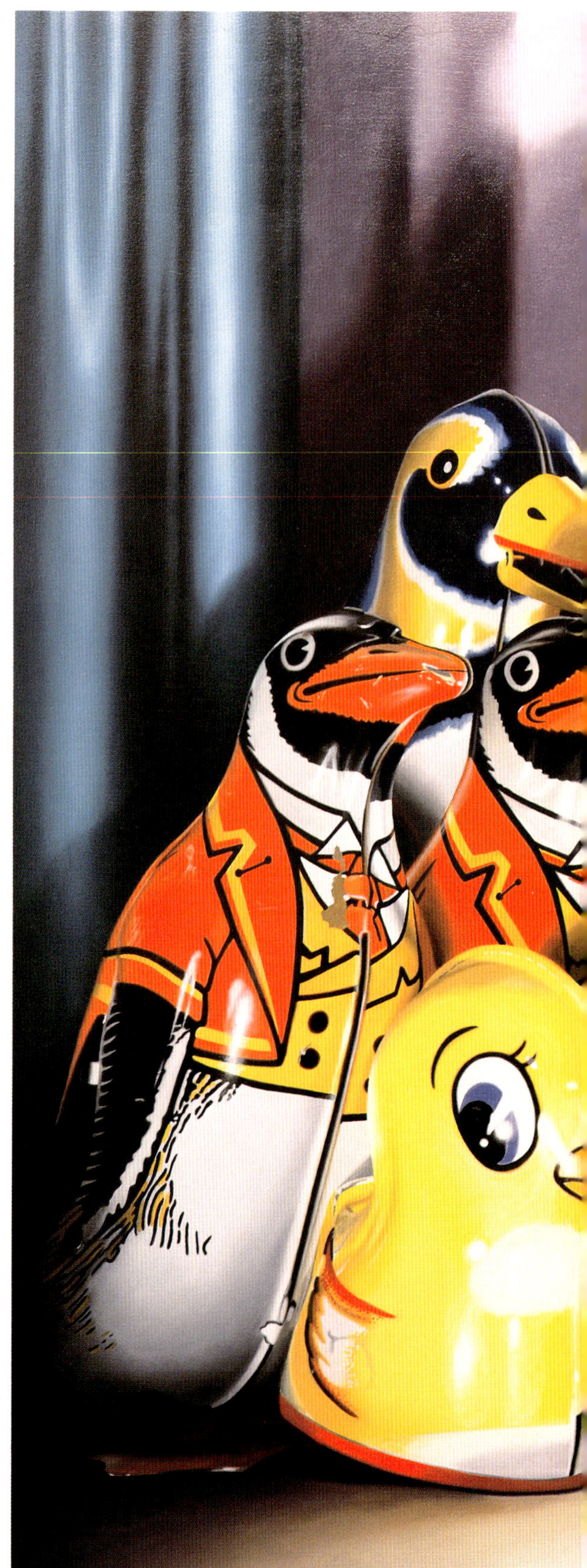

ABOVE: 148. Study for *Ta-Daa*. 1985. Colored pencil on board, 39½ × 56½″. Private collection, New York

RIGHT: 149. *Ta-Daa*. 1985. Oil on canvas, 72 × 108″. Private collection, New York

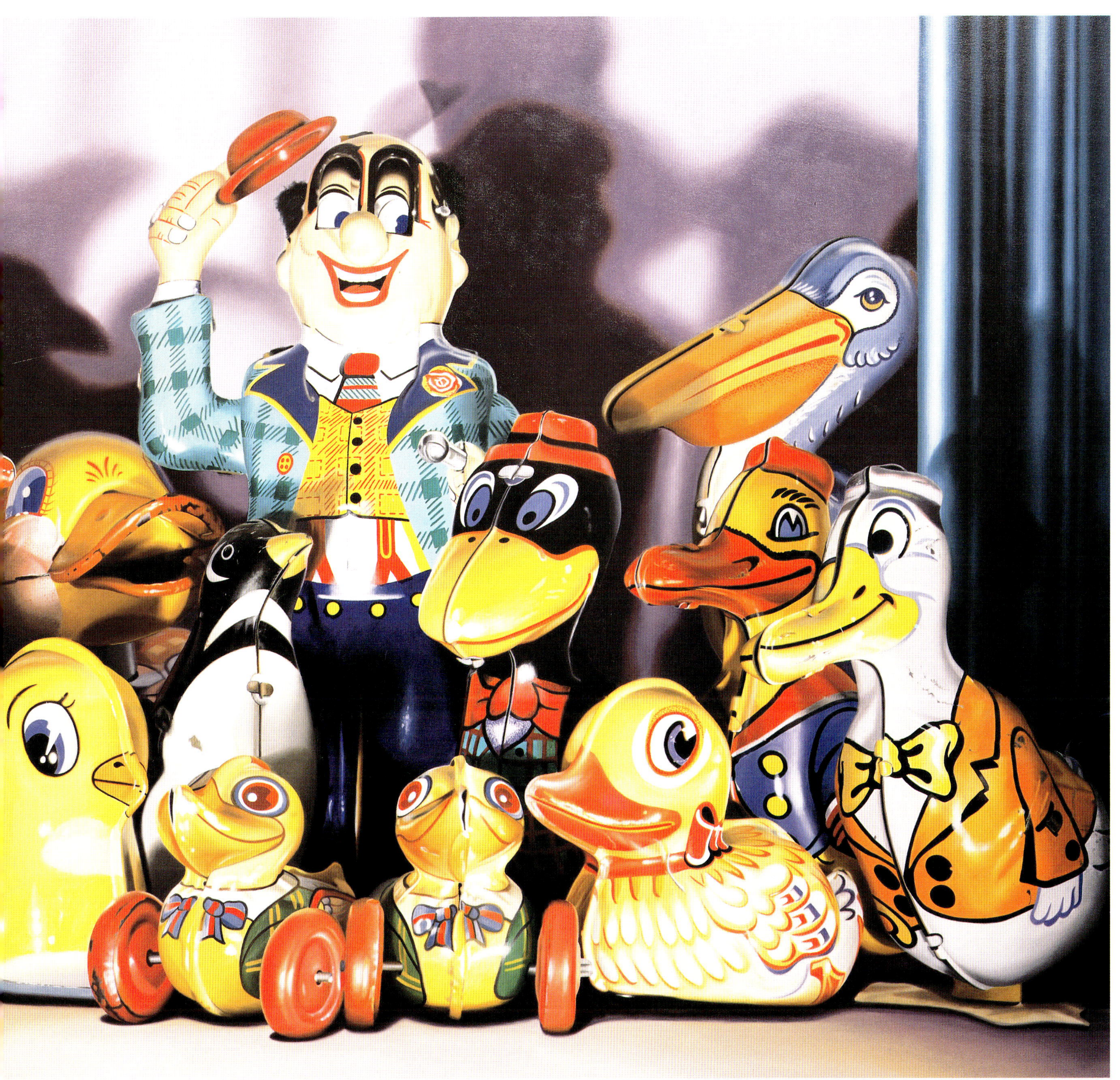

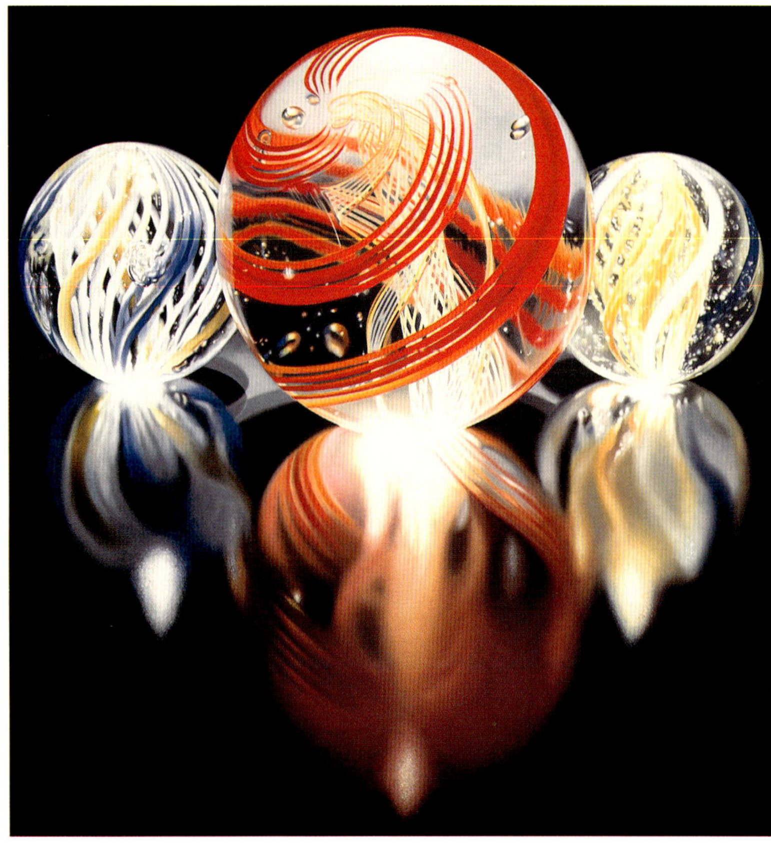

150. *Marbles XV*. 1985. Oil on canvas, 48 × 46½″. Private collection, New York

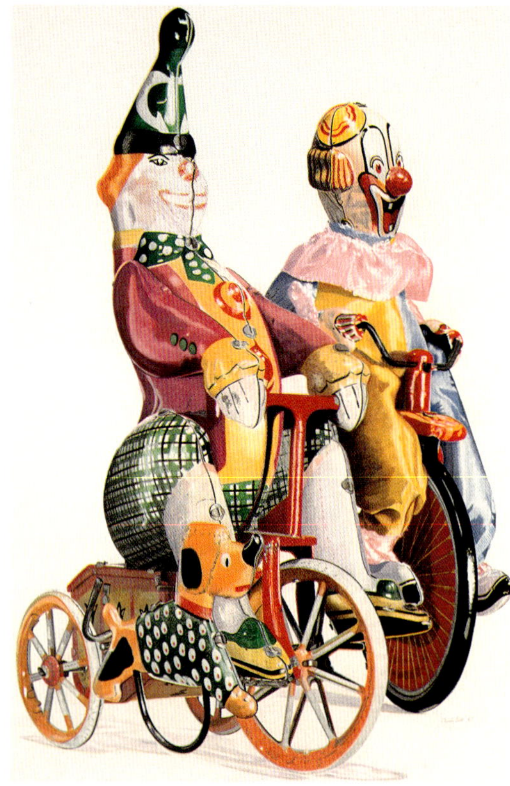

151. *Le Cirque*. 1985. Colored pencil on board, 60 × 40″. Private collection, Idaho

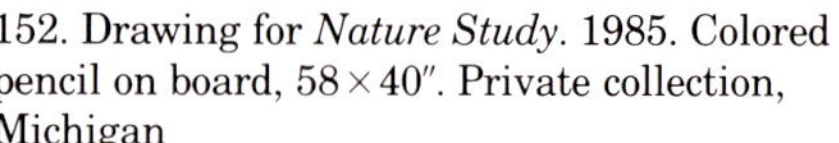

152. Drawing for *Nature Study*. 1985. Colored pencil on board, 58 × 40″. Private collection, Michigan

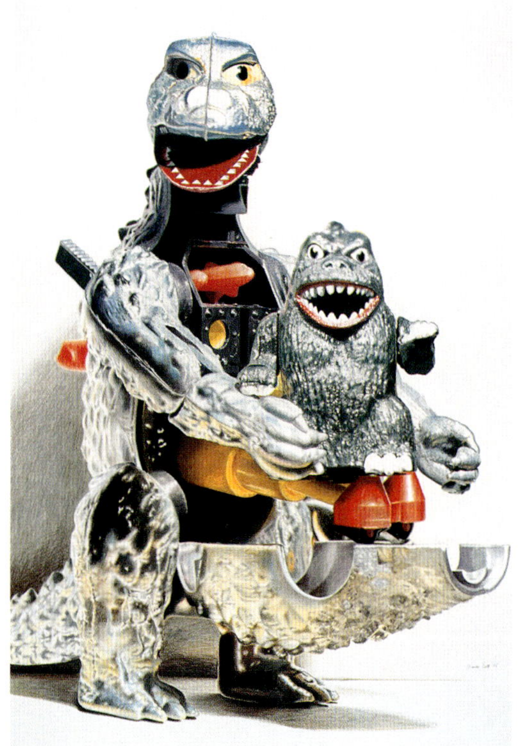

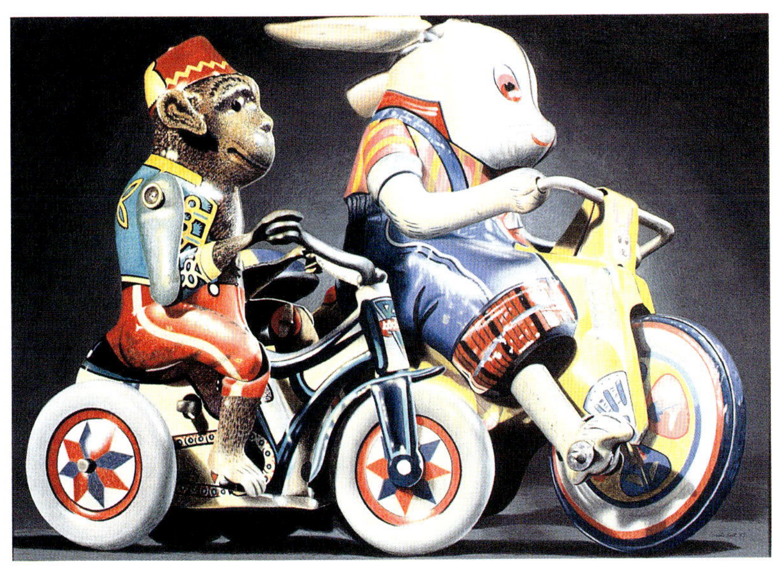

153. Study for *Bunny Cycle*. 1985. Colored pencil on black paper, 40 × 57″. Private collection, Illinois

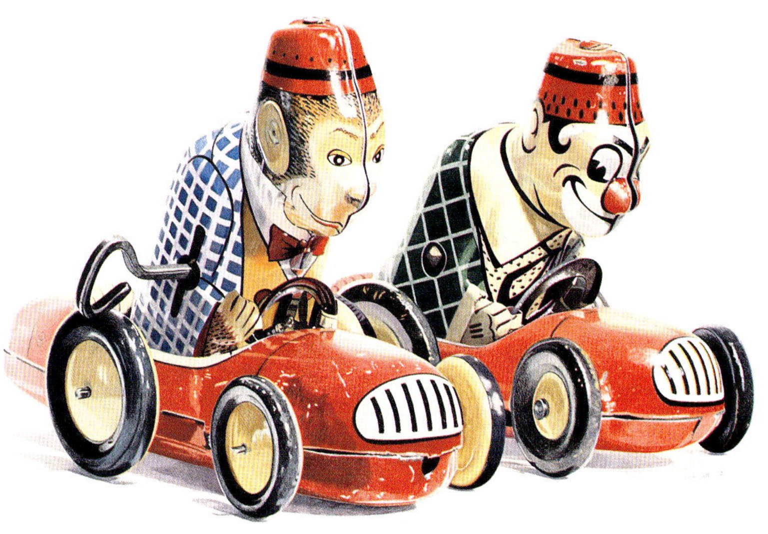

154. *Get Ready, Get Set*. 1985. Colored pencil on board, 40 × 60″. Private collection, New York

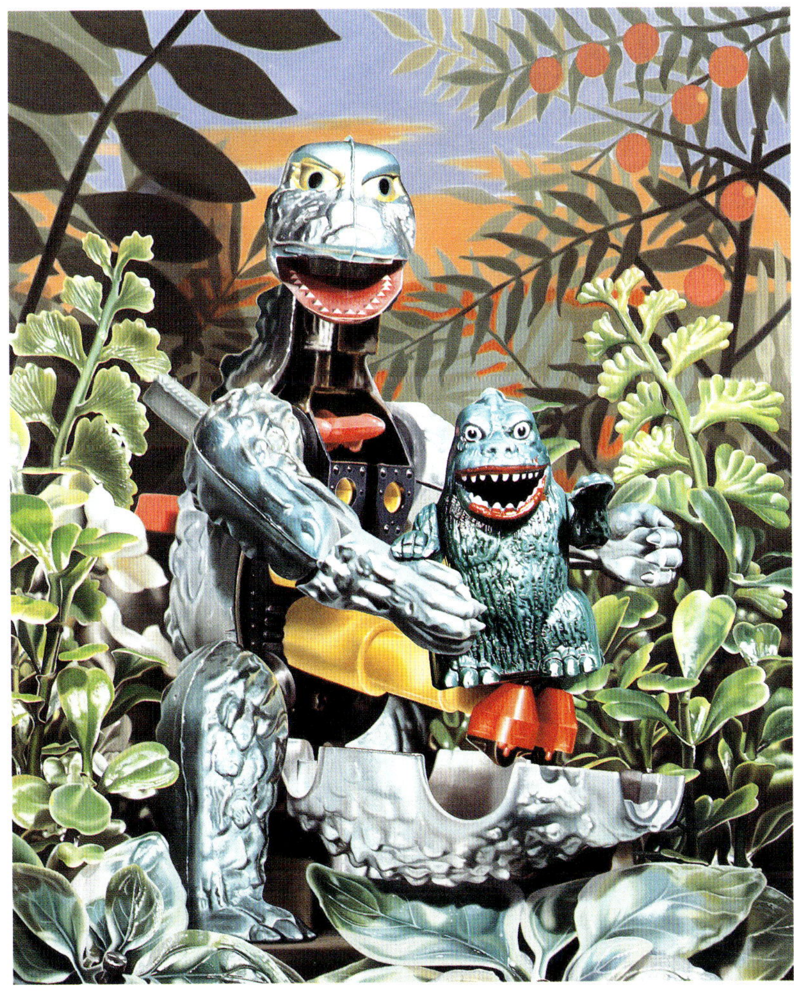

155. *Nature Study*. 1985. Oil on canvas, 72 × 60″. Collection the artist

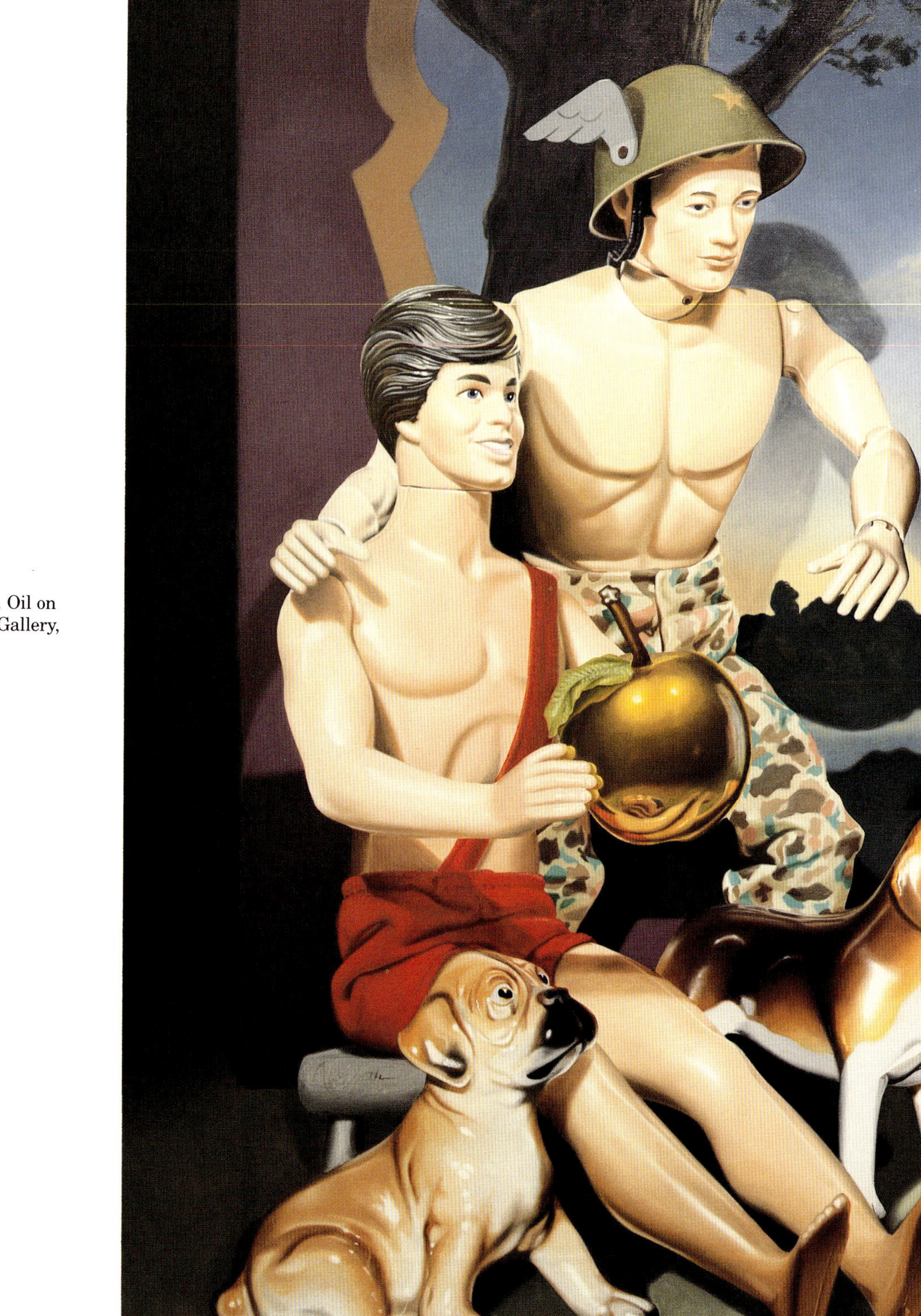

156. *The Judgement of Paris*. 1986. Oil on canvas, 72 × 120″. Louis K. Meisel Gallery, New York

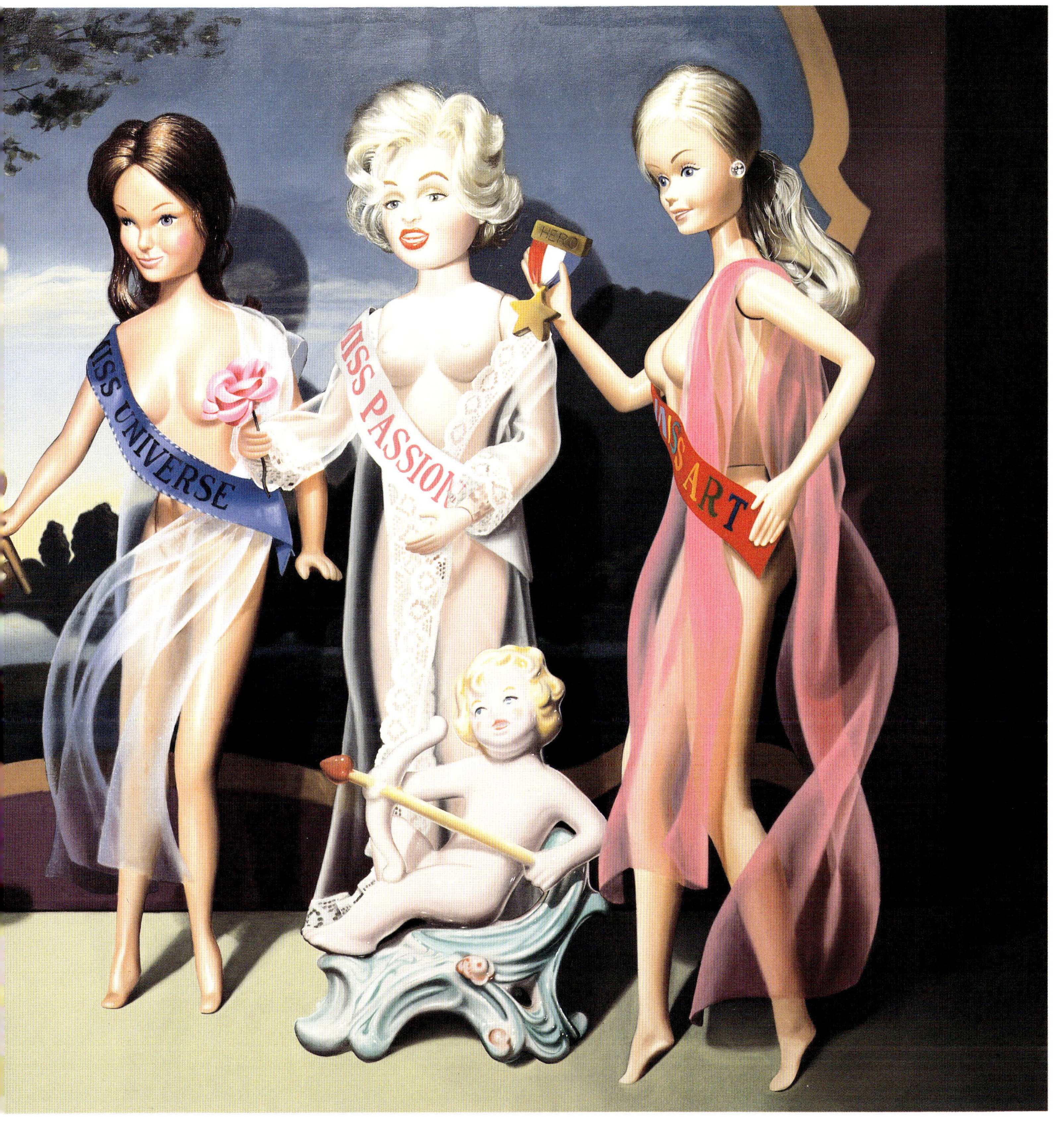
ISS UNIVERSE
ISS PASSION
HERO
ISS ART

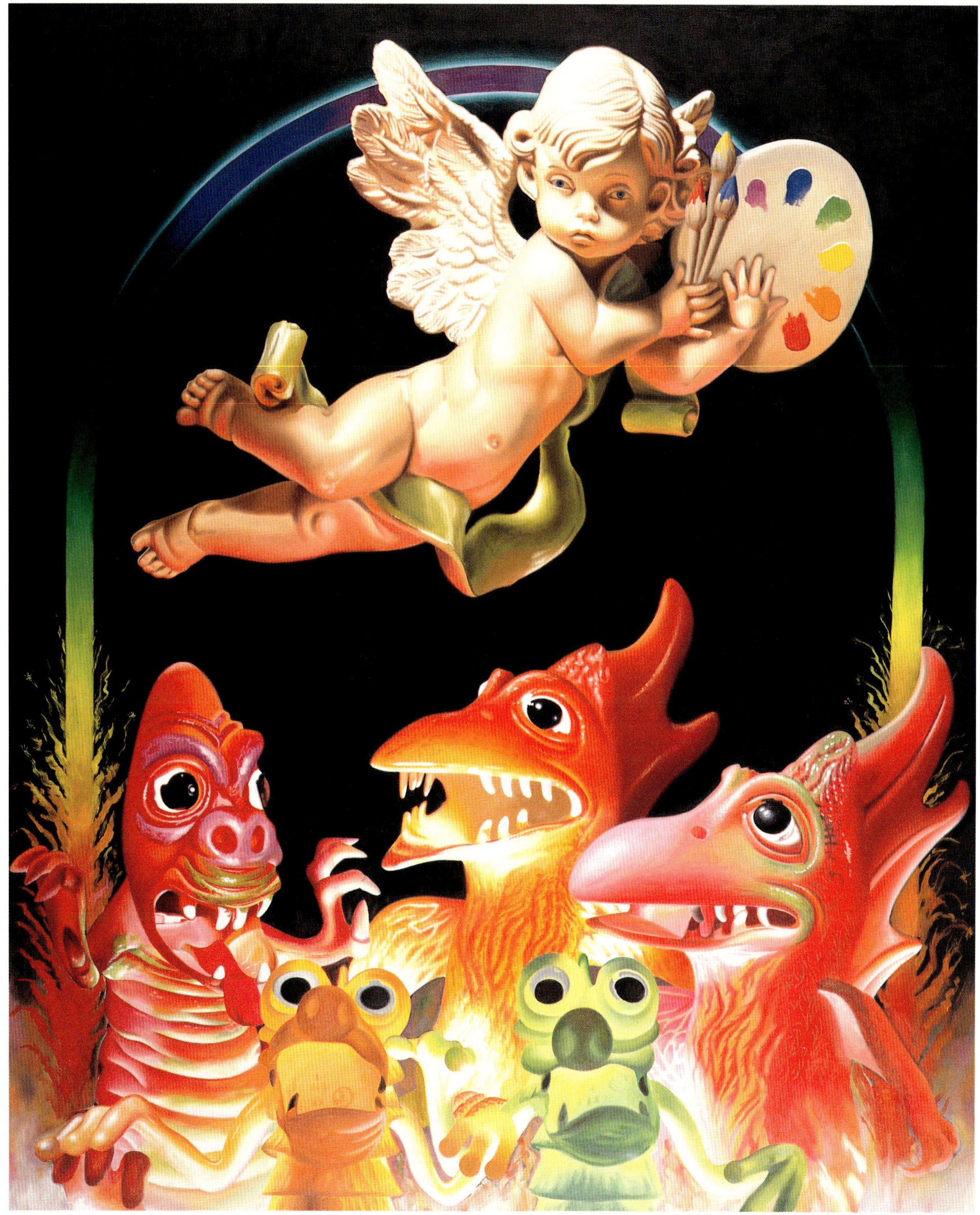

157. *Art Angel*. 1986. Oil on canvas, 72×60″. Collection Will Ching, New York

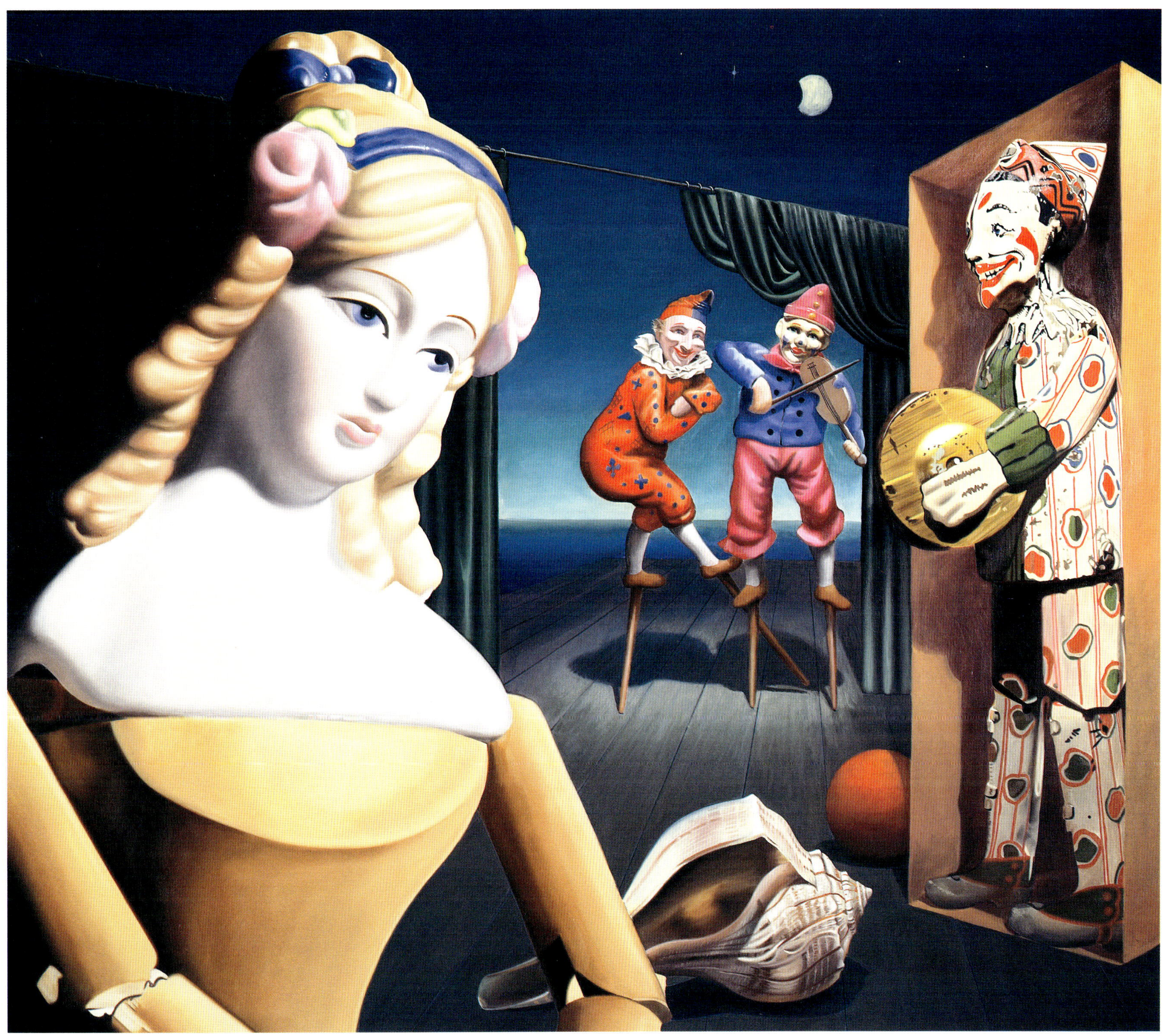

158. *Midsummer's Dream*. 1986. Oil on canvas, 60 × 72″. Louis K. Meisel Gallery, New York

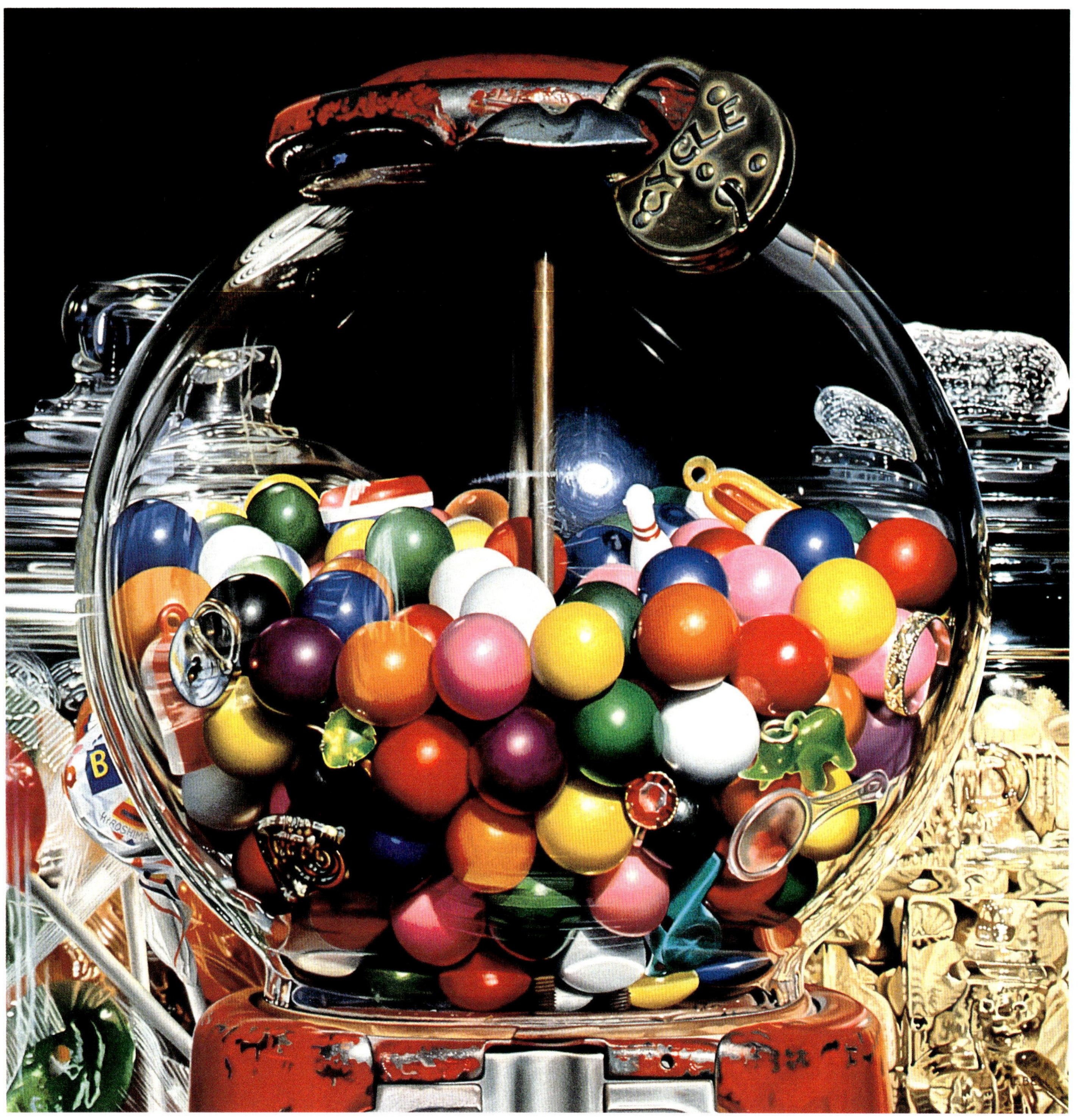

159. *Gumball XVII*. 1986. Oil on canvas, 66 × 66″. Hiroshima City Museum of Contemporary Art, Japan

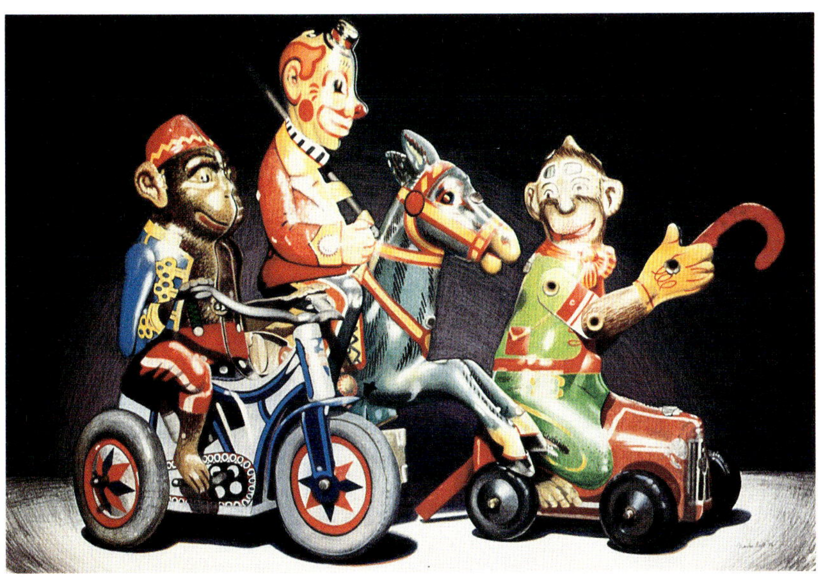

160. *Before the Journey*. 1986. Colored pencil on board, 39 × 58″. Collection Robert and Brenda Pangborn, Michigan

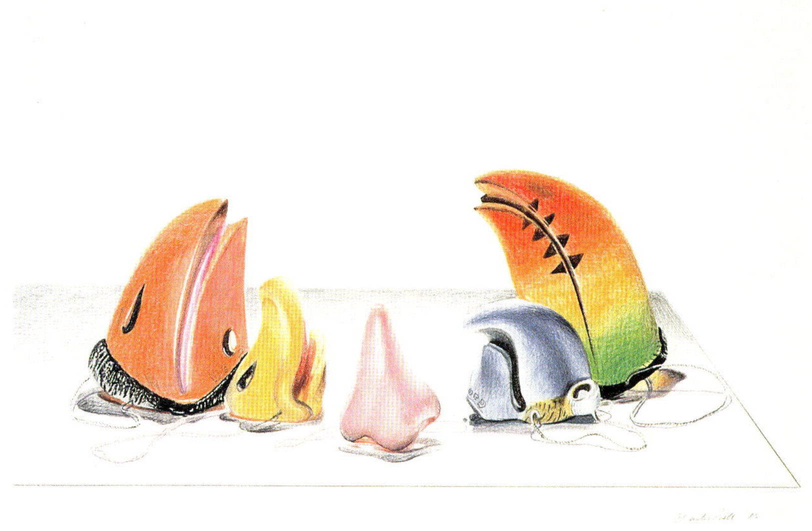

161. *Untitled (Nose Masks)*. 1986. Colored pencil on paper, 11¼ × 14¼″. Private collection, Portugal

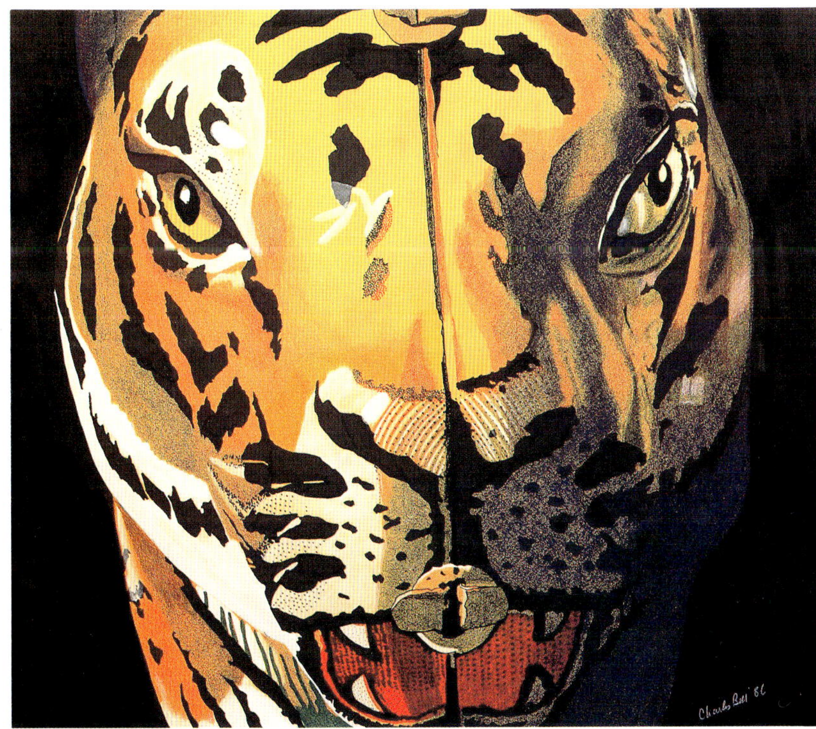

162. *Tiger*. 1986. Colored pencil and gouache on paper, 27½ × 31½″. Collection the artist

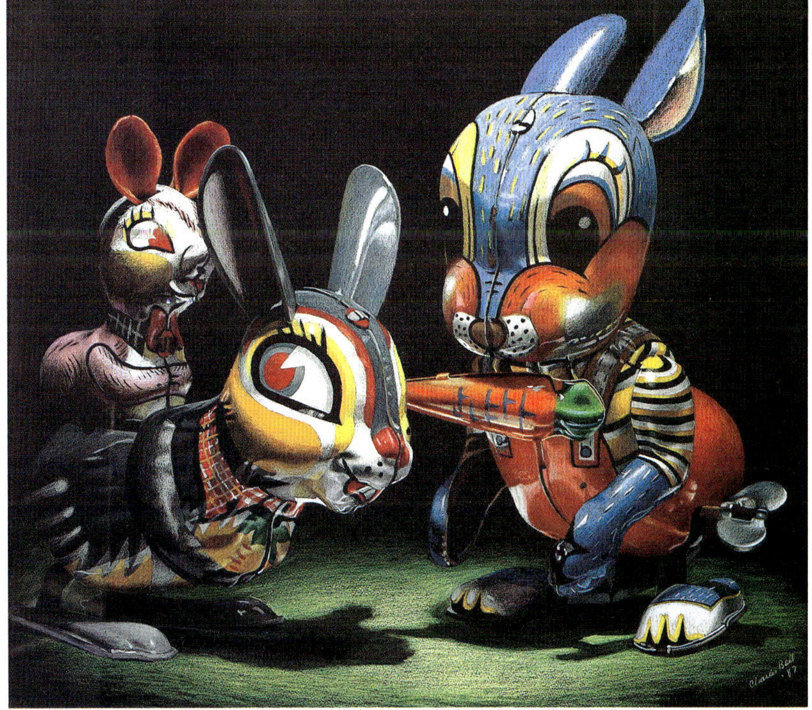

163. *Bridgehampton Bunnies*. 1987. Pastel and colored pencil on black paper, 26 × 30″. Collection Ari Ron Meisel, New York

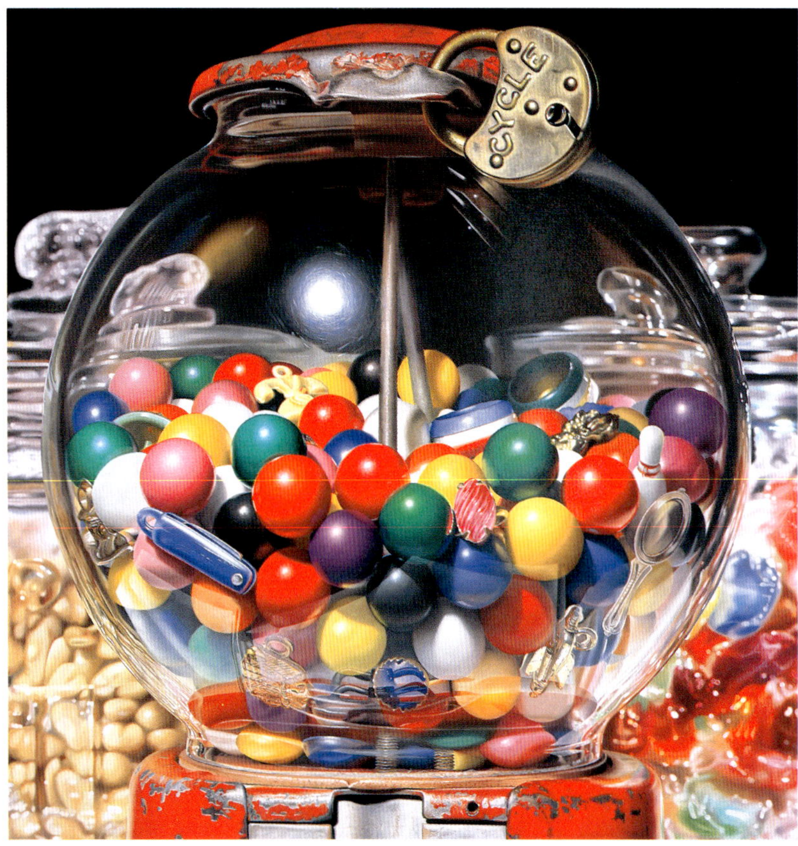

164. *Gumball XVIII*. 1986. Oil on canvas, 66 × 66″. Collection Douglas and Beverly Feurring, Florida

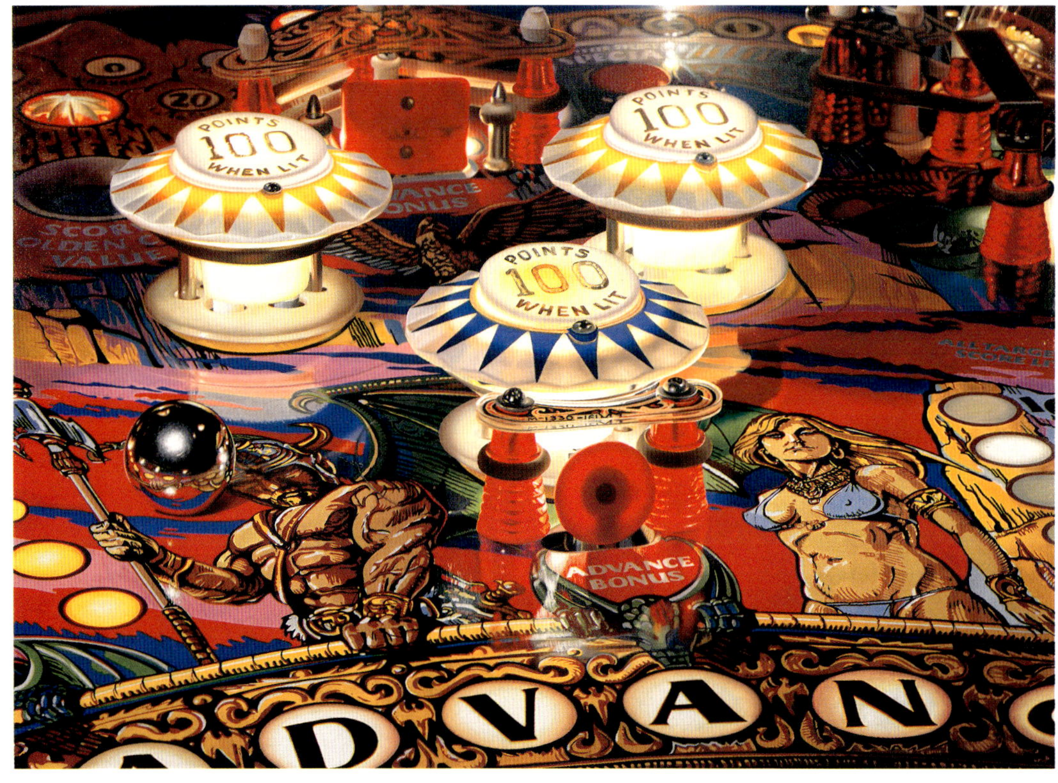

165. *Advance Bonus*. 1987. Oil on canvas, 60 × 84″. Private collection, California

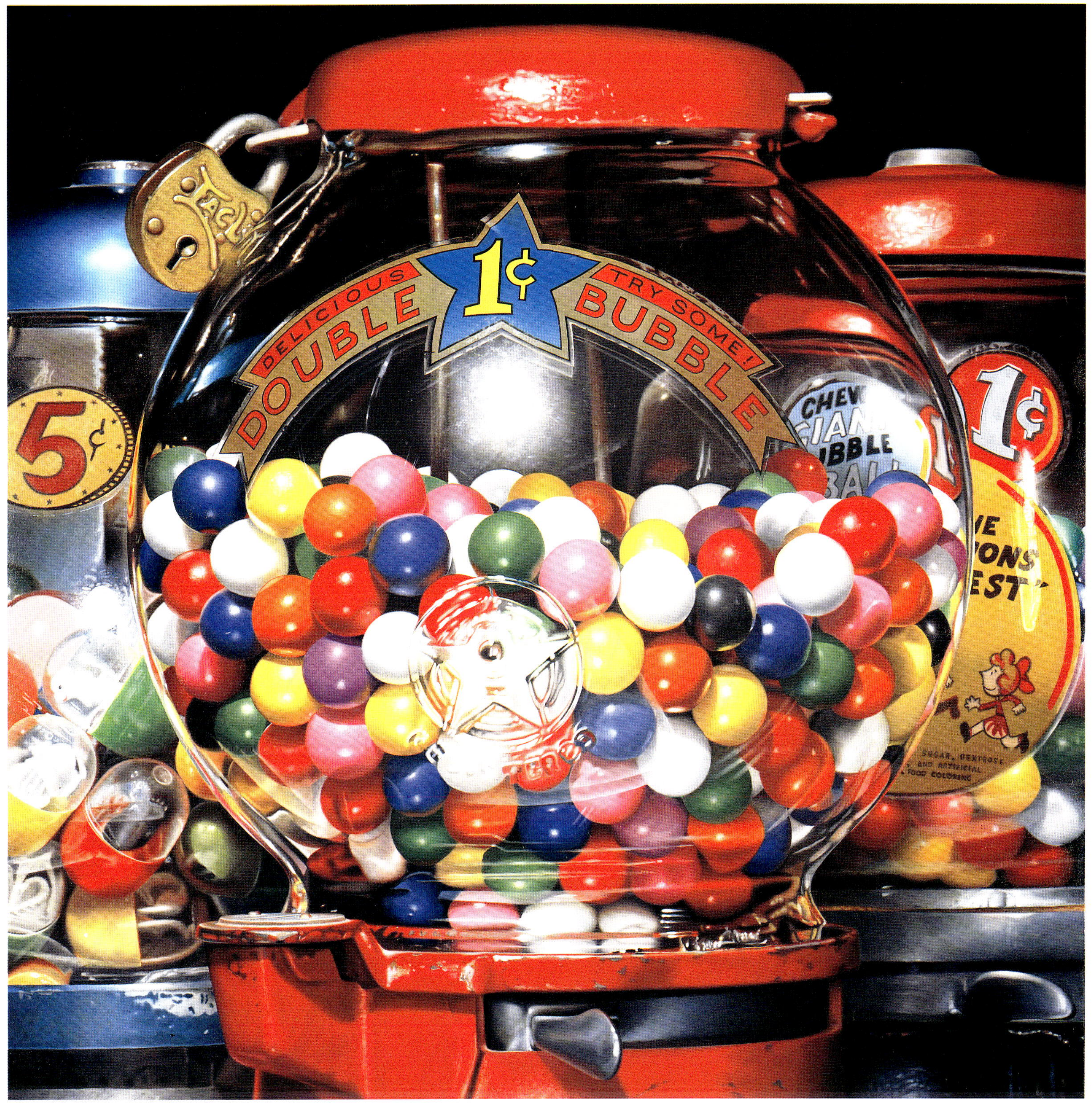

166. *"Double Bubble," Gumball XIX*. 1987. Oil on canvas, 72 × 72″. Private collection, Switzerland

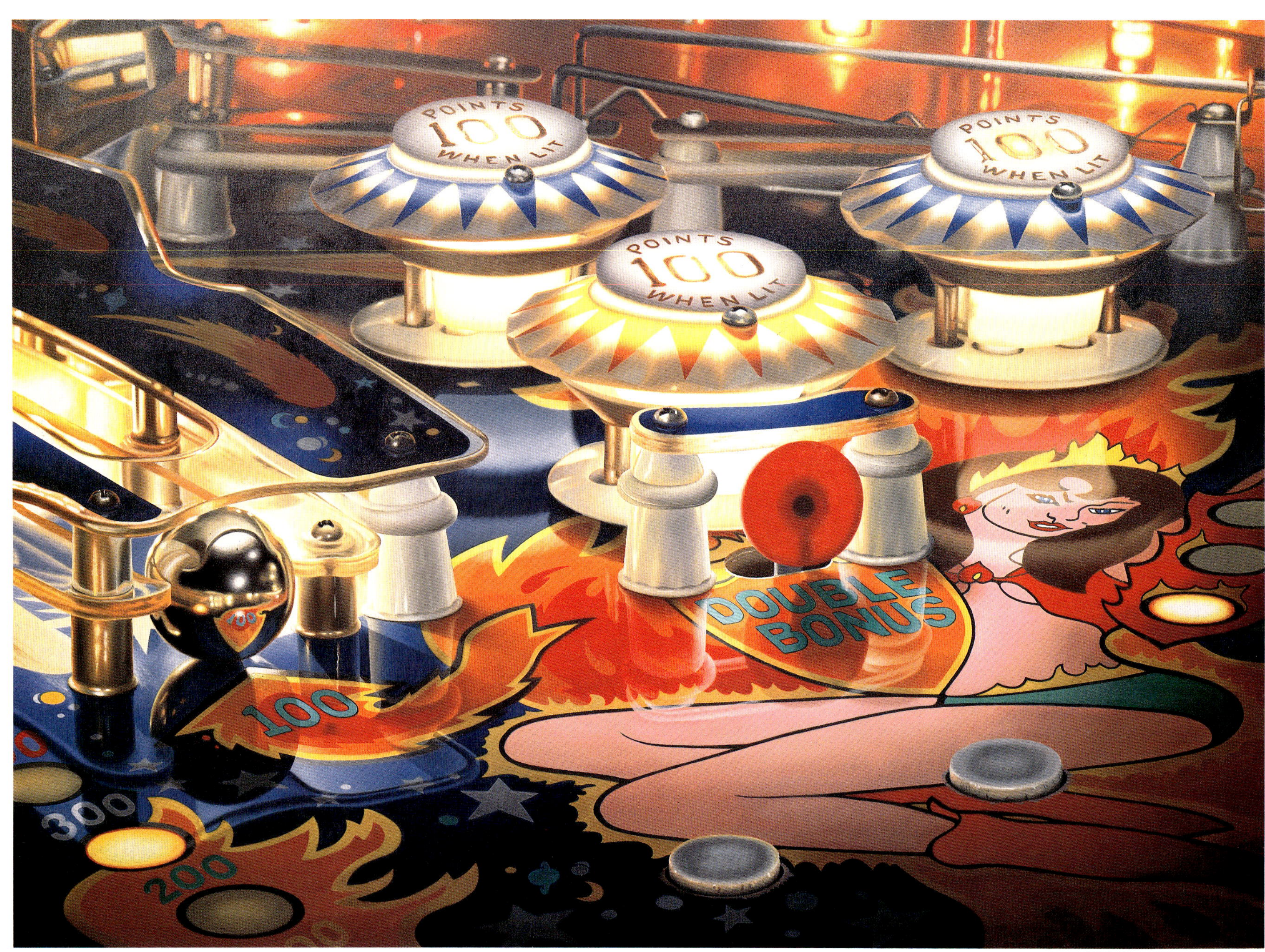

167. *Double Bonus*. 1987. Oil on canvas, 60 × 84″. Private collection, California

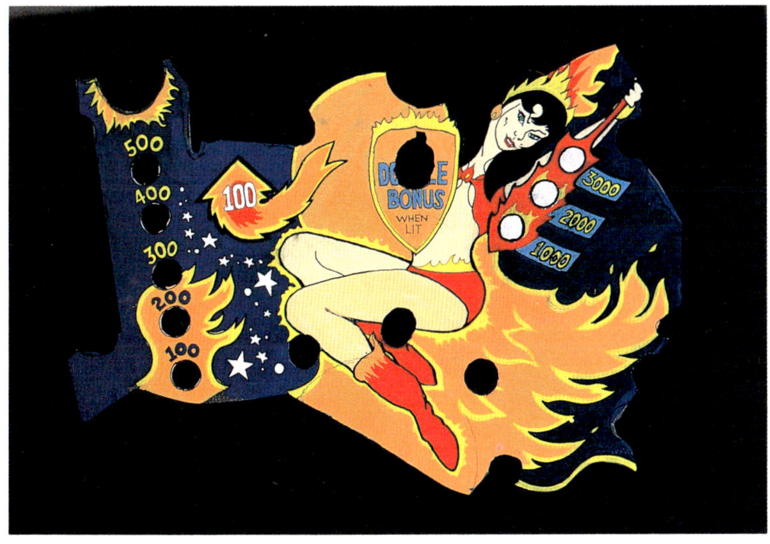

168. Study for *Double Bonus*. 1987. Acrylic on Mylar, 11 × 15″. Private collection, Michigan

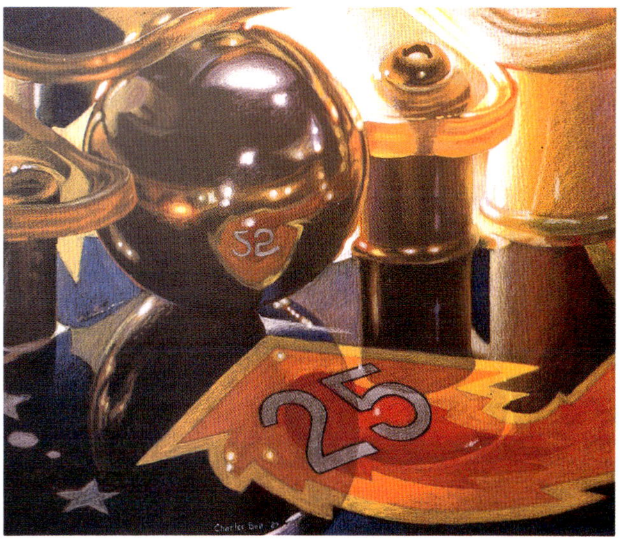

169. *25*. 1987. Conte crayon on paper, 17 × 24″. Private collection, California

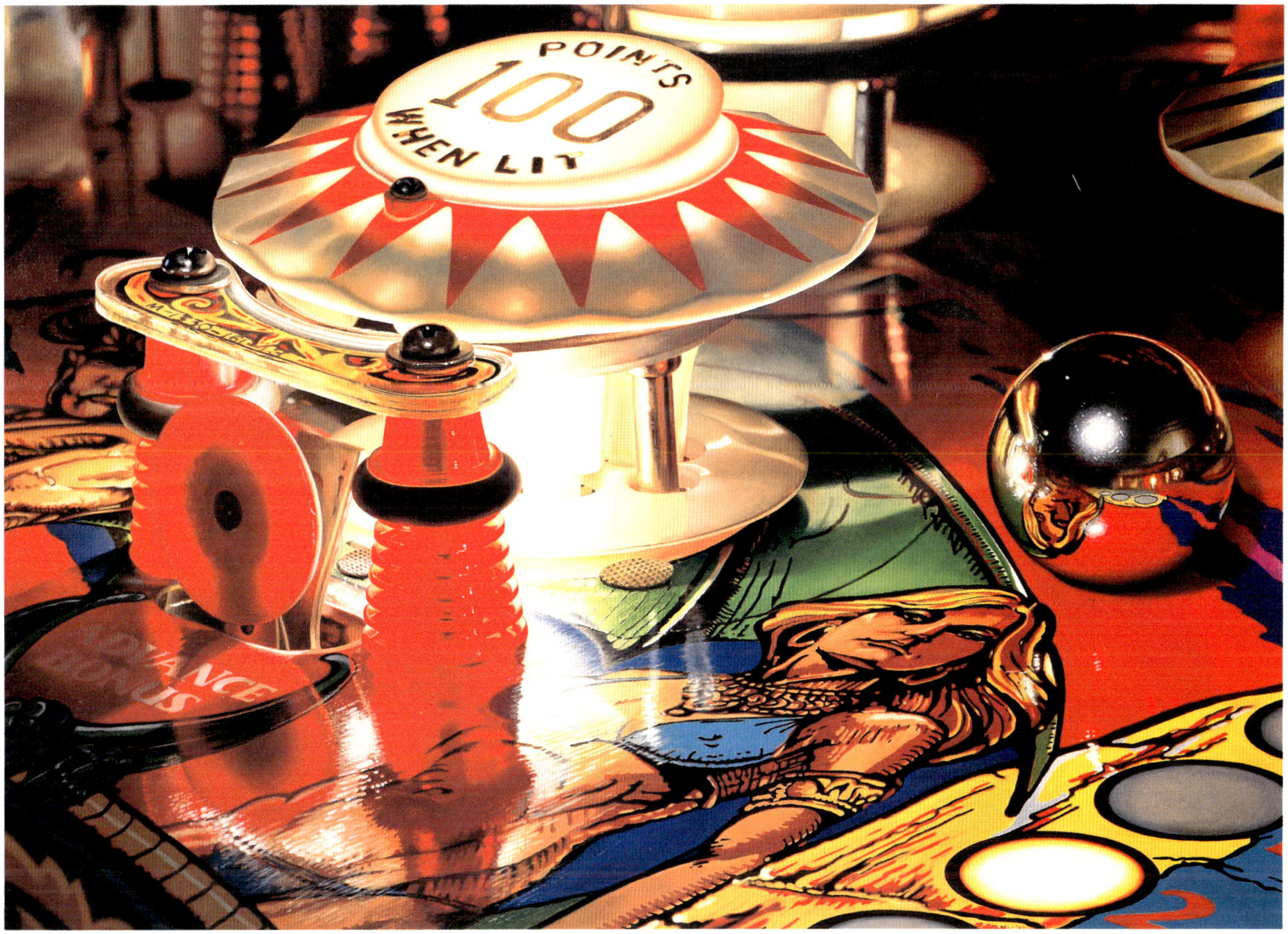

170. *Viking Strikes*. 1987. Oil on canvas, 42 × 60″. Collection Dale C. and Alexandra Zetlin Jones, New York

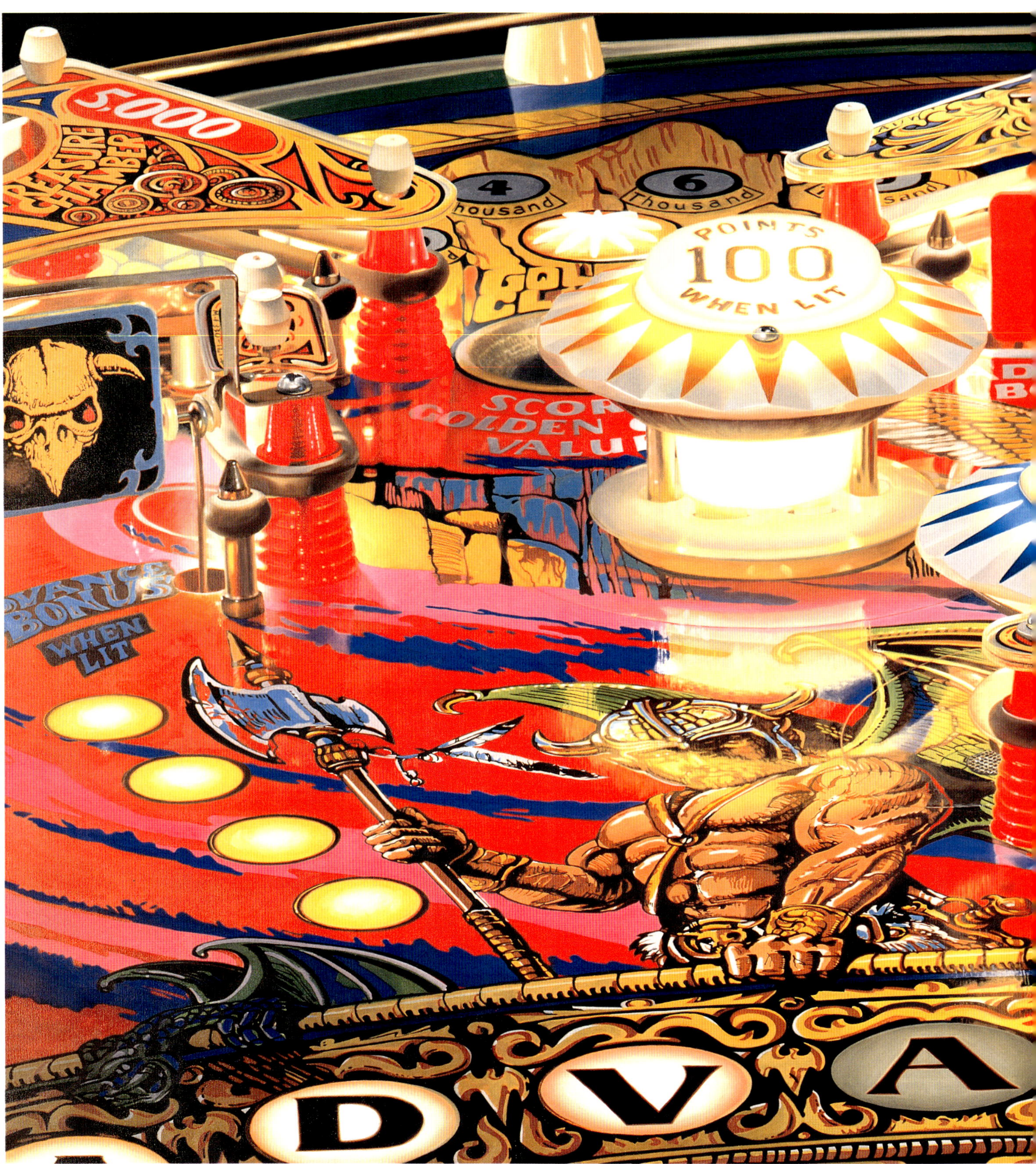
5,000
4
Thousand
6
Thousand
POINTS
100
WHEN LIT
WHEN LIT
D
V
A

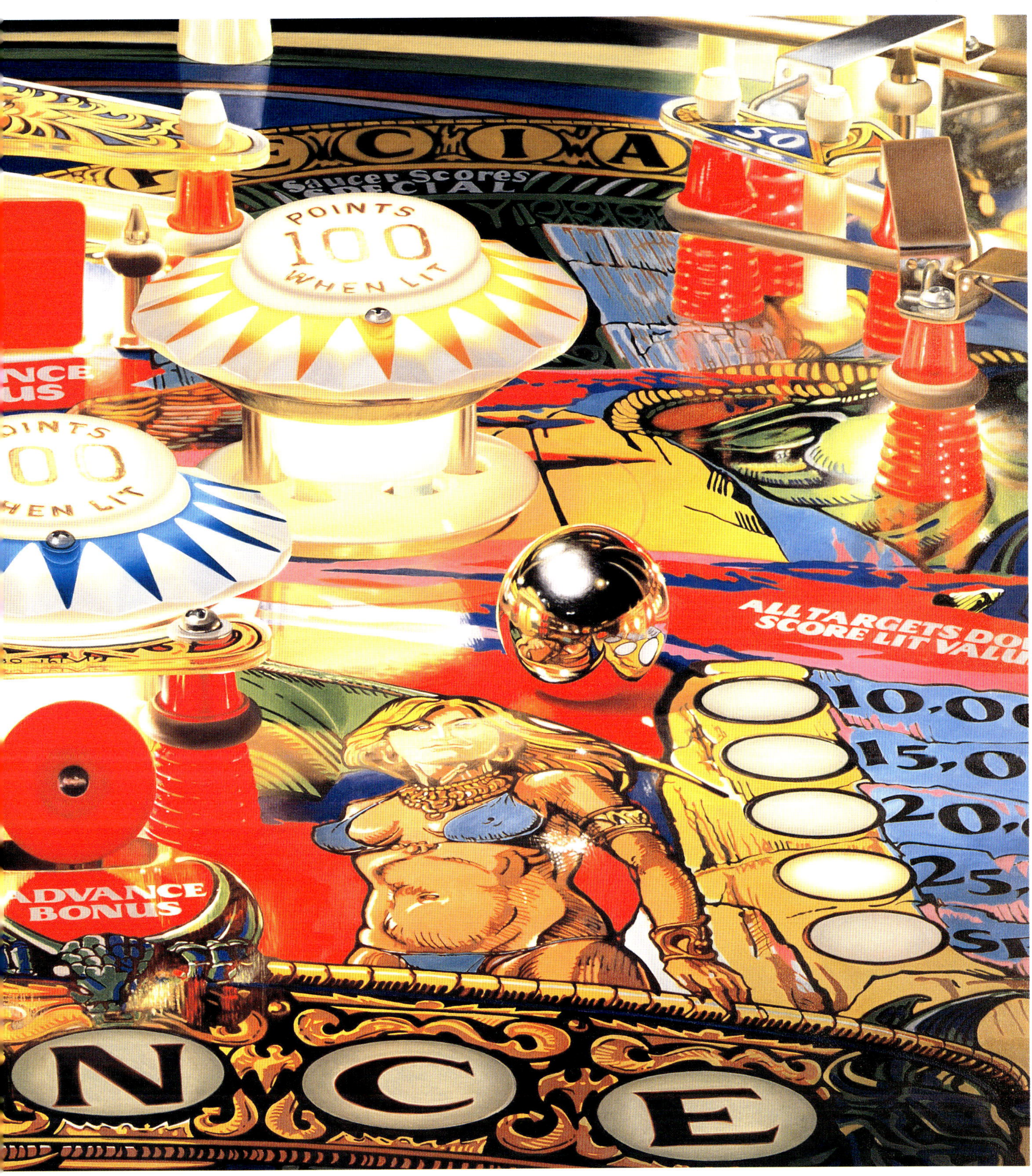

171. *Paragon*. 1988.
Oil on canvas, 50 × 96″.
Private collection,
Ontario

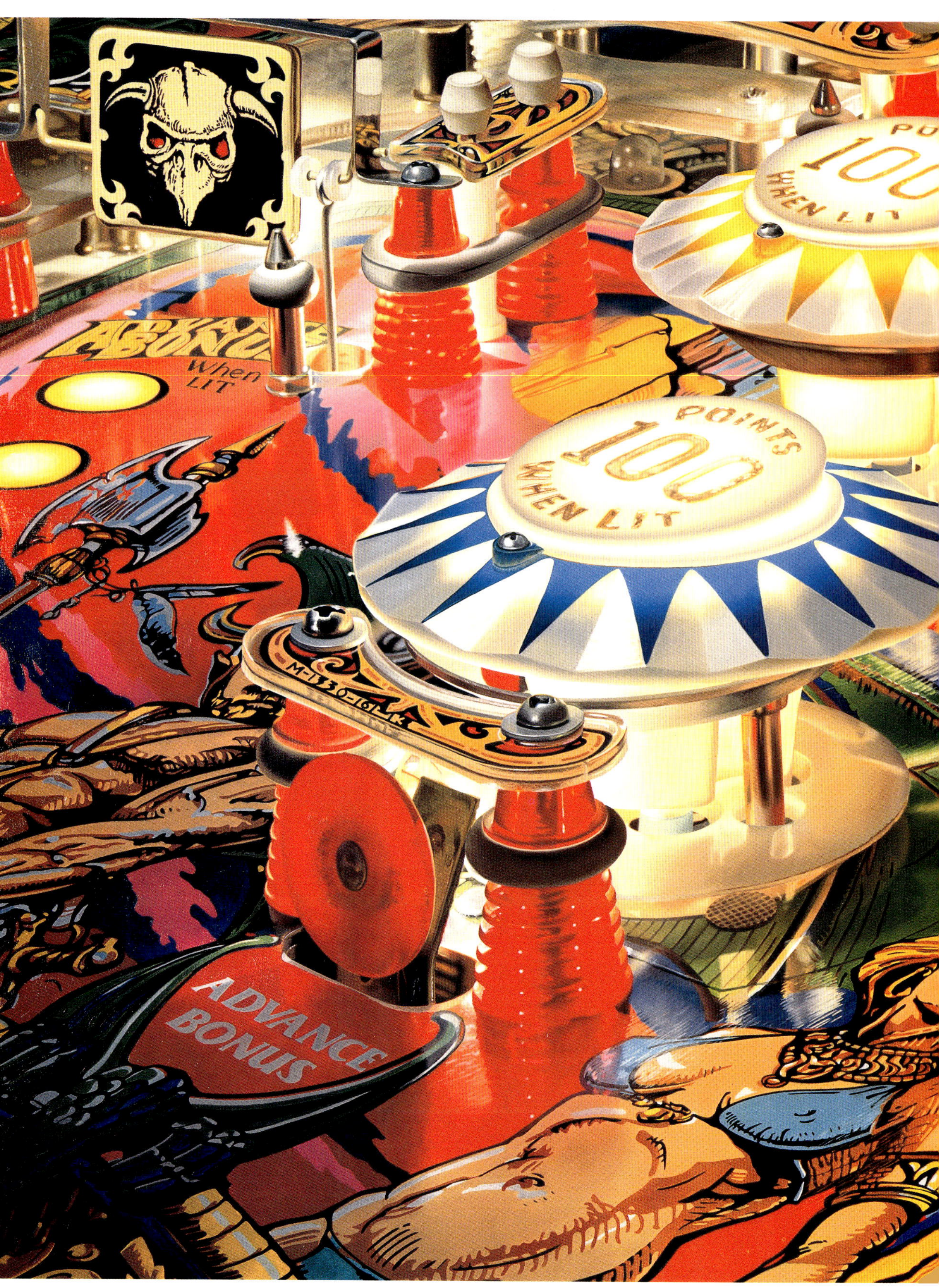
ADVANCE
BONUS
When
LIT
100
POINTS
WHEN LIT

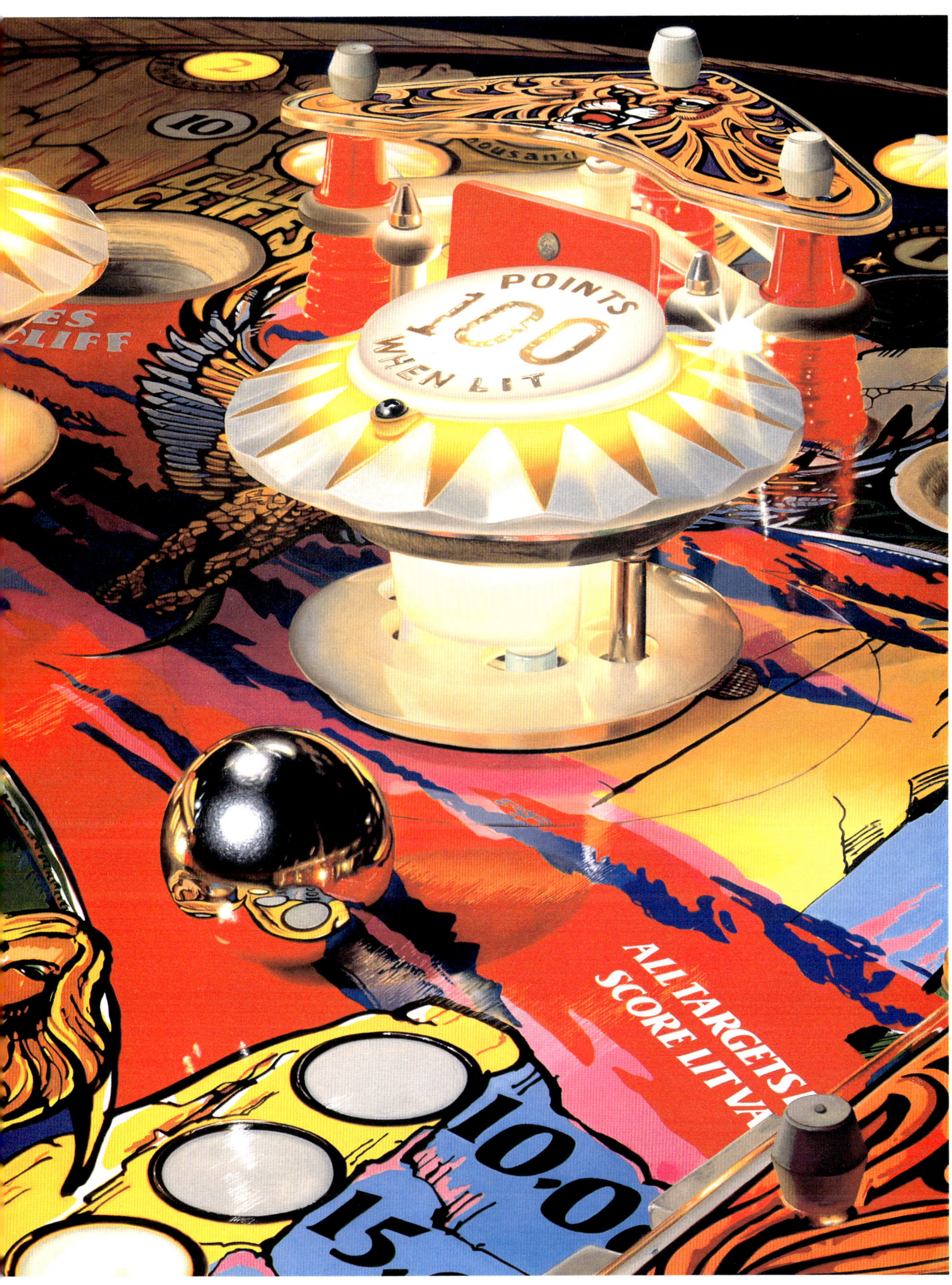

172. *1 to 4 Can Play.* 1988. Oil on canvas, 60 × 96″. Private collection, Switzerland

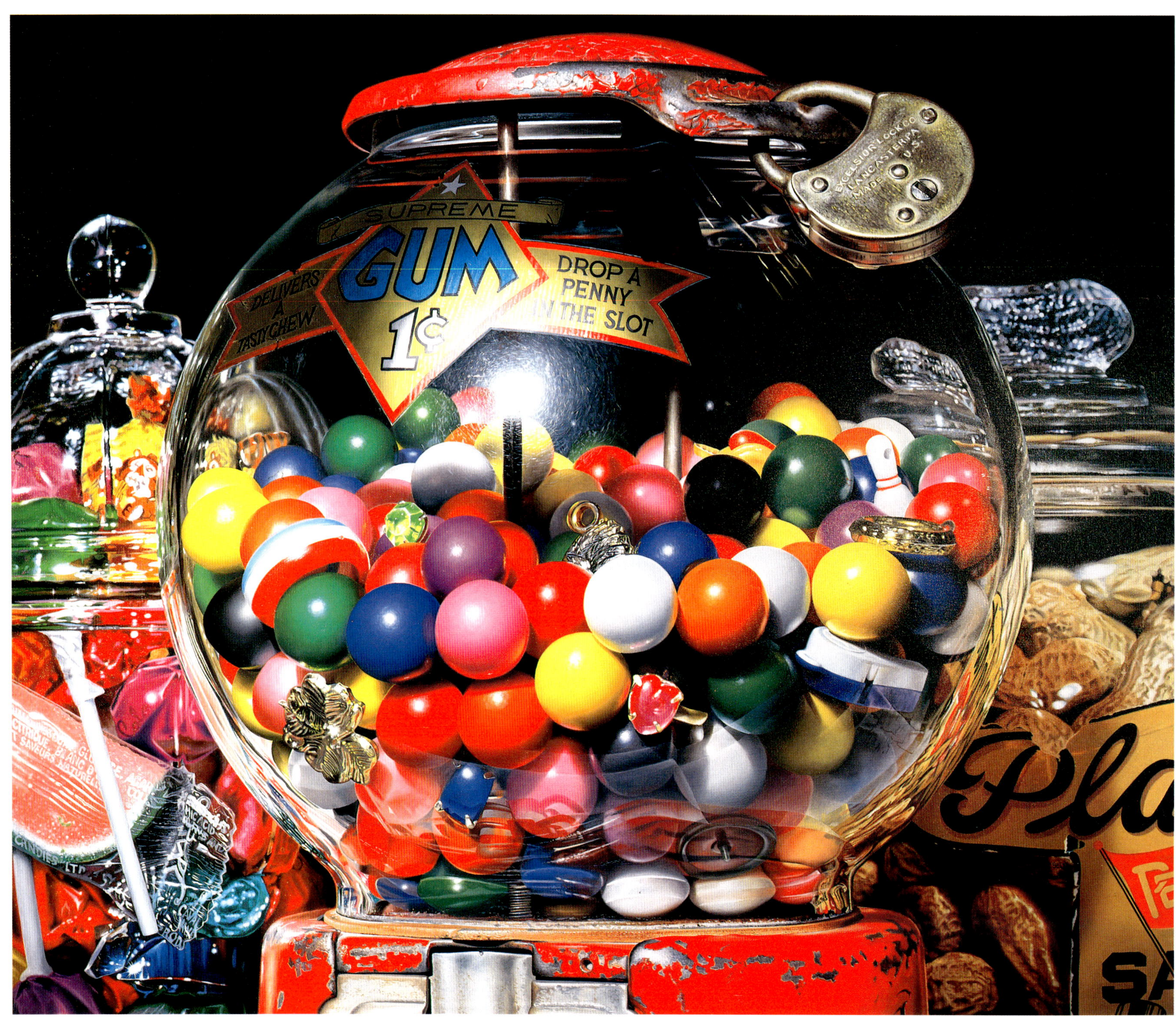

173. *"Drop a Penny in the Slot," Gumball XX.* 1988. Oil on canvas, 72 × 84″. Private collection, California

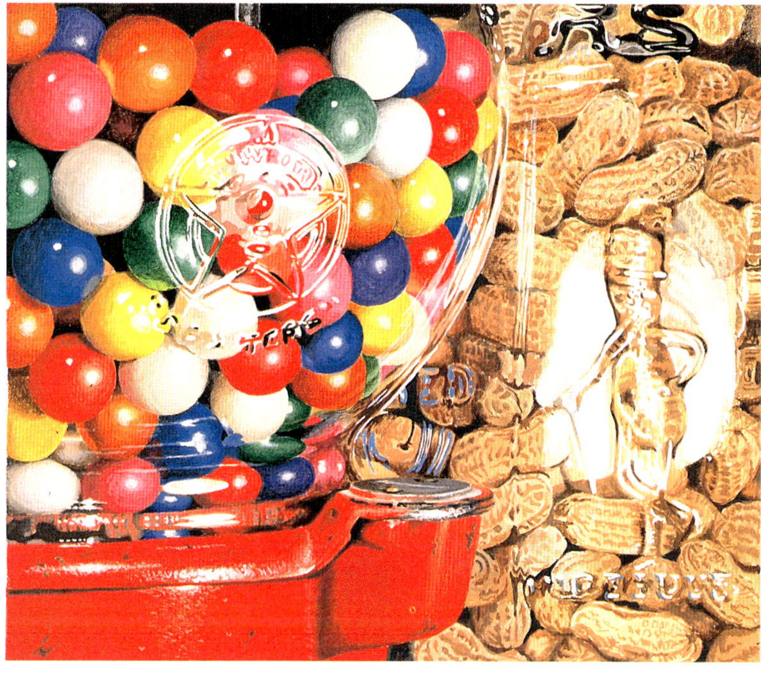

174. *"Andy's Mr. Peanut," Gumball XXII.* 1990. Watercolor, gouache, and pencil on paper, $7\frac{1}{2} \times 8\frac{3}{4}''$. Collection Bruce Vinokour, California

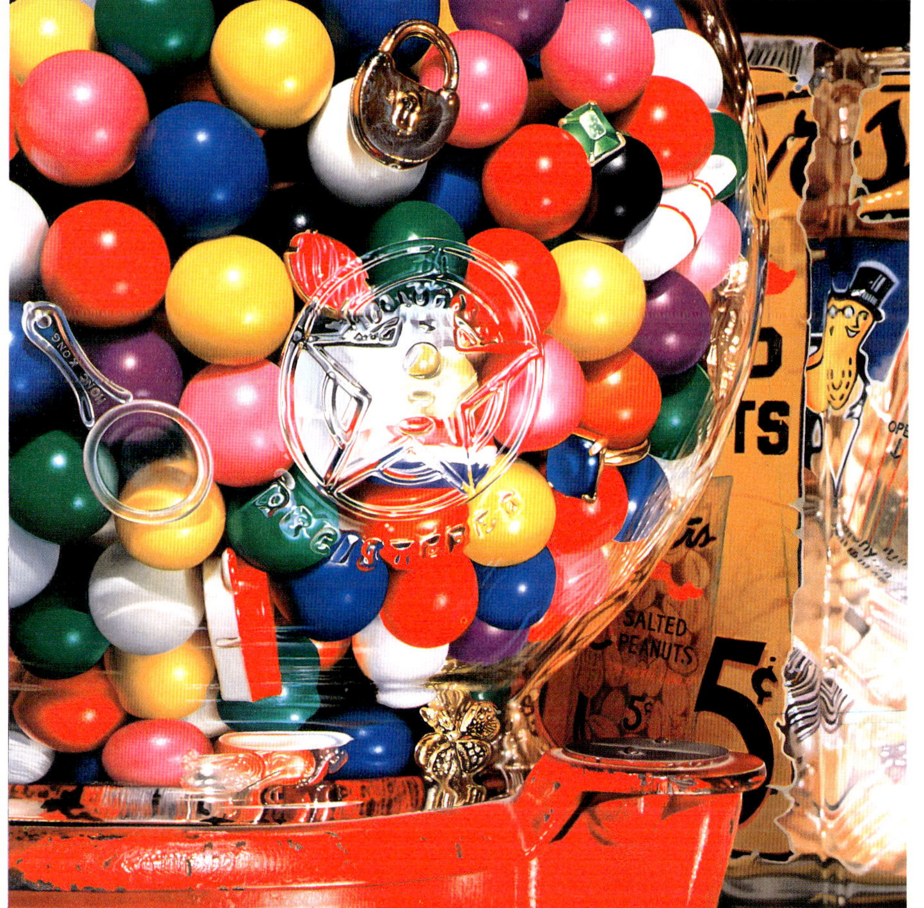

175. *"1 Cent—5 Cents," Gumball XXI.* 1988. Oil on canvas, $60 \times 60''$. Private collection, Pennsylvania

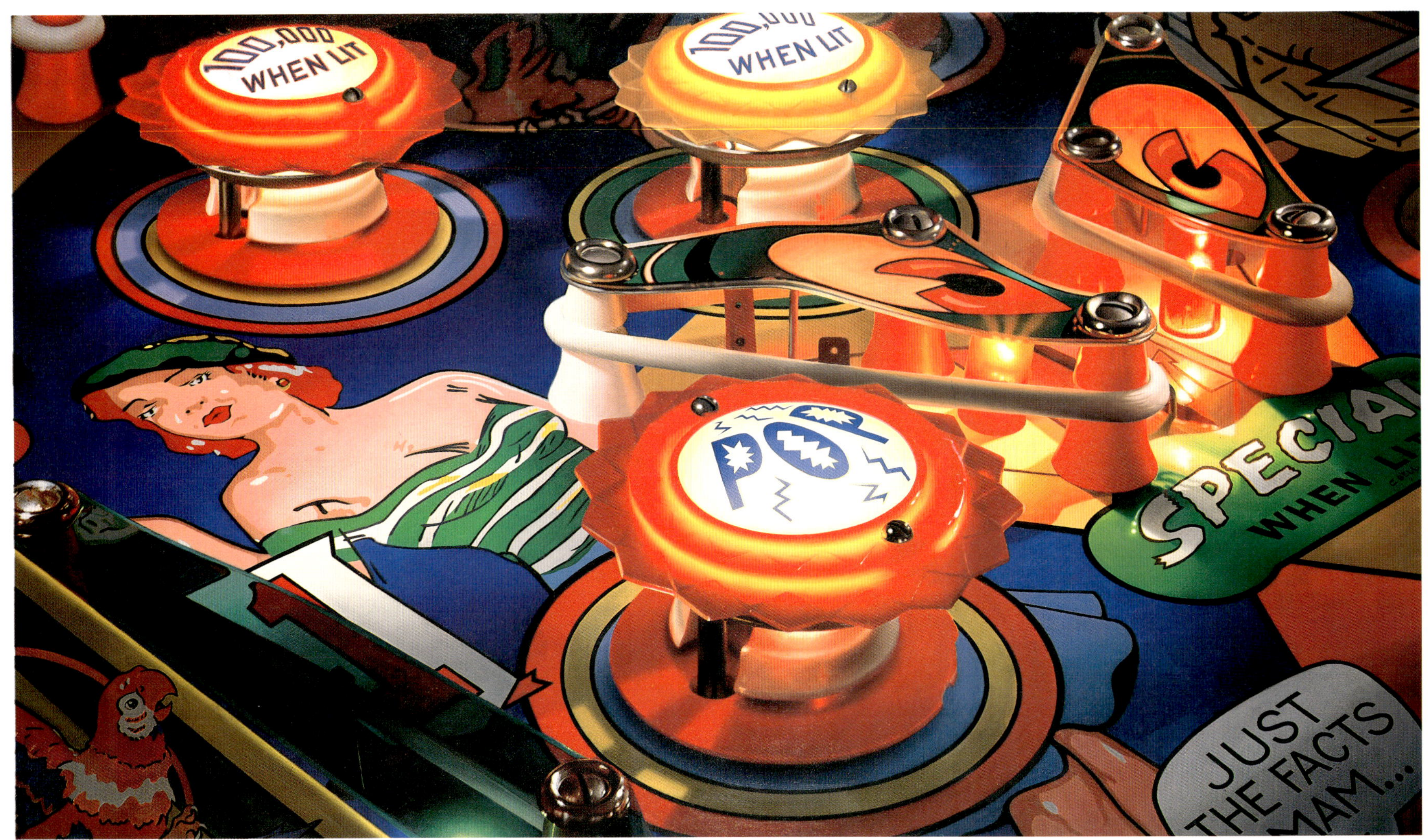

176. *Dragnet.* 1988. Oil on canvas, 46 × 80″. Private collection, Tennessee

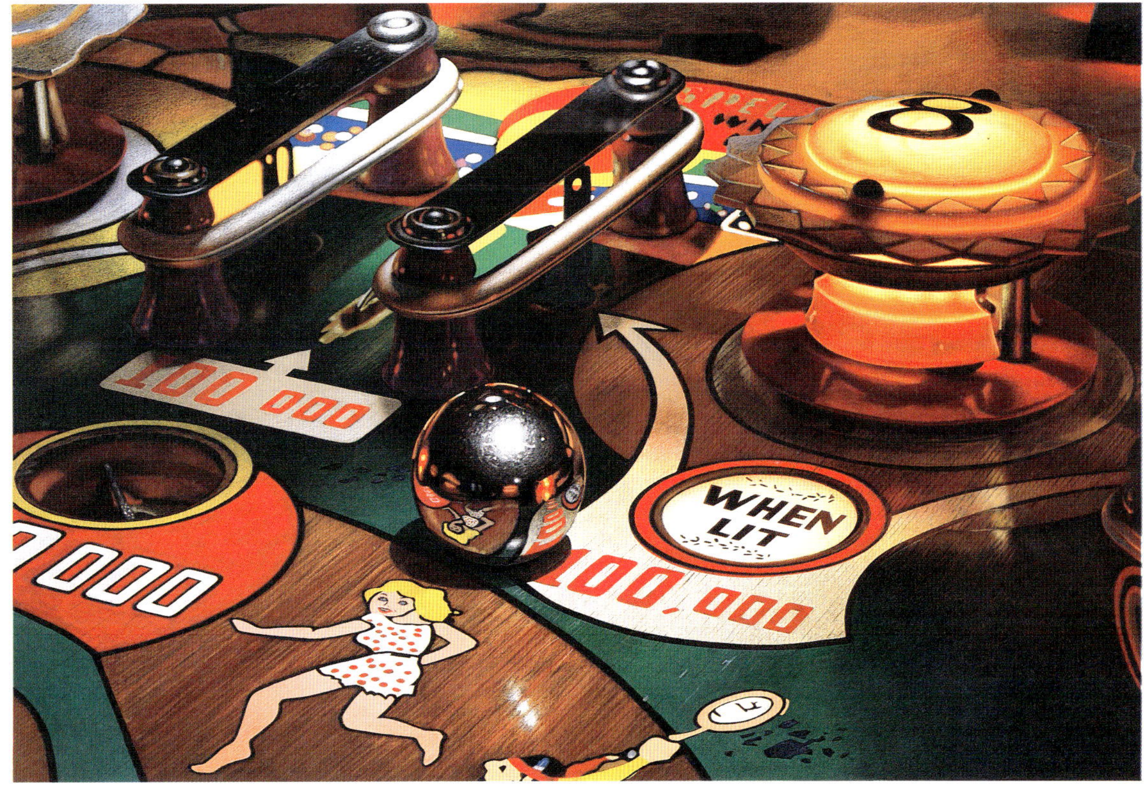

177. *100,000*. 1989. Colored pencil and gouache on black museum board, 36×54″. Collection Mr. and Mrs. Roger D. Hecht, Ohio

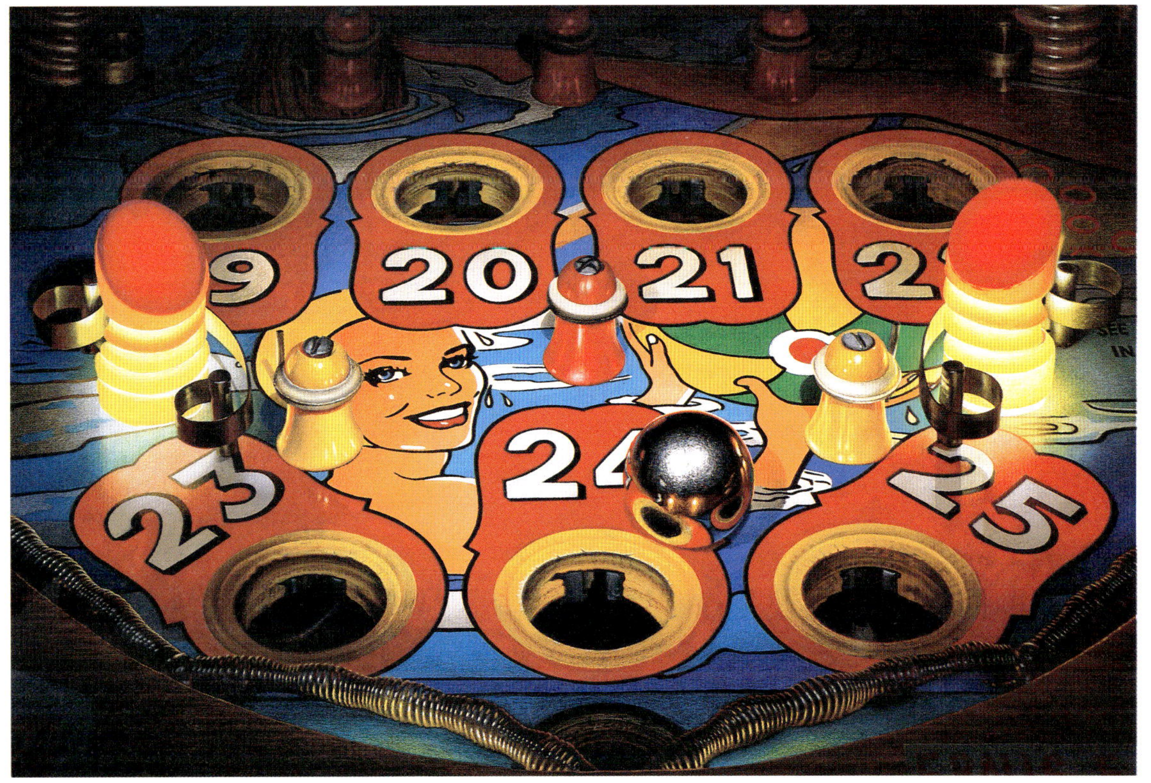

178. *Bingo!* 1989. Colored pencil and gouache on black museum board, 40×60″. Private collection, Pennsylvania

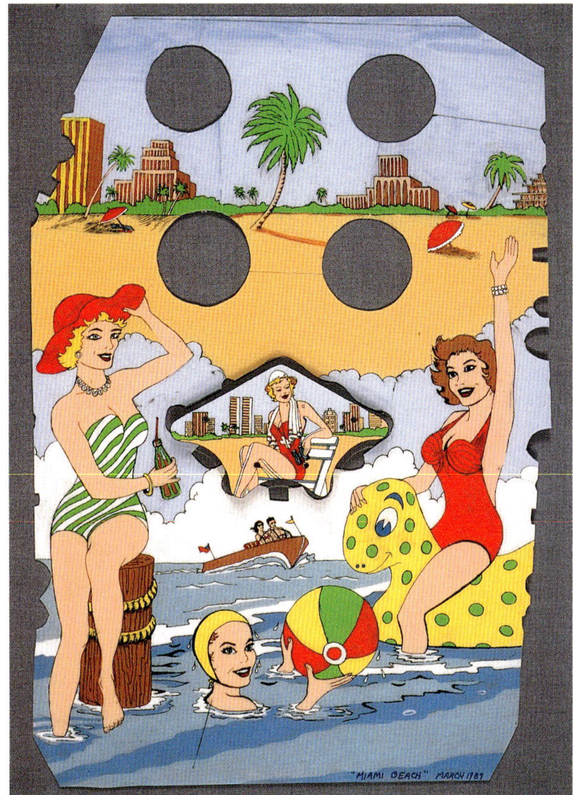

179. Study for *Miami Beach*. 1989. Acrylic on Mylar, 19¼ × 13½". Collection Louis K. and Susan Pear Meisel, New York

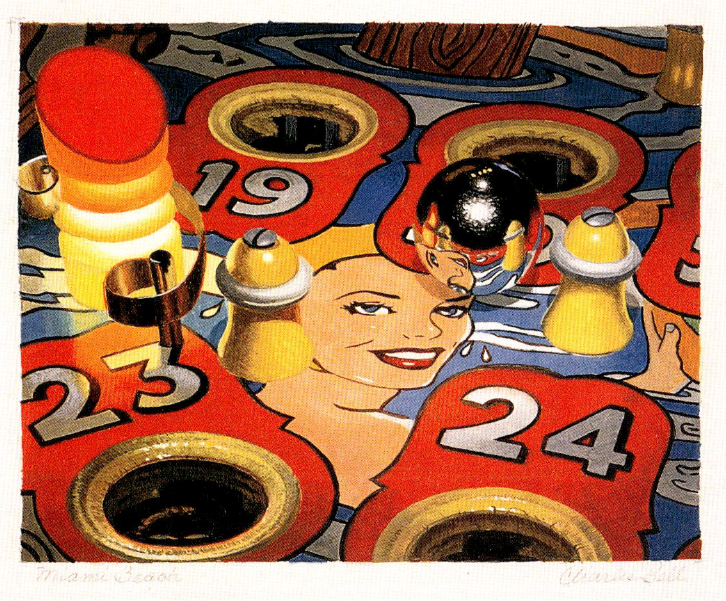

180. *Miami Beach Watercolor*. 1989. Watercolor and gouache on board, 4½ × 6". Collection Donna and Neil Weisman, New Jersey

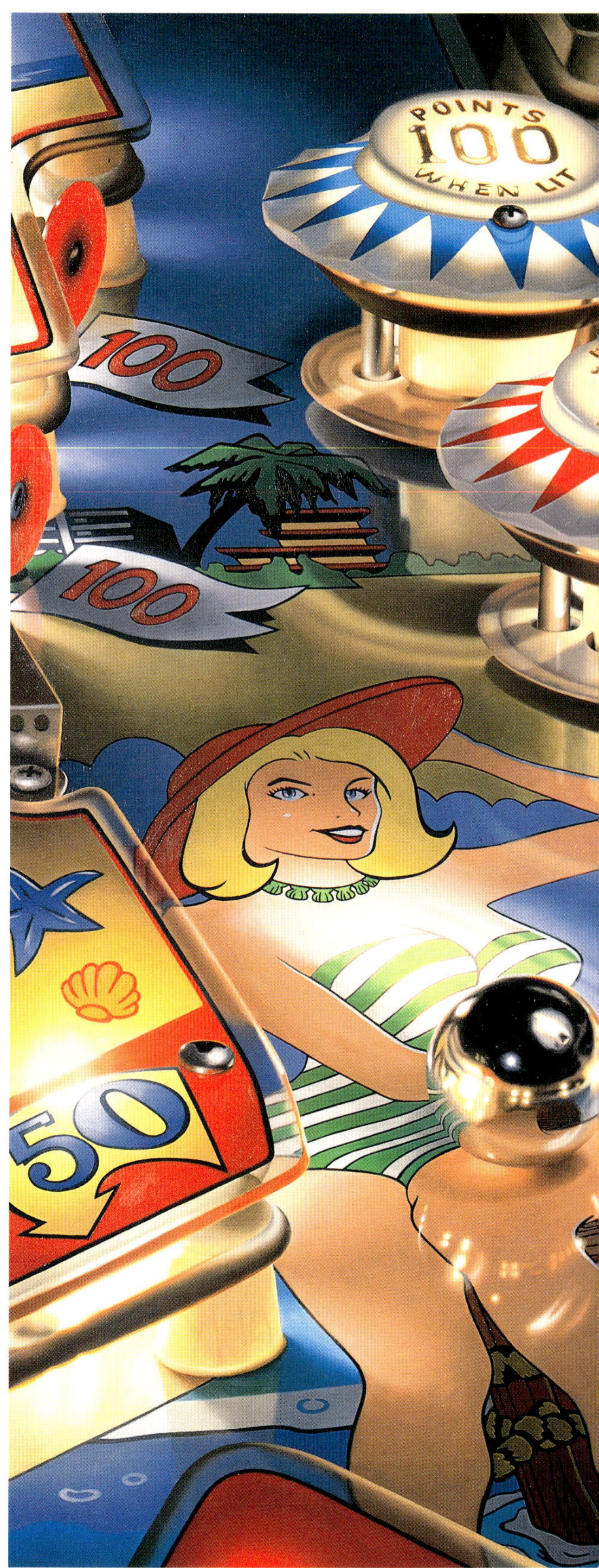

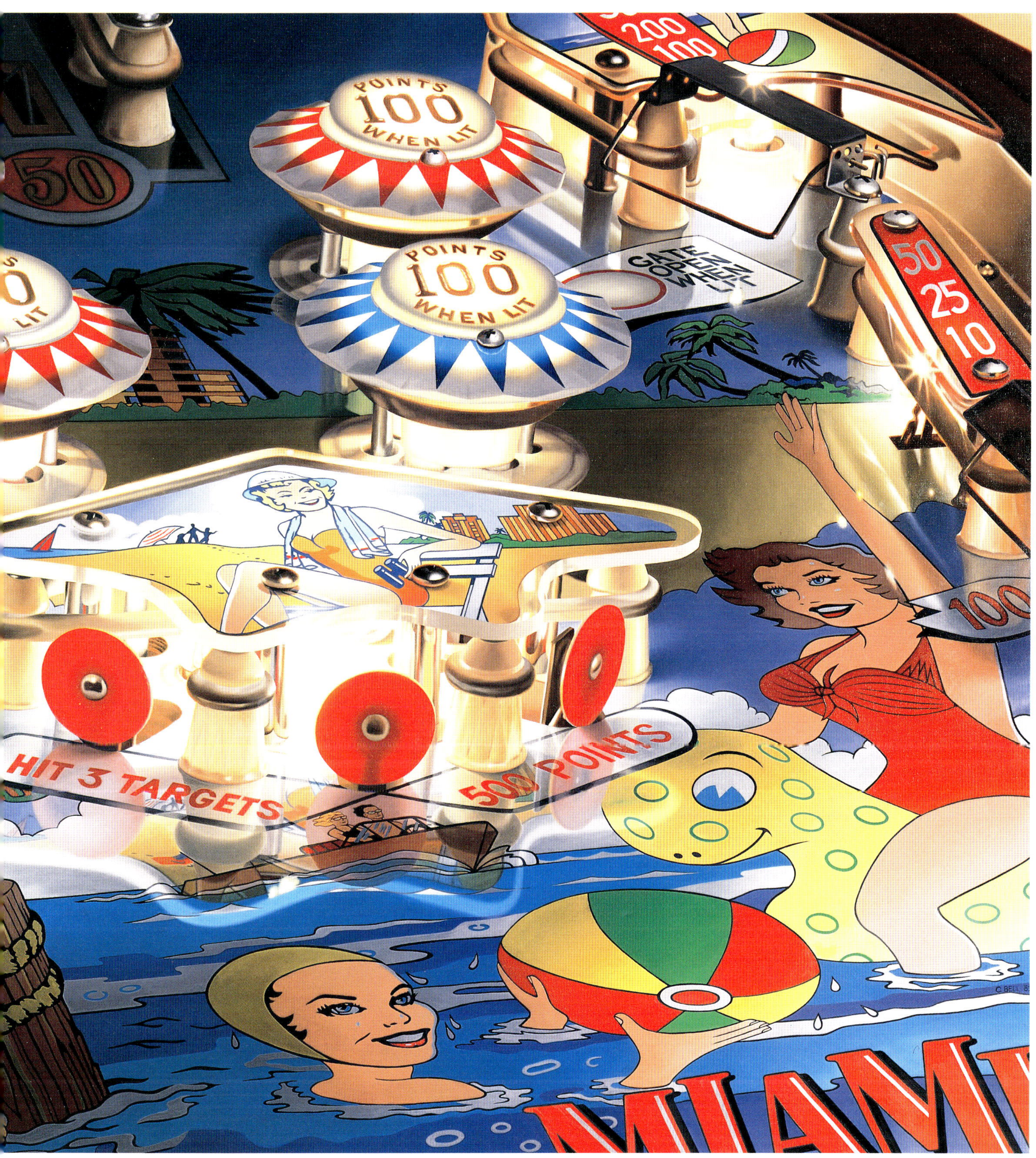

181. *Miami Beach*. 1989. Oil on canvas, 60 × 84″. Collection Louis, Susan, and Ari Meisel, New York

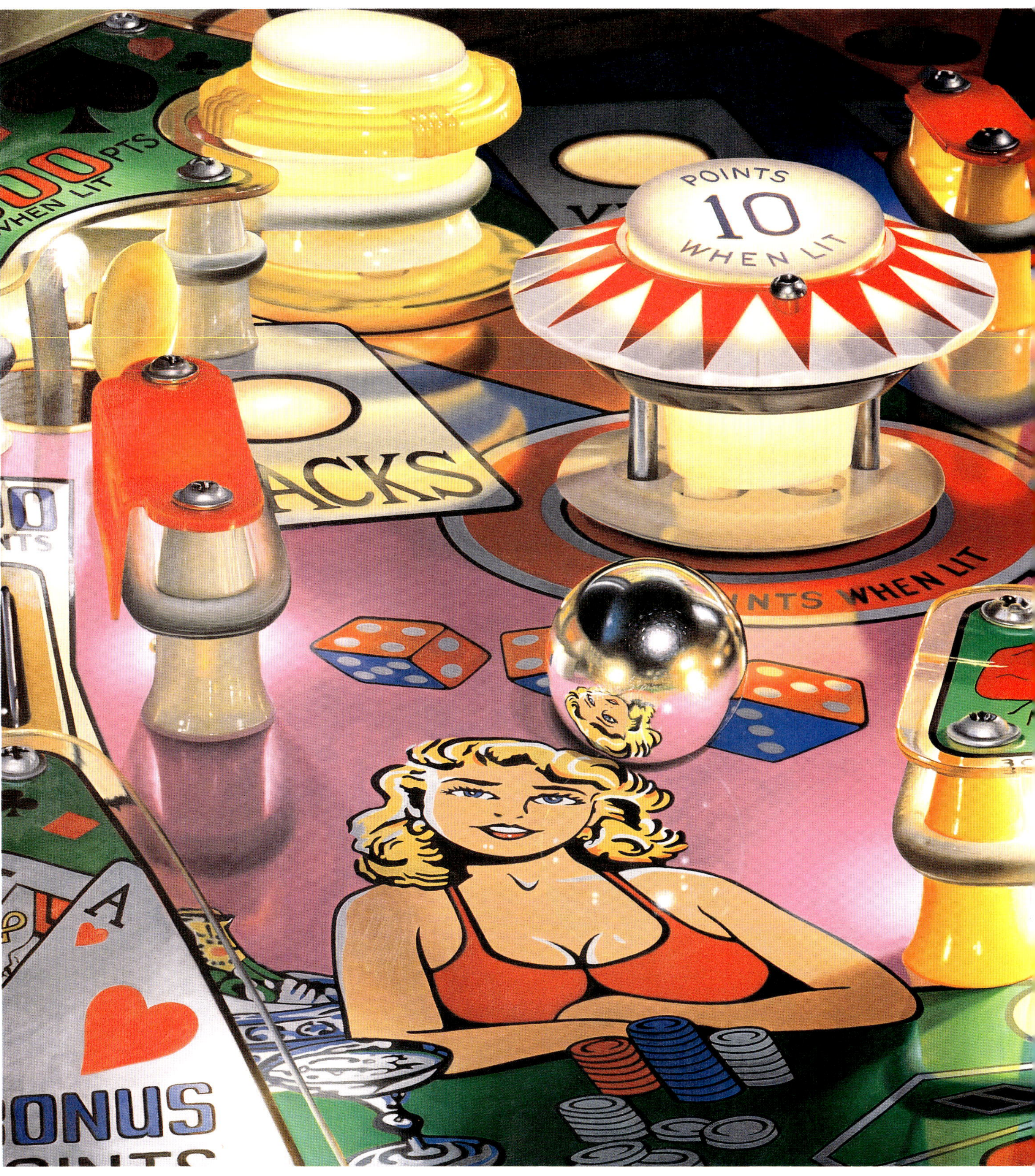
POINTS
10
WHEN LIT
PTS
WHEN LIT
ACKS
NTS WHEN LIT
BONUS

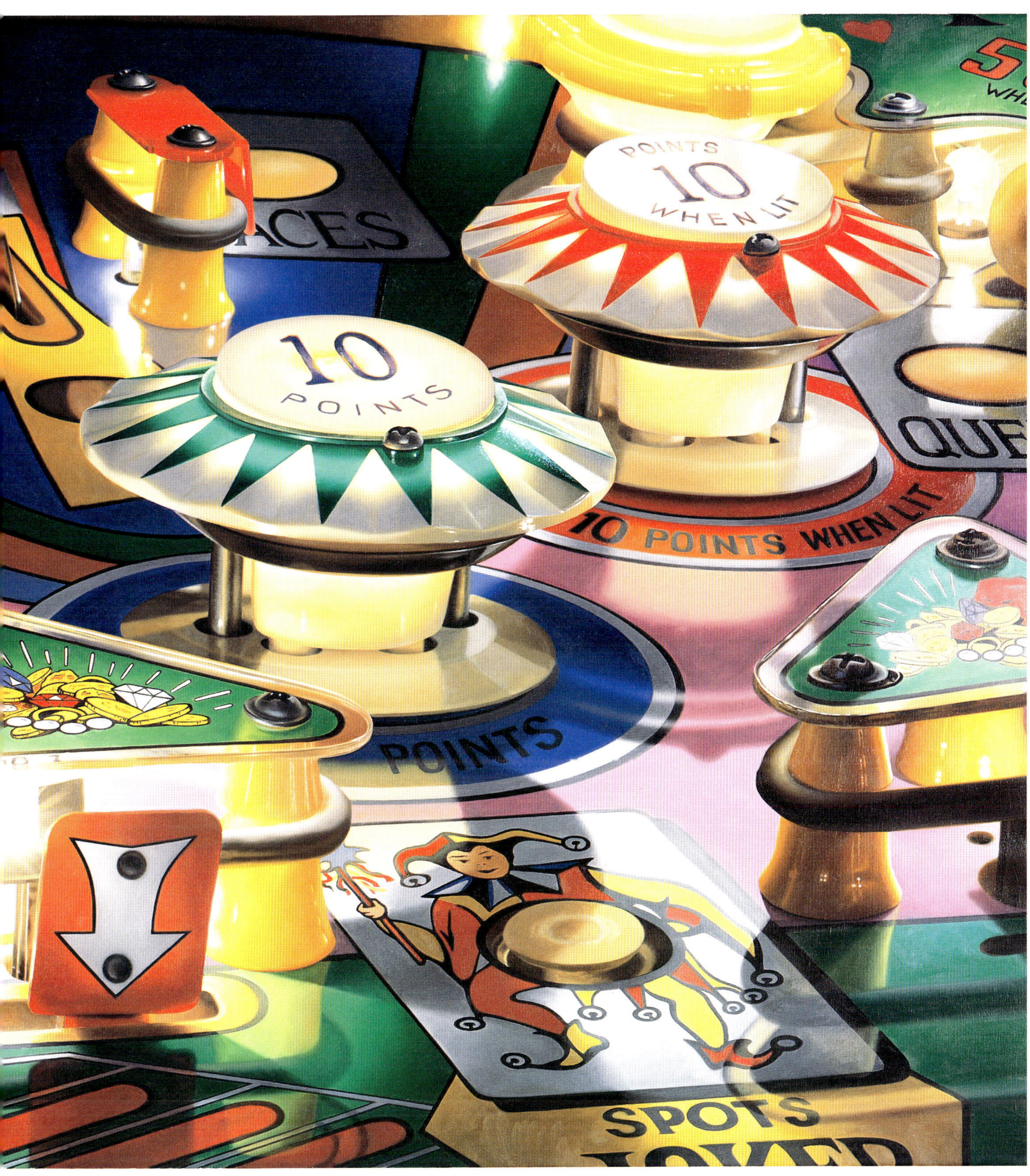

182. *Lucky Lady*. 1990.
Oil on canvas, 50 × 96″.
Collection Donna and
Neil Weisman, New
Jersey

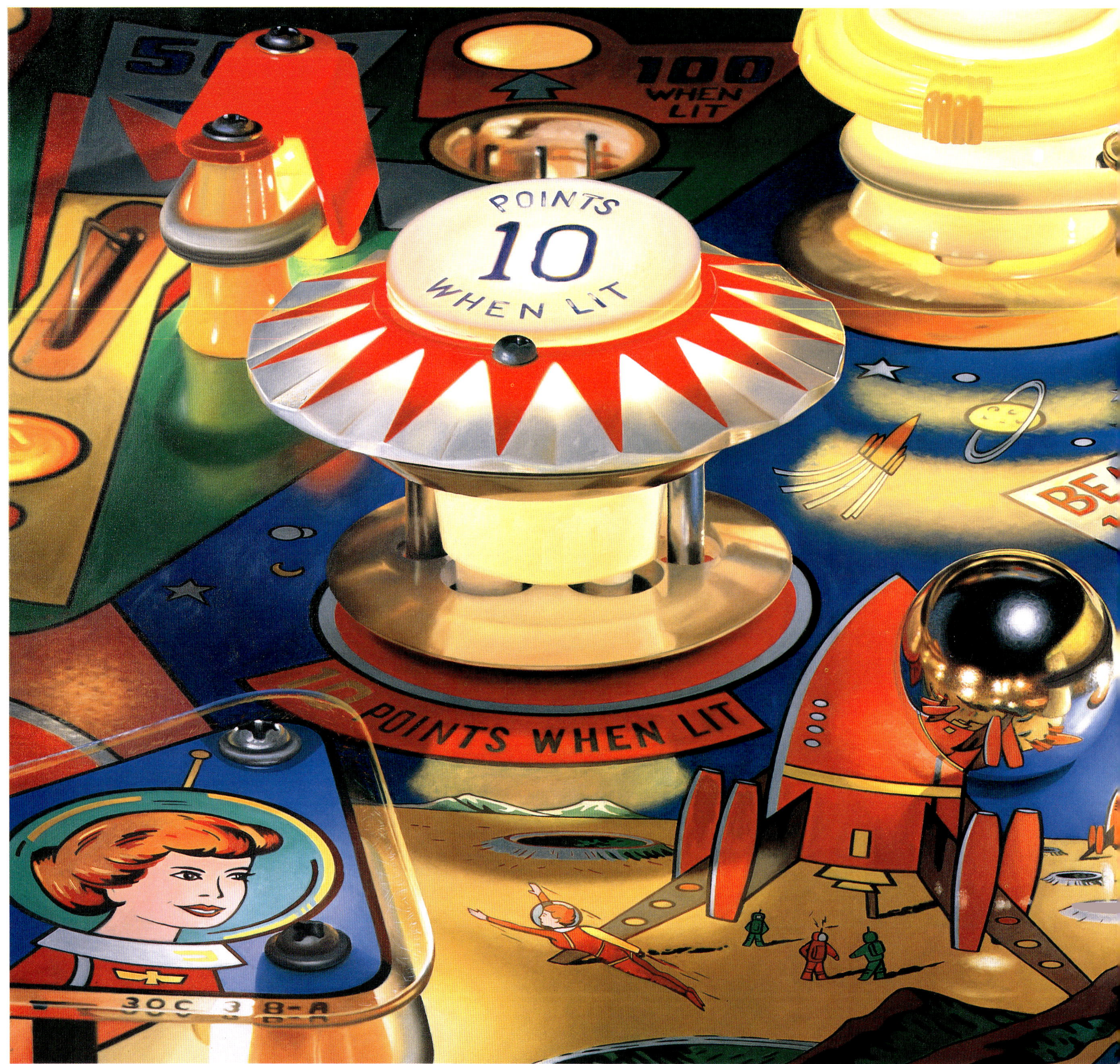
100
WHEN
LIT
POINTS
10
WHEN LIT
POINTS WHEN LIT
30C 3 8-A

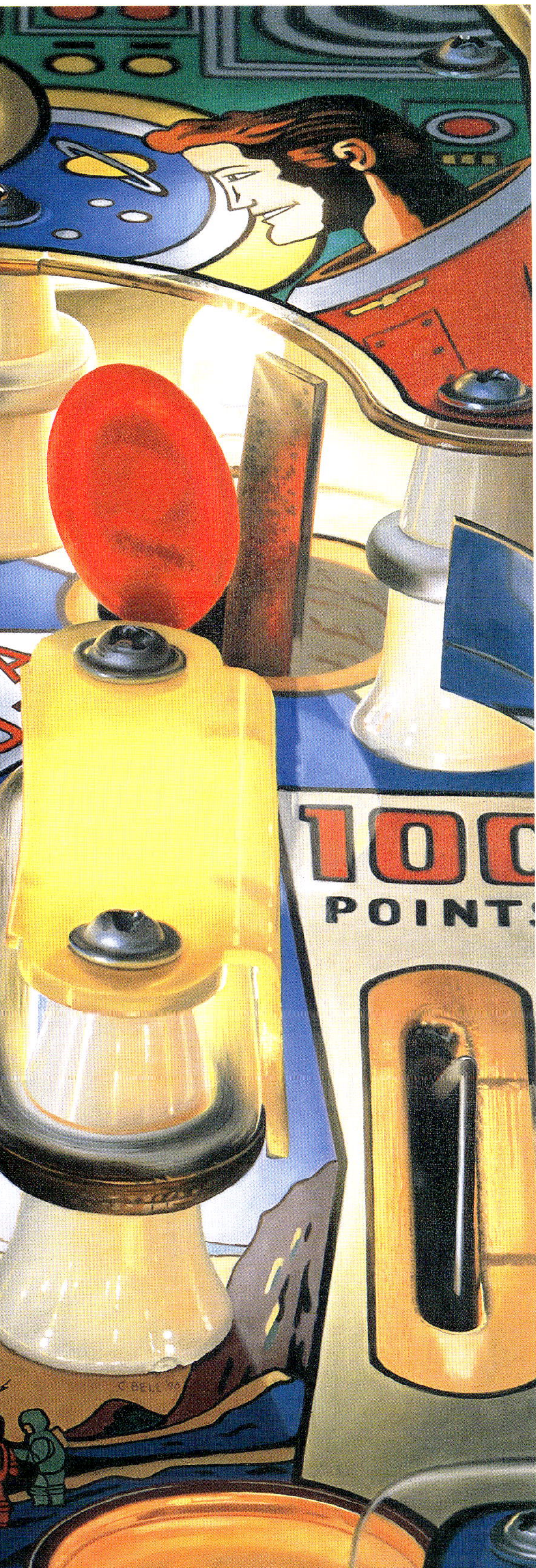

183. *Moon Mission*. 1990. Oil on canvas, 48 × 72″. Private collection, Ontario

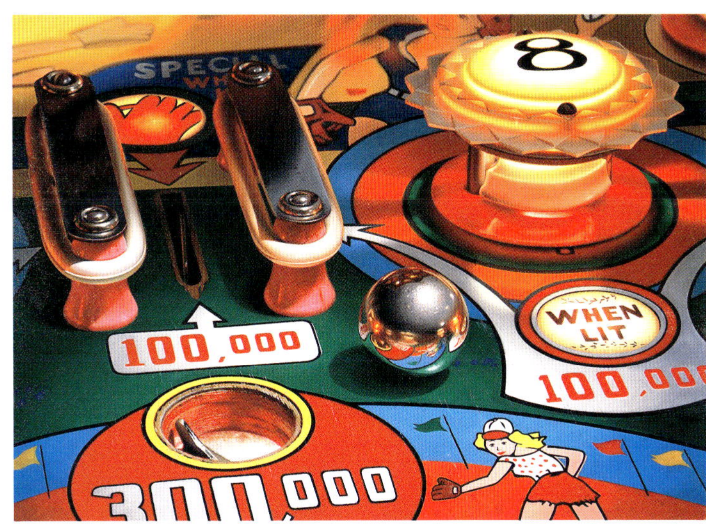

184. *Catcher*. 1988. Oil on canvas, 40 × 56″. Collection David and Jeanine Smith, California

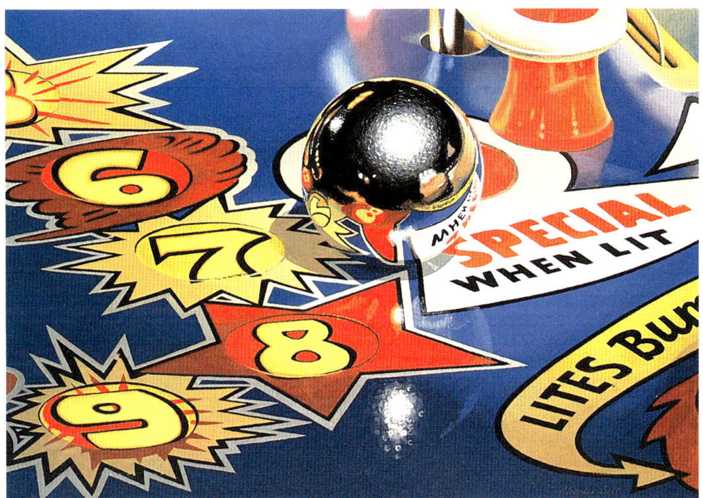

185. *5, 6, 7, 8, 9*. 1990. Gouache on paper, 11½ × 17¼″. PieperPower Companies, Inc., Wisconsin

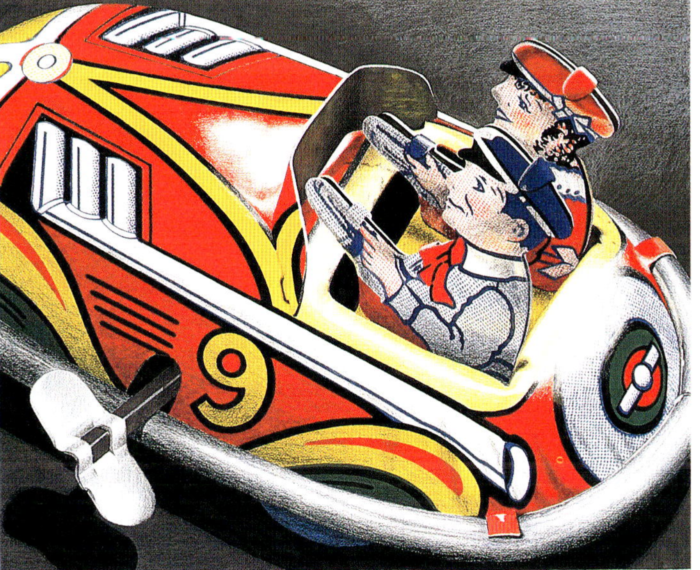

186. *Dodge 'Em*. 1990. Gouache and colored pencil on board, 24 × 30″. Private collection, Michigan

130

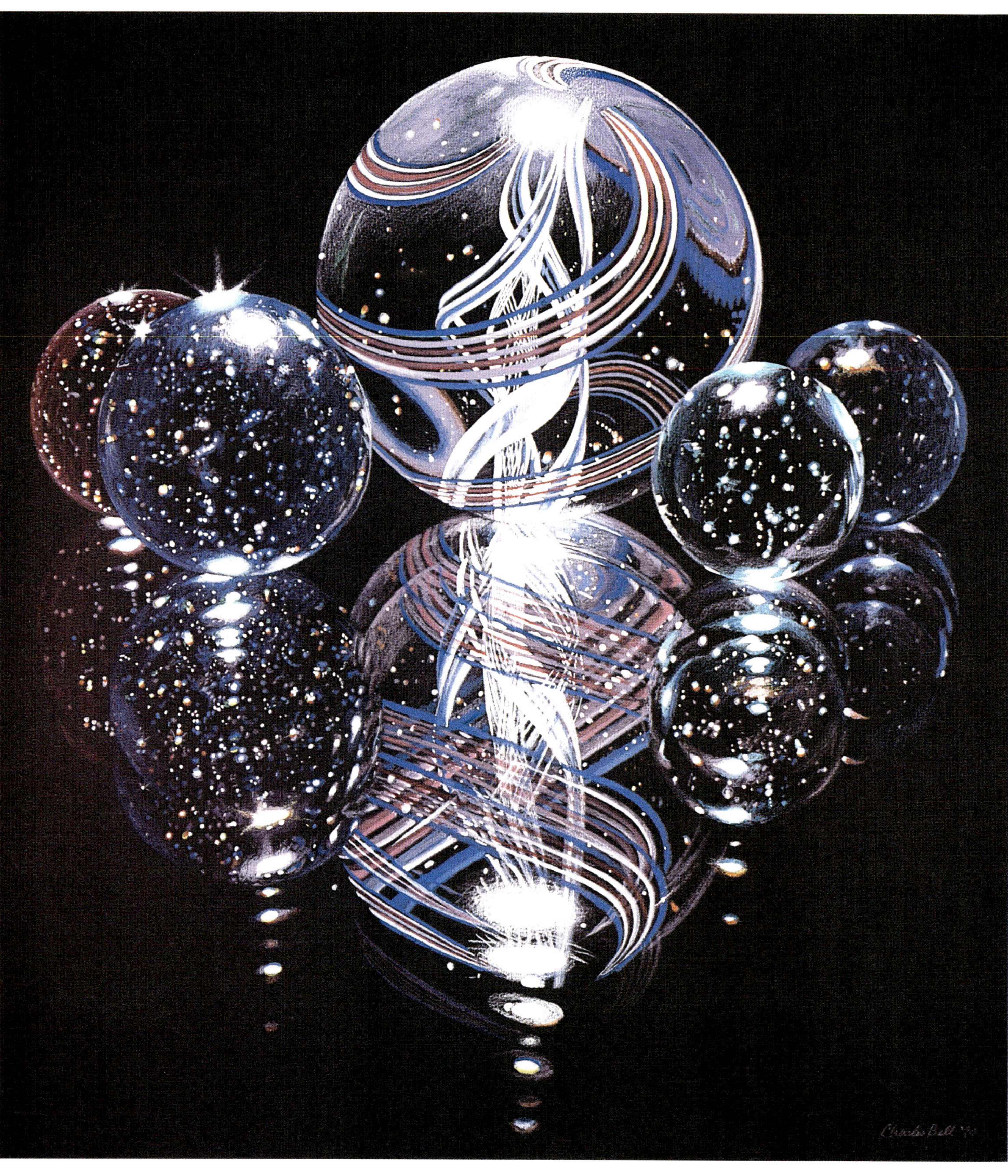

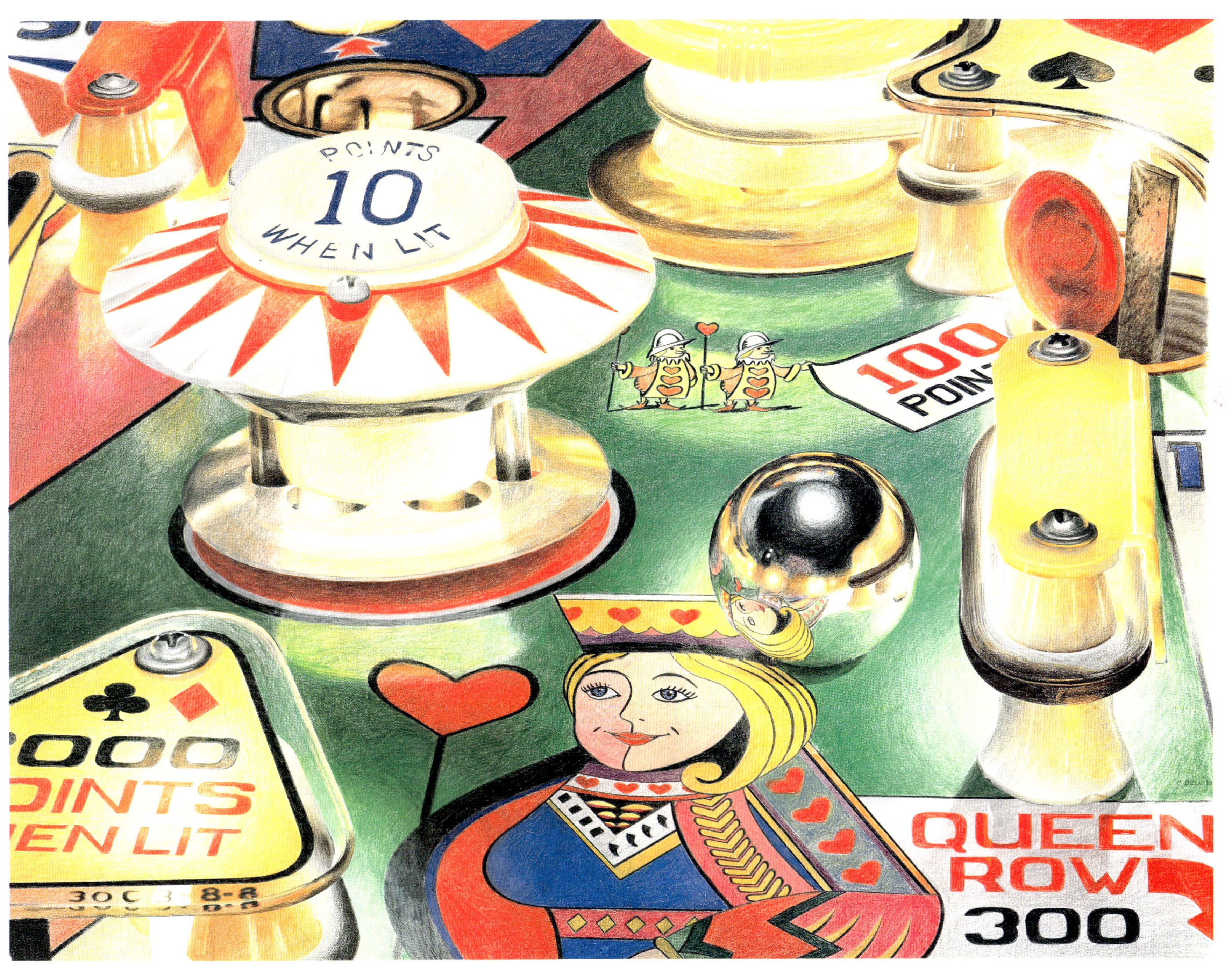

OPPOSITE: 187. *Clear Marbles*. 1990. Gouache and colored pencil on black paper, 21 × 19″. Private collection, Switzerland

ABOVE: 188. *Queen of Hearts*. 1990. Colored pencil on museum board, 38 × 50″. Louis K. Meisel Gallery, New York

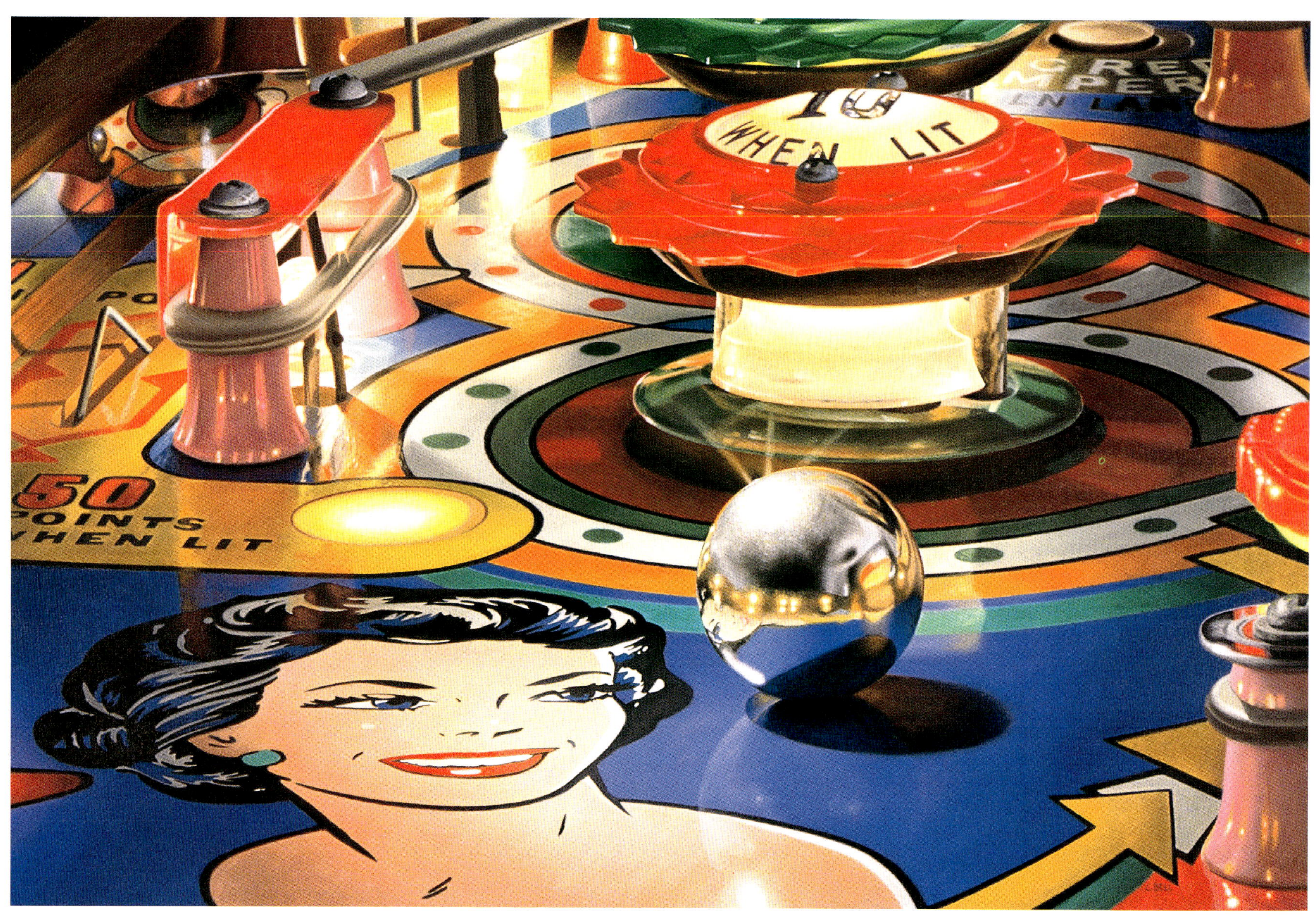

189. *50 Points When Lit.* 1990. Oil on canvas, 36 × 54″. Private collection, Michigan

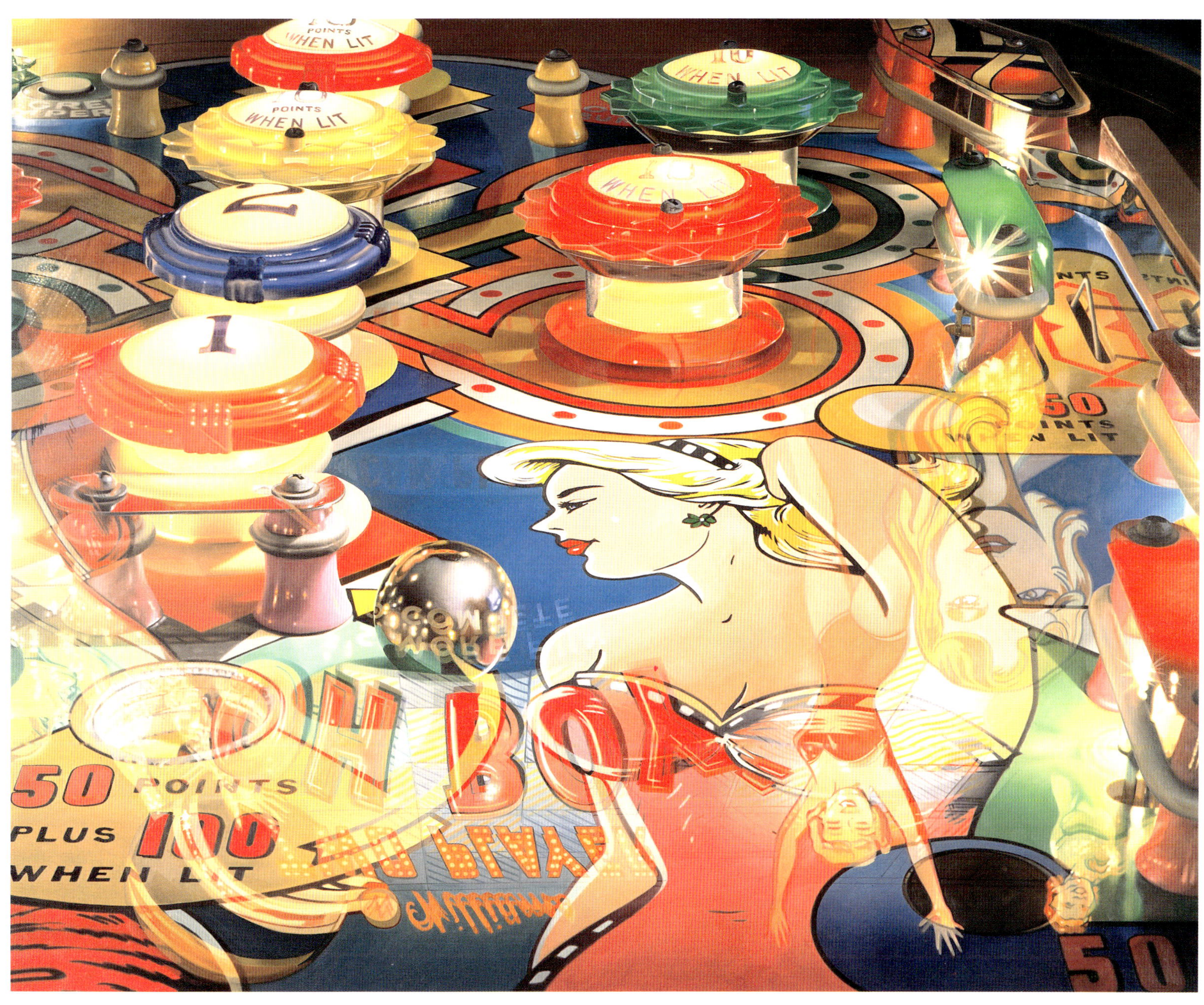

190. *Oh Boy*. 1990. Oil on canvas, 66 × 84″. Private collection, Ontario

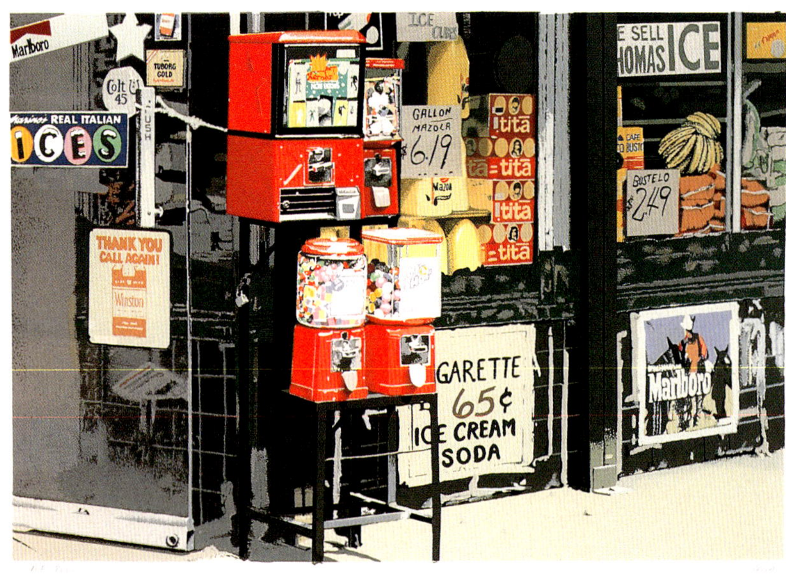

191. *Little Italy*. 1979. Serigraph on paper, 17 × 24¾″. Edition of 250

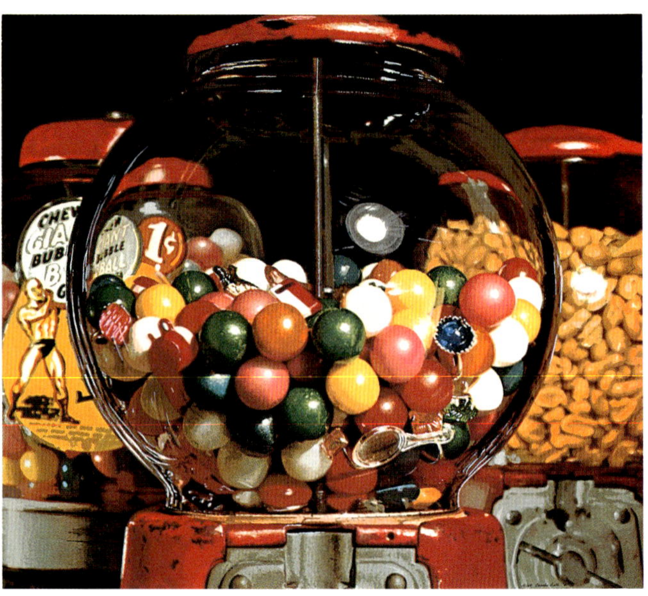

192. *The Ultimate Gumball*. 1981. Serigraph on Masonite, 46½ × 53¼″. Edition of 60

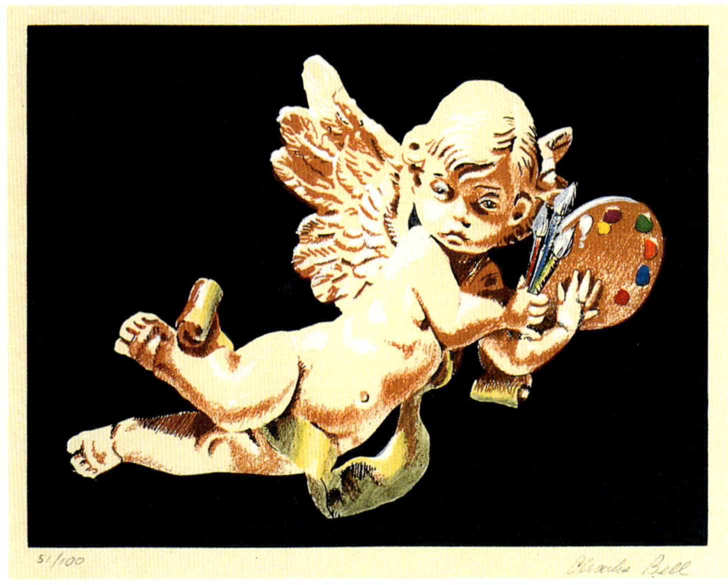

193. *Art Angel*. 1986. Serigraph on paper, 9 × 12″. Edition of 100

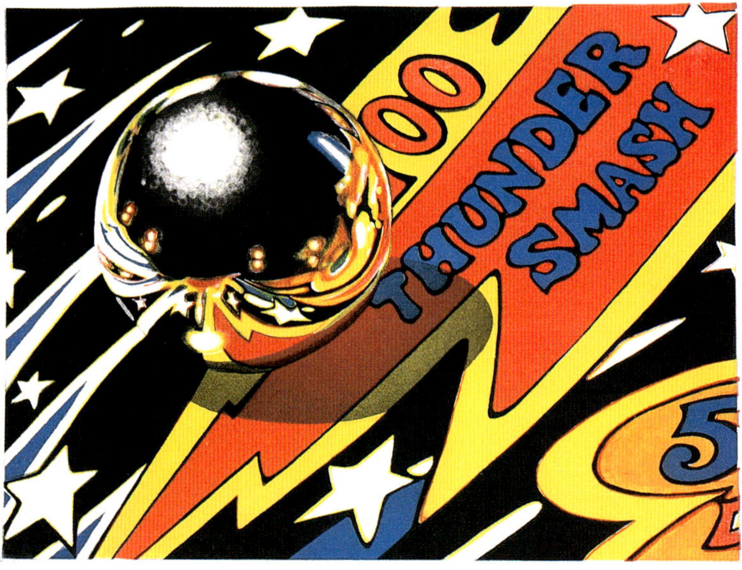

194. *Thunder Smash Fragment*. 1988. Aquatint etching on paper, 11½ × 15¾″. Edition of 25

The Prints
Figs. 191 to 195 illustrate all the editions of Charles Bell prints published through 1990.

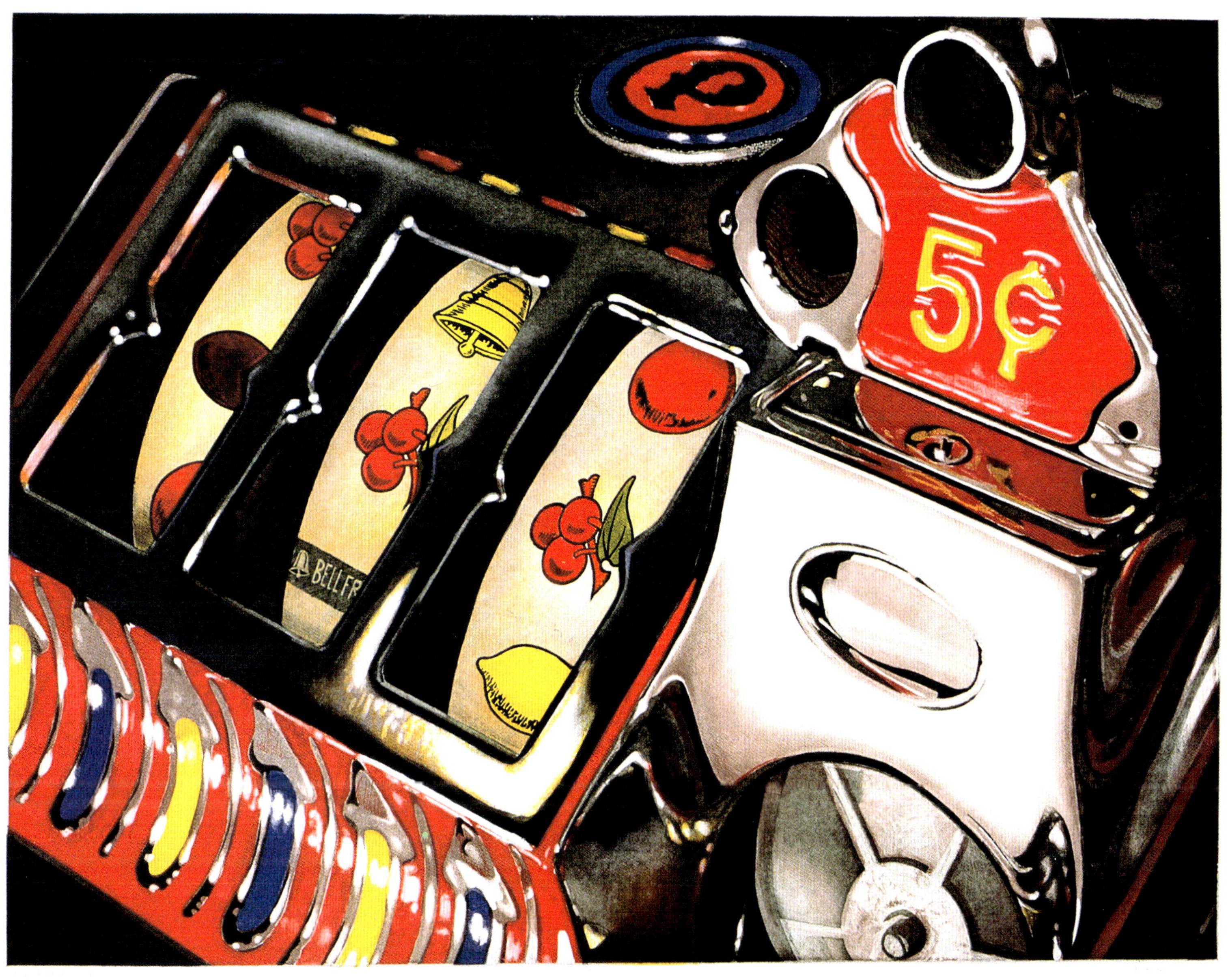

195. *5 Cent Slot*. 1990. Aquatint etching on paper, 29½ × 38½″. Edition of 30

CATALOGUE OF WORKS

Listed here, chronologically, are all the Charles Bell works from the years 1969 to 1990 that are illustrated in this volume. Entries for works in the Gumball, Marbles, and Pinball series contain both the title of the work and its number within the series.

1969
Raggedy Ann No. 1, fig. 48

1970
Raggedy Ann No. 2, unillustrated, see note, fig. 48
Raggedy Ann No. 3, fig. 49

1971
Skate, fig. 51
Raggedy Ann With Baseball, fig. 52
Gumball I, Gumball series no. 1, fig. 50

1972
Tinker Toy, fig. 53
Donald Duck, fig. 54
Buck Rogers, fig. 55
Lionel, fig. 56
Tops, fig. 57
Manikin Monkey, fig. 58
Bunny Cycle, fig. 59
Clown and Monkey, fig. 60

1973
Cat, fig. 61
Seaplane in Bathtub, fig. 62
Gumball II, Gumball series no. 2, fig. 63
Gumball III, Gumball series no. 3, fig. 64

1974
"Nation's Finest," Gumball IV, Gumball series no. 4, fig. 65
Fortune Teller, fig. 67
Horn and Hardart, fig. 66
"Thank You," Gumball V, Gumball series no. 5, fig. 68
Gumball VI, Gumball series no. 6, fig. 69
Bagels, fig. 70
Marbles, Marbles series no. 1, fig. 71

1975
Gumball VII, Gumball series no. 7, fig. 72
Gumball VIII, Gumball series no. 8, fig. 73
Gumball IX, Gumball series no. 9, fig. 74
"Sugar Daddy," Gumball X, Gumball series no. 10, fig. 75
Gumball Watercolor No. 1, Gumball series no. 11, fig. 76

1976
Gumball XI, Gumball series no. 12, fig. 78
"5 Cent Special," Gumball XII, Gumball series no. 13, fig. 77
Gumball Watercolor No. 2, Gumball series no. 14, fig. 79
Gumball Fragment No. 1, Gumball series no. 15, fig. 80
Gumball Fragment No. 2, Gumball series no. 16, fig. 81
"One Cent," Gumball Fragment No. 3, Gumball series no. 17, fig. 82
Scenic Overlook, fig. 83
Pinball No. 1, Pinball series no. 1, fig. 92

1977
The Wizard, Pinball series no. 2, fig. 85
Gin, Pinball series no. 3, fig. 86
Fire Ball 500 No. 1, Pinball series no. 4, fig. 87
Feel Them Bumpers, Pinball series no. 5, fig. 88
Double Advance, Pinball series no. 6, fig. 89

1978
The Ultimate Gumball, Gumball series no. 18, fig. 90
Thunder Smash Fragment, Pinball series no. 7, fig. 91
Toy Portrait Series I, fig. 84

1979
Captive Messenger, Pinball series no. 8, fig. 93
Little Italy (serigraph), fig. 191

1980
Captive Messenger No. 2, Pinball series no. 9, fig. 95
Gumball Section A, Gumball series no. 19, fig. 94
"Chicago" Pat. No. 1,910,193, fig. 96
Gumball XIV, Gumball series no. 20, fig. 99
Marbles I, Marbles series no. 2, fig. 97
Marbles, Marbles series no. 3, fig. 98

1981
1 Cent Win the Ring, Gumball series no. 21, fig. 100
Marbles II, Marbles series no. 4, fig. 101
Study for *Troupe* (Clowns and Seal), fig. 102
Puss in Boots (Cat Toy), fig. 103
100 Points When Lit, Pinball series no. 10, fig. 104
Rol-A-Top, fig. 105
5 Marbles and 465 West Broadway IV, Marbles series no. 5, fig. 106
The Ultimate Gumball (serigraph), fig. 192

1982
Marbles V, Marbles series no. 6, fig. 108
"Solitaire Blue," Marbles VI, Marbles series no. 7, fig. 107
Marbles VII, Marbles series no. 8, fig. 109
Marbles, Marbles series no. 9, fig. 110
Tinker Toys and Clown, fig. 111
Seaplane, fig. 112
Marbles VIII, Marbles series no. 10, fig. 118
Red Rider, fig. 117
Pace Bantam, fig. 114
"Columbus Star," Gumball Watercolor No. 3, Gumball series no. 22, fig. 113
"Captive Messenger," Pinball Watercolor No. 2, Pinball series no. 11, fig. 115
Gumball Watercolor No. 4, Gumball series no. 23, fig. 116
Solitaire Yellow, Marbles series no. 11, fig. 119
The Critics, fig. 121
Curtain Call, fig. 122
Marbles IX, Marbles series no. 12, fig. 120

1983
Celebrity, fig. 123
Trained Seal, fig. 124
Troupe, fig. 125
The Secret, fig. 126
Marbles X, Marbles series no. 13, fig. 127
Texas, fig. 128
Gumball XV, Gumball series no. 24, fig. 129
Uncle Harry, fig. 130

The Optimist, fig. 131
The Big Bad Wolf, fig. 132
Snow Scene, fig. 133
A Study for The Journey, fig. 134
Study (Roly-Poly), fig. 135
Circus Act, fig. 137
Lullaby, fig. 138

1984
Hot Pursuit, fig. 136
Marbles XI, Marbles series no. 14, fig. 139
Marbles XII, Marbles series no. 15, fig. 141
Marbles XIII, Marbles series no. 16, fig. 140
Night Fireball, Pinball series no. 12, fig. 142
Side Show, fig. 143
Clear Flippers and Release Fire Gods, Pinball series no. 13, fig. 144
Valentine, fig. 146

1985
"Glassies," Marbles XIV, Marbles series no. 17, fig. 145
"Pleasant Tasting," Gumball XVI, Gumball series no. 25, fig. 147
Study for *Ta-Daa,* fig. 148
Ta-Daa, fig. 149
Marbles XV, Marbles series no. 18, fig. 150
Study for *Bunny Cycle,* fig. 153
Drawing for *Nature Study,* fig. 152
Nature Study, fig. 155
Le Cirque, fig. 151
Get Ready, Get Set, fig. 154

1986
Art Angel, fig. 157
The Judgement of Paris, fig. 156
Gumball XVII, Gumball series no. 26, fig. 159
Midsummer's Dream, fig. 158
Gumball XVIII, Gumball series no. 27, fig. 164
Before the Journey, fig. 160
Untitled (Nose Masks), fig. 161
Tiger, fig. 162
Art Angel (serigraph), fig. 193

1987
Bridgehampton Bunnies, fig. 163
"Double Bubble," Gumball XIX, Gumball series no. 28, fig. 166
Advance Bonus, Pinball series no. 14, fig. 165
25, Pinball series no. 15, fig. 169
Double Bonus, Pinball series no. 16, fig. 167
Viking Strikes, Pinball series no. 17, fig. 170
Study for *Double Bonus,* fig. 168

1988
Paragon, Pinball series no. 18, fig. 171
1 to 4 Can Play, Pinball series no. 19, fig. 172
"Drop a Penny in the Slot," Gumball XX, Gumball series no. 29, fig. 173
Catcher, Pinball series no. 20, fig. 184
"1 Cent—5 Cents," Gumball XXI, Gumball series no. 30, fig. 175
Dragnet, Pinball series no. 21, fig. 176
Thunder Smash Fragment (aquatint etching), fig. 194

1989
100,000, Pinball series no. 22, fig. 177
Bingo!, Pinball series no. 23, fig. 178
Miami Beach, Pinball series no. 24, fig. 181
Miami Beach Watercolor, Pinball series no. 25, fig. 180
Study for *Miami Beach,* fig. 179

1990
"Andy's Mr. Peanut," Gumball XXII, Gumball series no. 31, fig. 174
Lucky Lady, Pinball series no. 26, fig. 182
Moon Mission, Pinball series no. 27, fig. 183
Queen of Hearts, Pinball series no. 28, fig. 188
Clear Marbles, Marbles series no. 19, fig. 187
50 Points When Lit, Pinball series no. 29, fig. 189
Dodge 'Em, fig. 186
5, 6, 7, 8, 9, Pinball series no. 30, fig. 185
Oh Boy, Pinball series no. 31, fig. 190
5 Cent Slot (aquatint etching), fig. 195

1991
Andy's Mr. Peanut (Major), fig. 1

BIOGRAPHY AND LIST OF EXHIBITIONS

1935 Born: Tulsa, Okla.

EDUCATION
1957 B.B.A., University of Oklahoma, Norman

SOLO EXHIBITIONS
1972 Meisel Gallery, New York
1974 Louis K. Meisel Gallery, New York
1976 Morgan Gallery, Shawnee Mission, Kans.
1977 Louis K. Meisel Gallery, New York
1980 Louis K. Meisel Gallery, New York
1983 Louis K. Meisel Gallery, New York
Hokin/Kaufman Gallery, Chicago, Ill.
1986 Louis K. Meisel Gallery, New York
1988 Modernism, San Francisco, Calif.
1989 Louis K. Meisel Gallery, New York

SELECTED GROUP EXHIBITIONS
1968 Setay Gallery, Beverly Hills, Calif.
"Society of Western Artists Annual Exhibition," M. H. de Young Memorial Museum, San Francisco, Calif.
1969 Greenwich Gallery, New York
Meisel Gallery, New York
1973 "East Coast/West Coast/New Realism," San Jose State University, Calif.
"Hyperréalistes américains," Galerie Arditti, Paris
1973–78 "Photo-Realism 1973: The Stuart M. Speiser Collection," traveling exhibition: Louis K. Meisel Gallery, New York; Herbert F. Johnson Museum of Art, Cornell University, Ithaca, N.Y.; Memorial Art Gallery of the University of Rochester, N.Y.; Addison Gallery of American Art, Andover, Mass.; Allentown Art Museum, Pa.; University of Colorado Art Museum, Boulder; University of Texas at Austin Art Museum; Witte Memorial Museum, San

Antonio, Tex.; Gibbes Art Gallery, Charleston, S.C.; Brooks Memorial Art Gallery, Memphis, Tenn.; Krannert Art Museum, University of Illinois, Champaign-Urbana; Helen Foresman Spencer Museum of Art, University of Kansas, Lawrence; Paine Art Center and Arboretum, Oshkosh, Wis.; Edwin A. Ulrich Museum, Wichita State University, Kans.; Tampa Bay Art Center, Fla.; Sewall Art Gallery, Rice University, Houston, Tex.; Tulane University Art Gallery, New Orleans, La.; Smithsonian Institution, Washington, D.C.

1974 "New/Photo Realism," Wadsworth Atheneum, Hartford, Conn.

"Tokyo Biennale '74," traveling exhibition, Japan: Tokyo Metropolitan Art Museum; Kyoto Municipal Art Museum; Aichi Prefectural Art Museum, Nagoya

1975 "The New Realism: Rip-Off or Reality?," Edwin A. Ulrich Museum, Wichita State University, Kans.

"Photo-Realists," Louis K. Meisel Gallery, New York

"39th Annual Midyear Show," The Butler Institute of American Art, Youngstown, Ohio

"Watercolors and Drawings—American Realists," Louis K. Meisel Gallery, New York

1975–76 "Photo Realism, American Paintings and Prints," traveling exhibition, New Zealand: Barrington Gallery, Auckland; Robert McDougall Art Gallery, Christchurch; Academy of Fine Arts, National Art Gallery, Wellington; Dunedin Public Art Gallery, Dunedin; Govett-Brewster Art Gallery, New Plymouth; Waikato Art Museum, Hamilton

1976 "New Accessions U.S.A.," Colorado Springs Fine Arts Center, Colorado Springs, Colo.

"Troisième foire internationale d'art contemporain," Grand Palais, Paris

"Washington International Art Fair," D.C. Armory, Washington, D.C.

1976–78 "Aspects of Realism," traveling exhibition sponsored by Rothmans of Pall Mall Canada Limited: Stratford Art Gallery, Ont.; Vancouver Centennial Museum, B.C.; Glenbow Alberta Institute, Calgary, Alta.; Mendel Art Gallery, Saskatoon, Sask.; Winnipeg Art Gallery, Man.; Edmonton Art Gallery, Alta.; Memorial University Art Gallery, St. John's, Newf.; Confederation Art Gallery, Charlottetown, P.E.I.; Musée d'Art Contemporain, Montréal, Que.; Dalhousie University Art Gallery, Halifax, N.S.; Windsor Art Gallery, Ont.; London Art Gallery and McIntosh Memorial Art Gallery, London, Ont.; Art Gallery of Hamilton, Ont.

1977 "New Realism," Jacksonville Art Museum, Fla.

"Recent Acquisitions," Solomon R. Guggenheim Museum, New York

"Washington International Art Fair," D.C. Armory, Washington, D.C.

"Works on Paper II," Louis K. Meisel Gallery, New York

1978 "Drawings Since 1960," University Art Gallery, Creighton University, Omaha, Nebr.

"Landscape/Cityscape," Brainerd Hall Art Gallery, State University College, Potsdam, N.Y.

"Painting and Sculpture Today, 1978," Indianapolis Museum of Art, Ind.

"Photo-Realism and Abstract Illusionism," Arts and Crafts Center of Pittsburgh, Pa.

"Photo-Realist Printmaking," Louis K. Meisel Gallery, New York

"Illusion and Reality: 10 New York Painters," Tolarno Galleries, Melbourne, Australia

"Washington International Art Fair," D.C. Armory, Washington, D.C.

1979 "Brooklyn '79," Community Gallery, Brooklyn Museum, New York

Middendorf Gallery, Washington, D.C.

"New York Now," Phoenix Art Museum, Ariz.

"Photo-Realism: Some Points of View," Jorgensen Gallery, University of Connecticut, Storrs

"Prospectus: Art in the Seventies," The Aldrich Museum of Contemporary Art, Ridgefield, Conn.

"Selections of Photo-Realist Paintings from N.Y.C. Galleries," Southern Alleghenies Museum of Art, Saint Francis College, Loretto, Pa.

"Washington International Art Fair," D.C. Armory, Washington, D.C.

1980 "New York Art Fair," 7th Regiment Armory, New York

"Photorealism Show," Kauffman Galleries, Houston, Tex.

"Still Life—A Selection of Contemporary Paintings," The Gallery, School of Art, Kent State University, Ohio; Tangeman Fine Arts Gallery, University of Cincinnati, Ohio

1980–81 "Assignment Aviation—The Stuart M. Speiser Photo-Realist Collection," National Air and Space Museum (Smithsonian Institution), Washington, D.C.

1981 "Cityscapes," The Graphics Gallery, Arnot Art Museum, Elmira, N.Y.

"New York Gallery Showcase," Oklahoma Art Center, Oklahoma City

"A Range of Contemporary Drawing," Sordoni Art Gallery, Wilkes College, Wilkes-Barre, Pa.

"Seven Photorealists—From New York Collections," Solomon R. Guggenheim Museum, New York

"Toyama Now '81," The Museum of Modern Art, Toyama, Japan

1981–83 "American Super Realism: From the Morton G. Neumann Family Collection," Genevieve and Donald Gilmore Art Center, Kalamazoo Institute of Arts, Mich.; Art Center, South Bend, Ind.; Springfield Art Museum, Mo.; Hood Museum of Art, Dartmouth College, Hanover, N.H.; DeCordova and Dana Museum and Park, Lincoln, Mass.; Des Moines Art Center, Iowa; Terra Museum of American Art, Evanston, Ill.

1982 "An Appreciation of Realism," Museum of Art, Munson-Williams-Proctor Institute, Utica, N.Y.

"Contemporary Realism," three-gallery exhibition: "Still Life," The Gallery at Hastings-on-Hudson, N.Y.; "Landscape," The Museum Gallery, White Plains Public Library, N.Y.; "The Figure," The Castle Gallery, College of New Rochelle, N.Y.

"The Long Island Collections, A Century of Art 1880–1980," Nassau County Museum of Fine Art, Roslyn, N.Y.

"Louis K. Meisel Gallery in Brussels," Galerie Isy Brachot, Brussels

"Photo-Réalisme Dix Ans Après," Galerie Isy Brachot, Paris

"Photographs by the Photorealists," Fort Wayne Museum of Art, Ind.; Cleveland Museum of Art, Ohio; Ball State University Art Gallery, Muncie, Ind.

"Still Life/Interiors," Contemporary Art Center, New Orleans, La.

1983 "The American Photorealists—An Anthology," Fischer Fine Art Limited, London

"Realism Now," The Museum of Modern Art, Saitama, Japan

"10th Anniversary Exhibition," Louis K.

Meisel Gallery, New York
"Toys," Greenville County Museum of Art, S.C.

1983–85 "American Art: Post–World War II Painting and Sculpture from the Solomon R. Guggenheim Museum," Birmingham Museum of Art, Ala.
"Assignment: Aviation—The Stuart M. Speiser Photo-Realist Collection," Smithsonian Institution traveling exhibition: Anchorage Historical & Fine Arts Museum, Alaska; Denver Museum of Natural History, Colo.; Maryland Science Center, Baltimore; Columbus Museum of Arts & Sciences, Ga.; Neville Public Museum, Green Bay, Wis.; The Dane G. Hansen Memorial Museum, Logan, Kans.; Longview Museum & Art Center, Tex.; Colorado Springs Fine Arts Center, Colo.; Springfield Art Museum, Mo.; Fine Arts Center at Cheekwood, Nashville, Tenn.; Historical & Creative Arts Center, Lufkin, Tex.; Amarillo Art Center, Tex.; Santa Fe Community College Art Gallery, Gainesville, Fla.

1984 "America Seen—Contemporary American Artists View America," Adams-Middleton Gallery, Dallas, Tex.
"Through the Looking Glass: Reflected Images in Contemporary Art," The Heckscher Museum, Huntington, N.Y.
"Aspects of Realism," Walter A. Moos Gallery, Toronto

1984–85 "New Realism," Robert L. Kidd Associates/Galleries, Birmingham, Mich.

1985 "American Realism: The Precise Image," traveling exhibition, Japan: The Isetan Museum of Art, Tokyo; the Daimaru Museum, Osaka; Yokohama Takashimaya Gallery

1985–87 "American Realism—Twentieth Century Drawings and Watercolors from the Glenn C. Janss Collection," San Francisco Museum of Modern Art, Calif.; DeCordova and Dana Museum and Park, Lincoln, Mass.; Archer M. Huntington Art Gallery, University of Texas, Austin; Mary & Leigh Block Gallery, Northwestern University, Evanston, Ill.; Williams College Museum of Art, Williamstown, Mass.; Akron Art Museum, Ohio; Madison Art Center, Wis.

1986 "Signs of the Times," traveling exhibition sponsored by Art Train, Detroit, Mich.

1987 "Art Against AIDS," Louis K. Meisel Gallery, New York
"Collector's Choice," Philbrook Art Center, Inc., Tulsa, Okla.
"Directions in American Realism," Fort Wayne Museum of Art, Ind.
"Realism: The New Generation," R. H. Love Modern, Chicago, Ill.
"Toys," Gallery Henoch, New York

1987–88 "Abstraction, Non-Objectivity and Realism: Twentieth-Century Paintings from the Solomon R. Guggenheim Museum," Picker Art Gallery, Colgate University, Hamilton, N.Y.
"Feasts," The Squibb Gallery, Princeton, N.J.

1988 "Art in the Armory," 69th Regimental Armory, New York
"ART/LA 88," Los Angeles Convention Center, Los Angeles, Calif.
"20th Anniversary (15 in SoHo)—Artists & Movements From Our First Two Decades," Louis K. Meisel Gallery, New York

1989 "Oklahoma Artists: Centennial Exhibition," Charles B. Goddard Center for Visual and Performing Arts, Ardmore, Okla.

1990 "Amerikansk Fotorealism," Art Now Gallery, Gothenburg, Sweden
"Collectors' Annual—Contemporary Art," Boca Raton Museum of Art, Fla.
"The 80's: A Post-Pop Generation," Southern Alleghenies Museum of Art, Loretto, Pa.
"Objects Observed—Contemporary Still Life," Gallery Henoch, New York
"Quickdraw—American Master Drawings Since 1959," Frank Bernarducci Gallery, New York
"Spotlight on Oklahoma: Eleven Oklahoma Artists," Oklahoma City Art Museum

1990–91 "Intaglio Printing in the 1980s," Jane Voorhees Zimmerli Art Museum, Rutgers, The State University of New Jersey, New Brunswick

PUBLIC COLLECTIONS

Akron Art Museum, Ohio
American Republic Insurance Company, Des Moines, Iowa
Cleveland Museum of Art, Ohio
Fort Wayne Museum of Art, Ind.
Solomon R. Guggenheim Museum, New York
Hiroshima City Museum of Contemporary Art, Japan
K & B Corporate Collection, New Orleans, La.
The Metropolitan Museum of Art, New York
Milwaukee Art Museum, Wis.
Philbrook Museum of Art, Tulsa, Okla.
Phoenix Art Museum, Ariz.
The Prudential Collection, Newark, N.J.
Stuart M. Speiser Collection, Smithsonian Institution, Washington, D.C.

BIBLIOGRAPHY

ARTICLES

Allen, Barbara. "In and Around," *Interview Magazine,* Nov., 1973, p. 36.

Beardsall, Judy. "Stuart M. Speiser Photorealist Collection," *Art Gallery Magazine,* vol. XVII, no. 1 (Oct., 1973), pp. 5, 29–34.

Sherman, Jack. "Art Review: Photo-Realism, Johnson Museum," *Ithaca Journal,* Nov. 13, 1973.

"Shop Around," *Evening Standard,* Mar. 30, 1973.
"The Speiser Collection of Photo Realism 1973," *Village Voice,* Sept. 20, 1973, p. 29.
The Art Gallery Scene, Oct., 1974, p. 8.
"Collection of Aviation Paintings at Gallery," *Andover* (Mass.) *Townsman,* Feb. 28, 1974.
Frank, Peter. "Charles Bell," *ARTnews,* Dec., 1974, p. 100.
Gruen, John. "Eight SoHo Shows," *The SoHo Weekly News,* Oct. 31, 1974, p. 16 ill.
Marticelli, Joseph. "Our Books and Yours," *Case and Comment,* vol. 79, no. 4 (July-Aug., 1974), p. 11, cover ill.
Walsh, Sally. "Paintings That Look Like Photos," *Rochester Democrat and Chronicle,* Jan. 17, 1974.
Bromhead, Peter. "Photorealism," *New Zealand Star,* July 22, 1975.
Curnow, Wynstan. "The Imagery of Now," *New Zealand Listener,* Sept. 13, 1975.
"First Exhibition of Photorealist Art in Auckland," *Auckland* (New Zealand) *Tourist Times,* July 22, 1975, p. 6.
Frackman, Noel. "Charles Bell," *Arts Magazine,* Jan., 1975, p. 11.
"Local Art Exhibition," *South Auckland* (New Zealand) *Carrier,* July 30, 1975.
Lucie-Smith, Edward. "Contemporary Art in America," *Illustrated London News,* Jan., 1975.

McNamara, T. J. "Photo-Realist Exhibition Makes Impact," *The Auckland* (New Zealand) *Star,* July 21, 1975.
______. "Photo-Realist Exhibition Makes Impact," *New Zealand Herald* (Auckland), July 23, 1975.
"Photo-Realism Exhibit Is Opening at Paine Sunday," *Oshkosh Daily Northwestern,* Apr. 17, 1975.
"Photo Realism Flies High at Paine," *Milwaukee Journal,* May, 1975.
"Photo Realism on the Way," *Western Leader, Auckland* (New Zealand) *Suborian,* July 21, 1975.
"Photo Realist Art To Be Shown in Dunedin," *The Evening Star* (Auckland, New Zealand), July 18, 1975.
"Photo-Realists at Paine," *Post Crescent View Magazine* (Appleton, Wis.), Apr. 27, 1975, pp. 5–6.
"Photorealism," *Northern Advocate* (Witangare, New Zealand), Aug. 4, 1975.
"Photorealism at Best," *The Christchurch Star* (Canterbury Province, New Zealand), Aug. 27, 1975.
"Photorealism Tours Our Big Centers," *Manawatu* (New Zealand) *Evening Standard,* July 30, 1975.
"Unique Art Exhibition," *City News* (New Zealand), July 23, 1975.
Artner, Alan. "Mirroring the Merits of a Showing of Photo-Realism," *Chicago Tribune,* Oct. 24, 1976.
Better Homes & Gardens, Aug., 1976, p. 35.
Brown, Gordon. "Group Show," *Arts Magazine,* Sept., 1976.
Fox, Mary. "Aspects of Realism," *Vancouver Sun,* Sept. 21, 1976.
Hoffman, Donald. *Kansas City Star,* May, 1976.
K. M. "Realism," *The New Art Examiner,* Nov., 1976.
Greenwood, Mark. "Toward a Definition of Realism: Reflections on the Rothmans Exhibition," *Arts/Canada,* vol. XXIV, no. 210–11 (Dec., 1976–Jan., 1977), pp. 62–63.
Battcock, Gregory. "Dinner for Eighty," *The SoHo Weekly News,* Nov. 10, 1977, pp. 26, 45.
Beardsall, Judy. "Charles Bell," *Arts Magazine,* Nov., 1977, p. 14.
Crossley, Mimi. "Review: Photo Realism," *Houston Post,* Dec. 9, 1977, p. 10E ill.
Edelson, Elihu. "New Realism at Museum Arouses Mixed Feelings," *Jacksonville* (Fla.) *Journal,* Feb., 1977.
Perreault, John. "Pin Ball Wizard," *The SoHo Weekly News,* Nov. 24, 1977, p. 26 ill.
Bongard, Willie. *Art Aktuell* (Cologne), Apr., 1978.
Harris, Helen. "Art and Antiques: The New Realists," *Town & Country,* Oct., 1978, pp. 242, 244, 246–47.
Mackie, Alwynne. "New Realism and the Photographic Look," *American Art Review* (Los Angeles), vol. 4, Nov. 6, 1978, pp. 72–79, 132–34, ills. pp. 76, 78.
Miller, Donald. " 'Center' Gets Lift From Exhibition," *Post-Gazette* (Pittsburgh), Oct., 1978.
Richard, Paul. "New Smithsonian Art: From 'The Sublime' to Photo Realism," *Washington Post,* Nov. 30, 1978, p. G 21.
The SoHo Weekly News, Apr., 1978, centerfold.
Veehoff, Cary. "Show Capsulizes Two Decades of Art," *Creightonian* (Omaha, Nebr.), vol. LVI, no. 7, Oct. 6, 1978.
Zimmer, William. "Review: Charles Bell," *Arts Magazine,* Jan., 1978, p. 24, ill. p. 25.
"Brooklyn Museum Showcases Borough Artists," *New York Daily News,* Jan. 31, 1979, p. WK 3 ill.
Louie, Elaine. "For Passionate Collectors," *House Beautiful,* Feb., 1979, pp. 56–57.
Bishop, Pete. "Gentlemen of the Jury," *The Pittsburgh Press Roto,* Feb. 10, 1980, ill. p. 18, pp. 19–20 ill.
"Contemporary and Modern Art To Be Offered June 10th at Christie's East," *Antiques & The Arts Weekly,* June 6, 1980, p. 38.
"Here Comes [sic] the Judges," *Oklahoma Art Gallery,* Summer, 1980, p. 38 ill., p. 41.
Mackenzie, David C. "Artist Charles Bell 'High Fashion' Now," *Tulsa World,* June 6, 1980, p. B1.
Forgey, Benjamin. "Aviation Art at Home in Its New Hangar," *The Washington Star,* May 21, 1981, pp. C–1 ill., C–4.
Karmel, Pepe. "Photographs by the Photorealists," *Art in America,* May, 1981, pp. 140–41.
"New York Gallery Showcase," *Artscape,* Oklahoma Art Center, Oklahoma City, Jan.–Feb., 1981, p. 2 ill.
Perreault, John. "Photorealing in the Years," *The SoHo Weekly News,* Oct. 20, 1981, p. 64.
Yoskowitz, Robert. "Review," *Arts Magazine,* Jan., 1981, p. 31.
Morera, Daniela. "Fotorealismo," *Vogue Italia,* Oct., 1982, pp. 634–39, 700.
Vogue (Italia) Bambini, April/May, 1982, p. 154.
Omni, Dec., 1983, ill. pp. 130–31.
Colby, Joy Hakanson. "New Realism Wins With Its Eye Appeal," *The Detroit News,* Dec. 23, 1984.
Jensen, Dean. "Collection by Pieper: Art for Business Sake," *Milwaukee Sentinel,* Mar. 13, 1984, part 4, pp. 1, 7 ill.
Omni, May, 1984, ill. pp. 56–57
Perreault, John. "Charles Bell," *Antique Toy World,* Chicago, Ill., vol. 14, no. 1, Jan., 1984, ill. front cover, pp. 8–12 ill.
Hofmann, Deborah. "Collecting Marbles Isn't Just Child's Play," *The New York Times,* June 20, 1985.
Reif, Rita. "Abstracts To Be Offered," *The New York Times,* Apr. 26, 1985.
______. "52 Modern Artworks Auctioned at Christie's," *The New York Times,* Nov. 7, 1985.
______. "Franz Kline's 'Untitled' Sold for $880,000 at Christie's," *The New York Times,* May 1, 1985.
Burdick, Marion. "A Feast for the Eyes Set at Squibb Gallery," *Time Off* (Princeton, N.J.), Dec. 2, 1987.
Ligocki, Gordon. "Photorealism Holds on to 1980s Audiences," *The Times* (Hammond, Ind.), July 3, 1987.
Bailey, Patricia Black. "ART/LA 88—The Business of Going International," *Art Today* (Wichita, Kans.), Winter, 1988–89, pp. 38–41, p. 40 ill.
National Air and Space Museum, Smithsonian Institution, Washington, D.C., Christmas card, 1988.
Papadopoulou, Bia. "Intellectual and Artistic Movements: American Photorealism," *Politea ("State") Magazine* (Athens), June, 1988, pp. 73 ill.–75.
Nob Hill Gazette (San Francisco, Calif.), Jan., 1989, cover ill.
"Oklahoma Artwork on Display," *The Daily Ardmoreite* (Ardmore, Okla.), Dec. 5, 1989.
"Oklahoma Artists," *The Outlook,* Charles B. Goddard Center for Visual and Performing Arts, Ardmore, Okla., Dec., 1989–Jan., 1990.

CATALOGUES

Hogan, Carroll Edwards. Introduction to *Hyperréalistes américains*. Galerie Arditti, Paris, Oct. 16–Nov. 30, 1973.

Meisel, Louis K. *Photo-Realism 1973: The Stuart M. Speiser Collection*. Louis K. Meisel Gallery, New York, 1973.

Radde, Bruce. Introduction to *East Coast/West Coast/New Realism*. San Jose State University, Calif., Apr. 24–May 18, 1973.

Chase, Linda. "Photo Realism." In *Tokyo Biennale '74*. Tokyo Metropolitan Museum of Art, 1974.

Cowart, Jack. *New/Photo Realism*. Wadsworth Atheneum, Hartford, Conn., Apr. 10–May 19, 1974.

Meisel, Susan Pear. *Watercolors and Drawings—American Realists*. Louis K. Meisel Gallery, New York, Jan., 1975.

39th Annual Midyear Show. Butler Institute of American Art, Youngstown, Ohio, June 29–Aug. 31, 1975.

Felluss, Elias A. Foreword to *Washington International Art Fair*. Washington, D.C., 1976.

Gervais, Daniel. Introduction to *Troisième Foire internationale d'art contemporain*. Grand Palais, Paris, Oct. 16–24, 1976.

Chase, Linda. "U.S.A." In *Aspects of Realism*. Rothmans of Pall Mall Canada Limited, June, 1976–Jan., 1978.

Dempsey, Bruce. Introduction to *New Realism*. Jacksonville Art Museum, Fla., 1977.

Felluss, Elias A. Foreword to *Washington International Art Fair*. Washington, D.C., 1977.

Meisel, Louis K. *Charles Bell*. Louis K. Meisel Gallery, New York, Nov. 5–26, 1977.

Garfield, Alan. Introduction to *Drawings Since 1960*. University Art Gallery, Creighton University, Omaha, Nebr., Sept. 30–Oct. 28, 1978.

Meisel, Louis K. Introduction to *Landscape/Cityscape*. Brainerd Hall Art Gallery, State University College, Potsdam, N.Y., Sept. 22–Oct. 22, 1978.

Meisel, Susan Pear. Introduction to *The Complete Guide to Photo-Realist Printmaking*. Louis K. Meisel Gallery, New York, Dec., 1978.

Yassin, Robert. Introduction to *Painting and Sculpture Today, 1978*. Indianapolis Museum of Art, Ind., June 15–July 30, 1978.

Felluss, Elias A. Introduction to *Washington International Art Fair '79*. Washington, D.C., May 2–7, 1979.

Frankel, Robert. Introduction to *New York Now*. Phoenix Art Museum, Ariz., Apr. 20–May 27, 1979.

Gerling, Steve. Introduction to *Photo-Realism: Some Points of View*. Jorgensen Gallery, University of Connecticut, Storrs, Mar. 19–Apr. 10, 1979.

Streuber, Michael. Introduction to *Selections of Photo-Realist Paintings from N.Y.C. Galleries*. Southern Alleghenies Museum of Art, Saint Francis College, Loretto, Pa., May 12–July 8, 1979.

Adams, Lowell. Introduction to *New York Gallery Showcase*. Oklahoma Art Center, Oklahoma City, Jan. 16–Feb. 22, 1981, pp. 30–33.

Cityscapes. The Column, Arnot Art Museum, Elmira, N.Y., July 1981.

Messer, Thomas M. "Photorealism." In *New Concepts for a New Art (Toyama Now '81)*. The Museum of Modern Art, Toyama, Japan, July 5–Sept. 23, 1981, ill. p. 25, pp. 107–10 ill.

A Range of Contemporary Drawing. Sordoni Art Gallery, Wilkes College, Wilkes-Barre, Pa., Aug. 31–Sept. 20, 1981.

Kayser, Thomas A., and Linda Chase. *Super Realism From the Morton G. Neumann Family Collection*. Kalamazoo Institute of Arts, Mich., Sept. 1–Nov. 1, 1981; The Art Center, Inc., South Bend, Ind., Nov. 22, 1981–Jan. 3, 1982; Springfield Art Museum, Mo., Jan. 16–Feb. 28, 1982; Dartmouth College Museum and Galleries, Hanover, N.H., Mar. 19–May 2, 1982; DeCordova and Dana Museum and Park, Lincoln, Mass., May 9–June 20, 1982; Des Moines Art Center, Iowa, July 6–Aug. 15, 1982; Terra Museum of American Art, Evanston, Ill., Nov. 4–Dec. 7, 1983, ill. p. 11.

Photo-Réalisme Dix Ans Après. Galerie Isy Brachot, Paris, Jan. 13–Mar. 6, 1982, ill. p. 20.

The American Photorealists—An Anthology, Fischer Fine Art Limited, London, May-June, 1983.

Chase, Linda, and Ronald McKnight Melvin. *American Super Realism From the Morton G. Neumann Family Collection*. Terra Museum of American Art, Evanston, Ill., Nov. 4–Dec. 7, 1983, ill. p. 11.

Perreault, John. *Charles Bell—Marbles & Toys*. Louis K. Meisel Gallery, New York, Mar., 1983.

Realism Now. The Museum of Modern Art, Saitama, Japan, Oct. 4–Dec. 4, 1983, p. 16 ill.

Martin, Alvin. *America Seen—Contemporary American Artists View America*. Adams-Middleton Gallery, Dallas, Tex., June-Sept., 1984.

Arthur, John. *American Realism: The Precise Image*. The Isetan Museum of Art, Tokyo, July 25–Aug. 19, 1985; The Daimaru Museum, Osaka, Oct. 9–28, 1985; Yokohama Takashimaya Gallery, Nov. 7–12, 1985, ill. p. 42.

Binai, Paul. Foreword to *The 80's: A Post Pop Generation*. Southern Alleghenies Museum of Art, Loretto, Pa., June 30–Sept. 9, 1990, p. 6 ill.

Selby, Roger L. Introduction to *Collectors' Annual—Contemporary Art*. Boca Raton Museum of Art, Fla., pp. 6, 7, ill. p. 13.

New Art in an Old City. The Virlane Foundation and the K & B Corporation Collections, New Orleans, La., pl. 26.

Hansen, Trudy V., and Phillip Dennis Cate. *Intaglio Printing in the 1980s*. Jane Voorhees Zimmerli Art Museum, Rutgers, The State University of New Jersey, New Brunswick, Dec. 9, 1990–Feb. 24, 1991.

BOOKS

Battcock, Gregory, ed. *Super Realism, A Critical Anthology*. New York: E. P. Dutton, 1975.

Kultermann, Udo. *Neue Formen des Bildes*. Tübingen, Germany: Verlag Ernst Wasmuth, 1975.

Who's Who in Amercan Art. New York: R. R. Bowker, 1976.

Krantz, Les, ed. *The New York Art Review*. New York: The Krantz Company Publishers, Inc., 1978.

Seeman, Helene Zucker, and Alanna Siegfried. *SoHo*. New York: Neal-Schuman, 1979.

Lindey, Christine. *Superrealist Painting & Sculpture*. New York: William Morrow & Co., Inc., 1980.

Meisel, Louis K. *Photorealism*. New York: Harry N. Abrams, Inc., 1980.

Krantz, Les, ed. *The New York Art Review*. New York: The Krantz Company Publishers, Inc., 1982.

Krantz, Les. *American Art Galleries*. New York and Oxford: Facts on File Publications, 1985.

______. *American Artists—An Illustrated Survey of Leading Contemporary Americans*. New York: Facts on File Publications, 1985.

Lucie-Smith, Edward. *American Art Now*. New York: William Morrow & Co., Inc., 1985.

Xuriguera, Gérard. *Les Figurations (de 1960 à nos jours)*. Paris: Editions Mayer, 1985.

Zanger, Virginia Vogel. *Face to Face*. Glenview, Ill.: Scott, Foresman and Company, 1985.

Martin, Alvin. *American Realism—Twentieth-Century Drawings and Watercolors—From the Glenn C. Janss Collection*. New York: San Francisco Museum of Modern Art in association with Harry N. Abrams, Inc., 1986.

Krantz, Les. *The New York Art Review*. Chicago: American References, Inc., 1988.

Farrell, Edmund, Ovida Clapp, and Karen Keuhner. *Patterns in Literature: America Reads—Classic Edition*. Glenview, Ill.: Scott, Foresman and Company, 1989.

Ward, John L. *American Realist Painting 1945–1980*. Ann Arbor: University of Michigan Press, 1989.

Levin, Richard I., and David S. Rubin. *Statistics for Management*. 5th ed. Englewood Cliffs, N.J.: Prentice-Hall, Inc., 1991.

INDEX

Page numbers are in roman type. Figures are so indicated. All works are by Bell unless otherwise indicated.